THE POST-WAR FINANCIAL PROBLEM
AND OTHER ESSAYS

THE POST-WAR
FINANCIAL PROBLEM

AND OTHER ESSAYS

BY

F. W. PAISH

LONDON
MACMILLAN & CO. LTD
1950

PRINTED IN GREAT BRITAIN

PREFACE

THERE is a pleasant story of two children who, asked
what they talked about on their walks, replied, " We looks,
and we talks about what we sees ". In the essays repub-
lished in this book I have in general endeavoured to follow
the example of these two young practitioners of the in-
ductive method.

The three earliest-written essays — " Banking Policy
and the Balance of International Payments", "Forecasting
Foreign Trade", and "Causes of Changes in Gold Supply"
— derive mainly from the experience obtained during my
service with the Standard Bank of South Africa, Ltd., in
Cape Town, especially during the years 1929 to 1932.
The first two of these essays are closely based on a paper,
read to the Association of University Teachers of Economics at Oxford in January 1936, which must have been
written in the later months of 1935. The concept of
marginal propensity to import was developed from direct
observation of the effects on the South African economy
first of a heavy fall in export prices and later of a flight
of capital, though the actual term " propensity " was
borrowed from Keynes' *The General Theory of Employment, Interest and Money*, first published in February 1936.

The next two essays, " Twenty Years of the Floating
Debt " and " British Floating Debt Policy ", arose from
a close study of the Floating Debt figures made for the purpose of estimating from time to time the changes in the
gold holdings of the Exchange Equalisation Account. At
the time, this attempt to read a meaning into the week to
week fluctuations in the Treasury bill figures had something

v

of the excitement of a detective story ; but on re-reading at any rate the earlier of these two essays, I find the prolonged examination of minutiae rather wearisome, though it may prove useful to anyone wishing to make a detailed study of the financial history of the period.

Except for the short note on " Capital Value and Income ", which arose out of a discussion with a research student of mine, the late Dr. G. B. Sanderson, the only other essay written before my temporary withdrawal from academic life in 1941 is " Economic Incentive in War-time ". This is in the main devoted to an early statement of the now universally recognised relationship between highly progressive taxation and a diminution of the incentive to work.

The five post-war essays, which form the first section of this book, all deal with different aspects of the imperfectly controlled post-war inflation in Britain. The first, which gives its title to the book, owes a great deal to the criticisms and suggestions of my colleagues on the Editorial Committee of the London and Cambridge Economic Service. It was an attempt, I think the first, to estimate, with the wholly inadequate data available in January 1947, what demands on the system were likely to be made by the post-war investment programme and how far they could be met out of voluntary saving. It is interesting to note that, while many of the individual items were wildly wrong (the export of capital, in particular, being hopelessly under-estimated), the estimates of total net investment have proved remarkably near the mark, and the need for a substantial Budget surplus to supplement private savings was in no way exaggerated. The second essay, based on a lecture delivered in the early spring of 1949, dealt with the dangers of the then current " Cheap Money Policy ", and provides a sequel to the earlier articles on the Floating Debt. Also published in August 1947 was the essay on " Planning and the Price System ". This is a plea for the use of the price system for carrying into effect whatever policies a Government may have, and of all the essays in this book is the one which reflects most clearly my own prejudices and beliefs. The fourth essay, on " Savings and Investment ", returns to the theme of the first, and carries the story down to about October 1948. In particular, it attempts to answer the question (on the whole fairly correctly) of why the marked disinflation portended by the November 1947 Budget and the contemporaneous cuts in the capital programme had been so much less marked than might have been expected. The last essay of the five, on " The Economics of Rent Restriction ", endeavours to suggest a way out of the impasse created by a particularly vicious example of the many attempts made to restrain inflation by imposing maximum prices for particular goods and services.

The next chapter in the story cannot yet be written. The rising level of Government expenditure and the difficulty of adding still further to the burden of taxation have caused the Government partially to abandon the use of the Budget as the main equilibrating instrument, and to turn instead to the attempt to inflate business savings by pegging both wage rates and dividends at a time when exports have been made more profitable through devaluation. Whether the strain imposed upon the Trades Unions by this policy will prove excessive, and how far the policy, even if successful, will be at the expense of incentive and mobility, it is still too soon to say. But if this latest attempt to expand savings fails, the only choice remaining will be between the restoration of drastic controls on consumption and an equally drastic cut in the capital programme, either by decree or through the mechanism of a rising rate of interest.

F. W. PAISH

May 1950

ACKNOWLEDGMENTS

I AM indebted to the London and Cambridge
Economic Service and to the editors of *Economica*, the
Westminster Bank Review, and *Lloyds Bank Review* for
authorisation to include in this volume various papers
which first appeared in their columns. " Forecasting
Foreign Trade " is reprinted from *Some Modern
Business Problems* by permission of the editor, Pro-
fessor Sir Arnold Plant, and the publishers, Messrs.
Longmans, Green & Co. Ltd.

F. W. P.

CONTENTS

THE POST-WAR FINANCIAL PROBLEM [1]

THE cost of the recent war was covered in three ways. Part of it was paid for out of current income; either, that is to say, by an increase in output, or by a reduction in consumption. A second part was covered by consumption of capital; and a third by contributions from overseas, notably Lend-Lease from the United States and gifts and mutual aid from Canada. The consumption of capital contributed to the cost of waging war in two ways; by the postponement of normal maintenance and replacement of buildings and equipment, and by drafts on overseas capital, whether by the sale of assets or by an increase in liabilities. In addition, the war destroyed physical capital, by enemy action; and the process of reconstruction is normally regarded as covering both the replacement of destroyed capital and the overtaking of arrears of normal maintenance and replacement. The rebuilding of overseas capital and the repayment of foreign debts are a separate and altogether longer-term problem.

The problem of reconstructing our internal capital losses cannot be considered in isolation from the creation of new capital. In many cases this is as urgent as the replacement of losses, and in some probably has priority. In considering how reconstruction can be financed, we must therefore take account of the whole range of capital expenditure contemplated during the reconstruction period. In the following discussion this period is taken arbitrarily

[1] Originally published under the title of " The Finance of Reconstruction" in the *Quarterly Bulletin of the London and Cambridge Economic Service*, February 1947.

as ten years from the end of 1945. It is to be hoped that by the end of the year 1955 the great bulk, at least, of our internal capital losses will have been made good.

In the following discussion no attempt has been made to compile a complete list of the many plans for capital development which have been put forward on greater or less authority. Instead, two figures have been calculated for the capital needs of the ten-year period : one puts each item at a bare minimum level, and therefore almost certainly under-estimates the total ; the other is a fair guess, low rather than high, at the needs which are likely to develop. It is assumed in both cases (1) that war-time losses will be made good, (2) that 3 million houses will be built during the ten years, (3) that industry as a whole (including nationalised concerns) will make no demands for new money capital, but will meet capital extensions out of undistributed profits, in accordance with the practice of recent years. The "bare minimum" figure and the "likely" figures are both the merest estimates, and both are likely to be lower than the sum of all the plans under serious consideration at the present time.

An estimate of internal physical destruction is given in Table 12 of the Statistical Material presented during the Washington Negotiations (Cmd. 6707). This puts total damage to property at £860 millions, equal to £1450 millions at current (end 1945) replacement costs. This seems to be a gross figure, that is to say, it does not allow for war-time replacements. The White Paper on National Income and Expenditure of the United Kingdom, 1938–45 (Cmd. 6784) puts the value of war-time restoration of buildings at £300 millions (Table 20, item 12). As we shall allow, in subsequent estimates, for other war damage made good, this is all we need deduct from the estimate of gross internal destruction, giving us a net figure of £1150 millions.

The other item in war destruction is our net loss of

shipping. Between 1939 and the end of 1945, the size of our merchant fleet fell by 4 million gross tons. Taking an average replacement cost of £75 per gross ton, the cost of building up our merchant fleet to its 1939 level would be about £300 millions.

Some estimate of the arrears of maintenance and replacement which have to be made good can be derived from information given in the White Paper on National Income and Expenditure of the United Kingdom, 1938–45 (figures in brackets denote the number of the item in Tables 20, 22, and 23 of that publication). For the six years 1940–45 the total sums allowed for depreciation and maintenance aggregate £3100 millions (85). Gross private capital formation in the same years is put at £1250 millions (88) and gross capital formation by public authorities for civil purposes at £574 millions (90), giving a total gross civil capital formation, public and private, of £1824 millions. This, however, includes the £315 millions restoration of war damage to buildings (12) already allowed for; the net figure is therefore £1509 millions. Deducting this from £3100 millions, we obtain an unused balance of depreciation and maintenance allowances of £1591 millions. We are also told that the net depletion of non-war capital assets of public authorities was £68 millions (73), so that we are left with a figure of over £1500 millions as the unused depreciation funds of private business. But these depreciation allowances will have been made mainly on the original cost of the assets, and it is reasonable to assume that the unspent balance will be quite inadequate to cover replacement and deferred maintenance at post-war prices. If we add 50 per cent to allow for increased prices we shall certainly be still much too low (the " Statistical Material " adds nearly 70 per cent to the 1938 cost of war damage to property to bring the replacement cost up to 1945 prices). This gives us £2250–£2500 millions as the cost of making good war-time depreciation of durable business assets and

£100-£120 millions for that of non-war assets of public authorities. It does not, however, include any allowance for the cost of building up business stocks of raw materials, goods in progress, and finished goods awaiting sale. This can hardly be put at less than £250 millions, and may well be at least £500 millions. We thus get a figure of £2500-£3000 millions for the total cost of restoring business assets to their pre-war level.

The treatment of the war-time depreciation of personally owned goods and chattels presents some difficulty. At first glance it is comparable to the depreciation of business property, and should be allowed for in the same way. But it is not obvious that a man who has made a suit last six years instead of three will replace it with two suits; the post-war demand is not increased by the sum of all purchases foregone during the war. (The same point arises with business assets, such as looms, which have continued in use when all their original value has been written off; but it is of greater importance in dealing with personal goods.) A more serious point, however, is that deferred consumption expenditure is indistinguishable from current consumption, and will appear in the national accounts as " consumption " and not as " saving ". If we wish our estimates of savings required to be of the same nature as " saving " in the National Income White Paper, we must omit this deferred consumption altogether, bearing in mind that, over the ten years, there will be a desire to increase consumption (and reduce savings) by anything from £750 millions to £1500 millions.

Now we must turn to the question of new capital construction. At the head of the list come the Government's housing plans. These are said to envisage the construction of houses at a maximum rate of 500,000 a year and of 4 millions in ten years from V.E.-day. Even if we discount this figure somewhat, and envisage house construction only at an average rate equal to that of the immediate pre-war years, we get an average of 300,000 a year (in addition to the replacement of destroyed houses included above) and a total of 3 millions for the period from January 1946. The present cost of building seems to average about £1300 a house for the minimum size permitted. Since the total to be built before 1955 will presumably include some larger houses, I think that £1100 per house is a minimum figure for the average cost for the whole period ; and the cost might well be as high as £1500. These estimates include cost of site preparation and of connection to existing services, but not the provision of new public utilities, which is included in the next paragraph. Both figures are slightly reduced by repayments of capital costs out of rent—*i.e.* out of increased consumption expenditure. This effect is ignored. This gives us figures of £3300 millions or £4500 millions.

Next we have other new capital creation by public authorities. In view of the need for new schools, and the public works which will be required for the new housing estates, I think that a total estimate of £1000-£1250 millions for the period is modest.

It is equally difficult to estimate the total requirements for new capital construction by industry, including nationalised industries. All one can say is that the White Paper puts non-personal private saving at £210 millions in 1945 (43), and explains that this consists of the undistributed net profits of companies. If this figure continues to rise slowly during the coming years, it would be conservative to estimate an average of £220 millions a year for the next ten years, or a total of £2200 millions for the period. If we further assume that on balance industry makes no demands on outside money but restricts its capital expenditure to its own savings, we can put its creation of new capital down at the same figure. Whatever figure is chosen will balance with the corresponding saving on the other side of the account.

There remains a small group of other capital requirements by the Government. Although we cannot hope to go far towards rebuilding our foreign investments during the next ten years, we may be obliged to export some capital on balance, leaving out of account our drafts on the American loans. In the last five years of the period capital repayments on the United States and Canadian loans will require nearly £20 millions a year; we are to begin paying £5 millions a year off the Argentine debt immediately; and capital repayments on our other sterling debts must sooner or later begin at a fairly substantial rate. It must be remembered, of course, that at present these debts are still increasing. On the other hand, we have already found it impossible to conduct our international trade without granting some foreign credits, largely on Government account. All in all, the net export of capital, before taking into account the U.S. and Canadian loans, may be anything from zero to £500 millions. In addition, there may be fairly substantial sums for compensation for war damage in Malaya, Burma, Malta, and other parts of the Empire which may have to be found by the British Government. The estimate here ranges from £50 millions to £200 millions. Finally, there is the cost of deficits on the ordinary Budget for the period. For the first quarter of 1946 this was about £85 millions. For the year 1946–47 the estimated deficit is rather over £700 millions, after taking credit for £150 millions for the sale of surplus war stores. If for convenience we omit these in order to show them as a contra item, this gives us an estimated deficit of over £850 millions for the year, or about £950 millions for the period from the beginning of 1946 to March 1947. It now seems likely that the deficit realised will be appreciably less than this, but it would almost certainly be to err on the side of optimism to put the fifteen months' deficit, apart from the sale of war stores, at £450 millions, and perhaps equally optimistic to assume that the ordinary

Budget will be balanced, without the aid of sales of war stores, in 1947–48 and subsequent years. £800 millions would be more likely. This gives a minimum capital requirement of £11,050 millions, and a " likely " requirement of quite £14,020 millions — say £11,000 millions and £14,000 millions in round figures. (See Table I.)

There are certain resources available to help towards the meeting of these claims. We have excluded the proceeds of sales of surplus war stores from the Budget, so we must allow for them here. The yield for 1946–47 was shown in the Budget estimates at £150 millions. No doubt this covers a large proportion of the most easily realised of the assets, but there must be large additional amounts which will still be held at the end of the year, including the Government's half of the remaining old stocks of Empire wool and a good many large assets, such as factories, which will be sold off in due course. Let us put the total to be sold or released for peace-time purposes at £350-£500 millions in all.

Next we have the United States and Canadian loans. We have already allowed for some capital repayments on these loans, so that we can count their full value as a net addition to resources during the period. This gives us £1100 millions for the U.S. loan and credit and £300 millions for the Canadian credit. Thus we have in all some £1750-£1900 millions of real resources to put against our gross capital requirements.

Of the balance we can probably rely on a part to be saved by public authorities other than the Central Government. There may be a substantial surplus on the working of these extra-budgetary funds, and especially on the unemployment insurance fund. In 1945 this fund alone increased its reserves by £69 millions, and, provided that unemployment continues to be at a low level, this surplus is likely to increase when the new rates come into force. On the other hand, the other insurance funds may show a deficit during the early years of the new Insurance Act. It would probably be optimistic to put the national savings through the

B

channel of the extra-budgetary funds at £120 millions a year, or £1200 millions for the ten years ; a " likely " figure would be £400 millions. A further £2200 millions we have already estimated as the savings through additions to company reserves.

The balance still outstanding is anything from £5750 millions to £9670 millions. If national income is maintained at the 1945 level of £8500 millions, the proportion of net personal saving required to national income is at least 6¾ per cent, and perhaps 11½ per cent. In 1938, out of a national income of £4600 millions, the White Paper puts personal net savings at £140 millions, or just over 3 per cent. When we bear in mind the desire to make up for deferred consumption, mentioned above, this low percentage may perhaps be taken as " normal " for the post-war years. We should thus need an increase of 120-270 per cent in the rate of personal saving as compared with this norm. *Saving must certainly be nearly more than doubled, and probably quadrupled.*

While even the higher figure is much less than the rate of net personal saving achieved during the last years of the war, its maintenance during peace will be no easy matter. Most changes since before the war are calculated to reduce the rate of voluntary saving. The more equal distribution of net incomes, largely as a result of taxation for social services ; the losses of internal and overseas capital and the consequent, if temporary, reduction in national real income ; the widespread possession of unspent past savings, representing not investments but merely postponed consumption ; perhaps, also, the low rate of interest, causing an increased tendency among the growing number of the elderly to consume their capital — all these will tend to diminish saving or to increase capital consumption. On the other side stand the devoted workers of the National Savings movement and the hope that in some at least of those who have saved for the first time during the war the habit will persist; and the effect of the gain to national income from full employment. He would be an optimist who would expect these to do more than balance the factors on the other side, and maintain voluntary net personal saving at the pre-war proportion of national income, giving a post-war rate of about £260 millions a year. There thus remains a gap to be filled of £315-£707 millions a year. The position is summarised in the following table:

TABLE I

THE FINANCE OF RECONSTRUCTION — 1946–55

ESTIMATED AGGREGATE POSITION

(£ Mn.)

Requirements for Capital	Mini-mum	Likely	Sources of Capital	Maxi-mum	Likely
Restoration of War Damage:			*Public Authorities :*		
On land . . .	1,150	1,150	Surplus war		
Shipping . .	300	300	stocks .	500	350
Deferred Maintenance and			U.S. loan and		
Replacement :			credit .	1,100	1,100
Public authorities			Canadian		
(non-industrial) .	100	120	credit .	300	300
Business . .	2,500	3,000	*Extra-budgetary*		
New Capital :			*Funds* . .	1,200	400
Housing . . .	3,300	4,500	*Business Savings :*		
Other public authori-			Undistributed		
ties (non-industrial)	1,000	1,250	profits .	2,200	2,200
Business . .	2,200	2,200	" *Normal* " *Per-*		
Overseas :			*sonal Savings*		
Colonial war damage	50	200	(3 per cent) .	2,600	2,600
Exports and repay-					
ments of capital .	0	500	Extra savings		
Budget Deficit . .	450	800	needed . .	3,150 as a min.	7,070 likely
TOTAL .	11,050	14,020	TOTAL .	11,050	14,020

Before discussing ways of filling this gap, it will help to make the position clearer if we examine separately the requirements and resources of each of the three sectors of the system — the personal sector, the business sector, and the public authorities sector. This will involve a somewhat arbitrary division of unrepaired war damage and of war damage compensation, but it is not thought that the errors will be so serious as materially to affect the general picture. The estimates are based on the " likely " columns of the previous table. No attempt is made to separate war damage compensation received but unspent from compensation still to be received. This makes no difference to the general position, for neither the compensation received already nor that still to be received can be spent unless and until it is saved by other parts of the community. Nor, so long as its cheap money policy obliges the Government to support the long-term capital market, does the fact that some of the money received has been invested in long-dated securities absolve the Government from the obligation of finding the means of taking these securities up when their owners wish to sell them in order to finance capital re-creation. This also holds true of the unspent depreciation and reserve funds which their owners may wish to use for reconstruction. If there are insufficient new savings to take them up at existing prices, the Government must either take them up itself or create additional money for others to take them up with, if it wishes to prevent the rate of interest from rising. Thus the cheap money policy throws the whole responsibility of finding the necessary resources upon the Government.

TABLE II

THE FINANCE OF RECONSTRUCTION — 1946–55

ESTIMATED POSITION OF DIFFERENT SECTORS

(£ Mn.)

PERSONAL SECTOR

Requirements for Capital:		Sources of Capital:	
War damage . . .	600	War damage compensa-	
New houses bought .	1000	tion	500
Surplus	2250	Post-war credits . .	750
		" Normal " savings . .	2600
TOTAL . .	3850	TOTAL . .	3850

BUSINESS SECTOR

Requirements for Capital:			Sources of Capital:	
War damage—			War damage compensation	500
On land	500		E.P.T. refunds	175
At sea	300		Unused war-time reserves	1200
		800	Unused depreciation and	
Deferred maintenance and			maintenance funds	*1800
replacement		3000	New additions to reserve	2200
New capital creation		2200	Deficit	125
TOTAL		6000	TOTAL	6000

PUBLIC AUTHORITIES SECTOR

Requirements for Capital:			Sources of Capital:	
War damage	50		Surplus war stocks	350
Deferred maintenance			U.S. and Canadian loans	1,400
and replacement	120		Extra-budgetary funds	400
New houses	3500		Surplus from Personal	
Other non-industrial			Sector	2,250
capital	1250		Additional savings needed	6,945
Foreign debt retirement	500			
		5,420		
War damage payments—				
Home	1000			
Abroad	200			
		1,200		
E.P.T. refunds	175			
Post-war credits	750			
		925		
Budget deficits		800		
Sales of securities by business sector—				
Unused war-time reserves	1200			
Unused depreciation and maintenance funds	1800			
		3,000		
TOTAL		11,345	TOTAL	11,345

* Including £300 millions for the unused proceeds of net sales of stocks.

If the estimates given in Table II are even approximately correct, it would appear that, assuming a continuation of the cheap money policy and the continued right of holders to sell securities in the market, the private sector, taken as a whole, will have more than enough, and the business sector very nearly enough, liquid resources to finance their own needs for capital. This does not mean, of course, that all individual persons or companies will be able to finance their capital requirements out of their own resources, for within each group there must obviously be great disparities between the possession of liquid resources and the need for additional capital assets; still less does it mean that there will be little demand for making new capital issues on the market, for a large proportion of these in any case consists of the re-sale of securities already issued by companies. But it does mean that to attempt to enforce priorities merely by means of the control of capital issues under the Borrowing (Control and Guarantees) Act would be quite unsuccessful, and might well enable businesses with liquid assets to obtain priority over more essential though less liquid concerns.

We are now in a position to commence consideration of the possible ways in which the gap between the country's requirements of capital for reconstruction and its probable level of voluntary saving can be closed. A possible way would be for the Government to cease to give direct or indirect support to the long-term capital market, and for the supply of and demand for long-term capital to be equated through the mechanism of a rise in interest rates. On the one side this would check the diversion of savings into the purchase of durable consumers' goods, and on the other it would discourage the demand for capital, especially for the creation of highly durable assets where the interest charge is a high proportion of annual cost, and probably in particular the demand for capital to finance housing. Priority would thus go automatically to those uses able to bear the highest rate of interest, which are, from one point of view, those things which the community most wants quickly. One effect would almost certainly be a sharp reduction in the rate of long-term capital creation and a corresponding increase in the flow of goods and services for early consumption.

It is, of course, extremely unlikely that the Government would adopt this method of equating the supply and demand for capital. To do so would not only substitute priorities fixed by the wishes of individuals for those considered desirable by the Government, but would greatly raise the cost of servicing the National Debt and complicate the budgetary problem. But it is important that the Government, in deciding its own priorities, should not be itself deceived by the artificially low rate of interest which it has created. Real capital, as distinguished from money capital, is extremely scarce — so scarce that it is doubtful if a long-term interest rate of, say, 6 per cent would be high enough to equate the scarcity of money capital with that of real capital. When taking its decisions about priorities for capital creation, the Government should act *as if* the money rate of interest was extremely high, and embark immediately only upon those schemes which it would still embark upon with a 6 per cent, or higher, rate of interest. In particular, it seems very probable from this criterion that the housing programme is over-ambitious. The country needs perhaps a million houses very urgently ; thereafter many of the additional new houses would merely replace older houses which, while less convenient, are still usable. It may be doubted if the country would really wish to build these additional houses at the rate contemplated if it realised what it was being asked to give up, either in the shape of additional productive capacity or of additional goods for immediate consumption, in order to obtain houses so rapidly.

A second possible course of action is to continue to keep interest rates low, while enforcing additional saving by means of the direct control of consumption, and investment priorities by the physical control of the creation and purchase of productive assets. How far, in the absence of any direct control on wage rates or the distribution of labour, and with a very partial control on the creation and distribution of producers' goods other than buildings, it will be possible to continue this policy indefinitely is a matter of opinion. But there can be little doubt that its indefinite continuation will involve a waste of man-power, both in Government service and still more in the service of the concerns which have to comply with Government instructions. The waste is especially serious in the case of higher executives, who have to spend so much of their time in obtaining licences and allocations, instead of thinking how to make more things better and cheaper. In addition, there is always the risk that the Government itself will not always make the wisest selection of priorities, even where it can enforce them. Have we then only a choice between a very sharp rise in interest rates and the indefinite continuation of controls, with the risk of open inflation should they break down?

There is, I believe, a third way which would permit the removal of the controls within a measurable time without a very great rise in interest rates, or, conversely, the maintenance of existing interest rates, together with a great lightening of the controls. The country is faced with the problem of having to save, during the period of reconstruction, some £300-£700 millions a year more than it wants to. The simplest and most straightforward way of enforcing saving is for the Government to do the saving on behalf of the community by means of an excess of Budget income over Budget expenditure. This method has the advantage that once it is started its effect is to some extent cumulative; for if an initial Budget surplus permits some withdrawal of control, the resulting reduction in the number of Government employees would bring a fall in Government expenditure and a larger surplus in the following year. The surplus would in the main be used to finance the capital requirements of the Government and local authorities; but some part of it might have to be employed in buying up or redeeming securities sold by the business sector to finance its share of reconstruction. This would enable the supply and demand for long-term securities to be equated without a further increase in the quantity of money. If, at the same time, the programme of capital creation were pruned of non-essentials, and especially if the housing programme were reduced to, say, two million houses over ten years, the Budget surplus would not need to be enormous ; an average of £300 millions a year might well be sufficient to secure many of the advantages suggested. Even this would raise problems of the maintenance of incentive to work, but it may be doubtful if the disincentive of high taxation, especially if much of it is indirect, is as serious as that of continued strict rationing ; while the release of man-power by the lightening of controls would reinforce the labour supply available for production.

CHEAP MONEY POLICY [1]

I N its simplest terms, a cheap money policy is a policy of driving down, or preventing a rise in, interest rates by increasing the quantity of money. The effects of an increase in the quantity of money are not always the same. They depend mainly on two things : first, the point in the system where the money is injected; and second, the state of business confidence ruling at the time. Money is parted with mainly for two purposes — spending and lending (under lending is included the purchase of variable dividend securities), and we can classify money held into two categories according to the use to which it is intended to put it — money-to-spend and money-to-lend. Now if we increase money-to-spend — if, for instance, each of us one morning found an official envelope on our breakfast plates containing ten one-pound notes, with a polite letter from the Government asking us to buy ourselves a present with it — the result will be a rapid increase in demand for goods and services. If there is widespread unemployment of resources at the time, this will normally lead to an increase in output with little or no rise in prices, and probably to an increased demand for capital to finance the increase in output and a tendency for interest rates to rise. Only if business confidence is at a very low ebb indeed will the shopkeepers or others whose stocks are depleted by the increase in demand use their extra receipts for repaying debts instead of buying new supplies, so that their creditors, in seeking new channels for investing the money repaid, will tend to force down the rate of interest. If, on the

[1] Originally published in *Economica*, August 1947.

other hand, resources are already fully employed, the increased demand will merely cause a rise in prices and, unless interest rates are raised sharply or other measures are taken to check it, will start or intensify a monetary inflation.

In contrast to this, when money-to-lend is injected into the system its immediate effect will be to reduce interest rates. Where business confidence is low, it may be a long time before the lower rates of interest encourage increased borrowing for expenditure on additional capital goods, and interest rates can be forced down a long way before any large part of the new money becomes money-to-spend. When, however, business confidence is high, the new money will be quickly borrowed and spent, with a resultant increase in output if there are many unemployed resources, and an increase in prices if there are not. In conditions of very high business confidence, it is possible that an increase in the supply of money-to-lend may very quickly induce a more than proportionate increase in the demand for it, and, if full employment has been reached, may generate a run-away inflation just as certainly and almost as quickly as an increase in money-to-spend. If, therefore, the increase in the quantity of money is designed to force interest rates down to a low level, the most favourable time is when unemployment is high and business confidence low.

In a developed monetary and banking system, the usual point for the initial injection of additional money is the central bank. By increasing the central bank's holdings of Government Securities or other assets it is possible to increase the total of bankers' deposits with the central bank and therefore the cash reserves of the commercial banks. Since banks do not normally use excess cash reserves to finance their own expenditures, these are almost invariably money-to-lend, and the banks' endeavours to find a profitable investment for them tend to reduce interest rates. Not all interest rates, however, will be affected equally. Even apart from those rates which are subject to a greater or smaller risk of default, there is an almost infinite series of interest rates varying with the contractual duration of the loan, from a few hours to the infinitely long. For our purposes it will suffice if we examine the effects of an increase in banks' cash reserves on three rates only — the Treasury bill rate, the rate for long-term gilt-edged securities, and the rate for overdrafts.

Let us take the bill rate first. The market for bills is a very limited one. The demand for them is almost entirely from banks and from discount houses financed on short-term bank loans. In London the banks, whether British banks or the London offices of overseas banks, always like to keep at least 20 per cent of their assets in bills and short loans against bills, whatever the rate of interest earned on them, and also find them the easiest and safest asset to expand quickly whenever they have a surplus of cash to invest. We thus find not only that bill rates are the first to fall as a result of an increase in banks' cash reserves, but that a large part of the demand will continue even if bill rates fall to a very low level. On the supply side, the available supply of commercial bills has in recent years been relatively small and insensitive to changes in the rate of interest, and though very recently there have been some signs of borrowers switching from overdrafts to London acceptances, the additional volume of finance bills so created is still absolutely small. The main variations in the volume of bills on the market are in Treasury bills, and by increasing the quantity of the banks' cash reserves and at the same time limiting supplies of Treasury bills, the Government can easily force the bill rate down to a level which barely covers the cost of carrying them. Up to 1931 the presence of foreign money on the London market made the demand for bills much more elastic, for if short-term interest rates fell in London relatively to overseas, overseas banks would withdraw part of their

balances to seek more profitable employment elsewhere.
But after 1931 international movements of short-term funds
largely ceased to be influenced by differences in interest
rates and were motivated almost entirely either by political
fears or by hopes or fears of changes in rates of exchange;
while since 1939 movements of capital have, of course,
been subject to control.

The power to force down rates of long-dated securities
is much more limited. While the security holdings of the
banks are absolutely large, they constitute only a small
fraction of those held by other institutions and the general
public. Any given expansion in the banks' holdings will
therefore have a much smaller effect on long-term rates
than it has on bill rates. Further, a fall in gilt-edged rates
will cause some holders to sell them in order to obtain a
larger yield in industrial debentures, preference shares, or
possibly ordinary shares, while even in periods of inactive
trade, low long-term rates will bring an increased willingness to finance the purchase or construction of highly
durable assets, such as houses, with borrowed money or
out of the proceeds of sales of securities. Even after 1931
the long-term capital market was probably less insulated
from rates abroad than was the short-term market, and
very low long-term rates were likely to increase the demand
by some of the remaining credit-worthy overseas borrowers
for new loans. All in all, while it is quite possible to force
long-term rates down a considerable way, it would be extremely difficult, if not impossible, to depress them, even
in the most favourable circumstances, to the levels reached
by short-term rates.

There is one further factor to be considered, which may
work in either direction. This is the effect of speculation.
So long as interest rates are falling and prices of securities
are rising, the movement will be assisted by those who
hope for capital profits from its continuation. The incentive to look to capital profits rather than to income is

increased by high rates of taxation on incomes without
corresponding taxes on capital profits. This incentive
reaches almost absurd levels in the case of the very rich
man paying surtax at maximum rate, for whom sixpennyworth of capital appreciation is worth a pound of gross
income. But as soon as the rise is checked, and security
prices look as if they are more likely to fall than to rise
further, speculation works in the opposite direction. When
interest rates are low, it takes several years even of gross
income to make up for the capital loss due to a small rise
in interest rates, while with high rates of tax the number
of years of net income lost by capital depreciation will be
very much larger. If we take a $2\frac{1}{2}$ per cent rate for irredeemable securities, and $\frac{1}{2}$ per cent as the gross rate obtainable on deposit account at a bank, the difference in annual
net yield, with income tax at 9s. in the pound, is only
£1 : 2s. The capital loss from a rise of only $\frac{1}{4}$ per cent in
the rate of interest, from $2\frac{1}{2}$ per cent to $2\frac{3}{4}$ per cent, is just
over £9. Thus even this small rise in the rate of interest
would wipe out the whole of the net yield on the securities
for over eight years, and if an investor expected a rise in
interest rates of even this magnitude within the next eight
years it would pay him better to keep his money on deposit
at a bank. For a very wealthy man, paying the maximum
rate of surtax on part of his income, the net yield is only
1s. 3d. per £100, or 1s. per £100 more than on bank
deposit. At this rate it would take him over 180 years to
make good the capital loss due to a rise of $\frac{1}{4}$ per cent in the
rate of interest. Thus a surtax payer cannot afford to take
the risk of capital depreciation unless it is balanced by an
at least equal chance of appreciation. The result of this is
that as soon as a further fall in interest rates becomes
unlikely, surtax payers and, to a somewhat smaller extent,
income tax payers, must take their profits, even if it means
getting only $\frac{1}{2}$ per cent interest on bank deposit for years
together. Thus a high level of security prices, reached

with the help of speculative purchases, may prove very difficult to consolidate once the rise ceases.

The third type of interest rate to be considered is the overdraft rate. Overdrafts, although repayable technically on demand, are rarely called in unless there is a serious change for the worse in the financial position of the borrower. They constitute a very convenient and economical form of borrowing, and, for a borrower with fluctuating requirements, may well prove cheaper than a loan for a fixed period at a much lower rate of interest. Thus the demand for overdrafts is not very much affected by moderate changes in the rate of interest, and is very much more dependent on the level of business activity. Overdraft rates have indeed fallen below their former minimum of 5 per cent as a result of competition between banks, but their level is similar to that of rates on industrial debentures rather than to bill rates. In the early stages of a cheap money policy a good deal of the money created comes back to the banks in repayment of overdrafts, and only when business activity has shown pronounced signs of recovery do overdrafts begin to expand. When they do, their expansion involves a more rapid conversion of the banks' money-to-lend into industry's money-to-spend, and is a sign that the credit expansion is now being converted into an expansion of money incomes.

Before leaving this general survey of the question, there are two other matters that must be mentioned. The first of these is not strictly relevant to the subject of this article, but since it has been widely discussed in the journals in the same connection it must be given some mention here. This is the question of changes in the holdings of securities by Government departments. There are now various large Government and semi-Government funds whose investment policy is presumably decided in accordance with the views of the Treasury. Of these, the most important are the Issue Department of the Bank of

England, the Exchange Equalisation Account, and the Unemployment Insurance Fund. What Government Securities are held in these funds is in itself purely a matter of interdepartmental finance. If, for instance, the Issue Department of the Bank of England, on which all profits have since 1928 gone to the Treasury, holds $2\frac{1}{2}$ per cent Treasury Stock instead of $\frac{1}{2}$ per cent Treasury bills, it only means that the Treasury pays out more interest during the year and gets back more profits on the note issue at the end of it. But while the actual composition of the assets in these funds is immaterial, changes in their composition can provide a convenient addition to the Treasury's technique for issuing and repaying loans, while at the same time making it difficult for observers to realise what it is doing. Thus if the departments surrender Treasury bills to the Treasury in exchange for long-dated securities, it looks like a funding loan, whereas nothing of any real importance has occurred; conversely, if the departments sell long-dated securities to the public and buy Treasury bills with the proceeds, thus enabling the Treasury to borrow less on short term from the banks, a funding operation has occurred, though the total of the Treasury's Floating Debt will be unchanged. Similarly, if the departments' holdings of long-dated securities are converted into Treasury bills issued for that purpose, it looks as if an expansion of the Floating Debt had occurred, whereas nothing real has happened; while if the departments sell their Treasury bills to the banks (or, more realistically, have them paid off out of the proceeds of additional Treasury Deposit Receipts [1]) and buy long-dated securities from the public with the proceeds, an unfunding operation has taken place although the Treasury returns show the Floating Debt as unchanged.

The Treasury seems habitually to use the departmental funds both to support the market for long-dated securities

---

[1] See below, p. 27.

and to facilitate the making of new long-dated issues and especially conversion operations. In the case of a new issue, the departments act as underwriters, taking up any amounts not absorbed by the public and selling them again gradually over a longer period. In a conversion operation their rôle is even more important. As the old loan approaches maturity it becomes equivalent to a bill, and, in view of its relatively high yield, becomes an attractive money market investment. Its yield for the remainder of its life, therefore, falls below the long-term rate, and all intelligent long-term investors sell it before maturity. But its new owners do not wish to hold long-term securities, and will therefore tend to take the cash option instead of converting into the new loan. Thus the Treasury will be faced with a poor response to its conversion offer, and will be obliged to find the cash to pay off a large part of the maturing loan. To prevent this, the Government departments buy up a large proportion of the maturing loan in the months before the conversion operation is due, convert their holdings into the new loan, and then (if they can) sell out the new loan gradually to the public, replacing it with Treasury bills in preparation for the next operation.

While it is interesting, and for some purposes important, to try to ascertain what the Treasury is really doing, as opposed to what it appears to be doing, it should be emphasised that all this is really only technique. What really matters from our point of view is what the effect of any such operations is on the volume of bank deposits, and this cannot be concealed by any such legerdemain. When the Treasury has to borrow more on short term from the banks in order to provide the departments with funds to support the long-term market, the effect will show in the bank figures, and if we confine our attention to these we shall not be misled.

There is one further consideration which must be taken into account in interpreting the effects of a rise in banks'

C

deposits, and that is the variations in the size of foreign short-term balances in London. In so far as these are held in Treasury bills there is little difficulty, for the Exchange Equalisation Account releases, or the Treasury issues, Treasury bills in return for the foreign exchange. But when the foreign balances are held in the form of bank deposits, the cash reserves and other assets of the banks must be allowed to increase sufficiently to create the necessary balances for the foreigner to hold; otherwise they will take balances away from residents and tend to reduce the quantity of money available for other purposes. The creation of additional bank deposits equal to the increase in foreign balances held in that form is therefore not inflationary but anti-deflationary.

Though there have been various periods of cheap money in this country, notably in the middle nineties of the last century, I do not think that we can trace the history of cheap money policy, in the sense of a forced expansion of credit designed to reduce rates of interest, back earlier than 1932. Until Britain's departure from the gold standard, banking policy had to be directed to safeguarding the gold reserve, while during the period between 1919 and 1925 policy was in general directed towards a return to the gold standard at par. But after 1931 the Bank was released from its preoccupation with foreign exchange rates and its gold stock, and was able to direct its policy in the light of purely internal considerations. On looking back from the standpoint of 1947, we can now see that the cheap money policy, so publicised at the time, was carried out, by present-day standards, with remarkable moderation. The conditions were exactly suitable for it — a low level of business confidence, a high level of unemployment, and virtual insulation from considerations of the effects of the policy on international movements of short-term capital. Yet the policy was enforced for less than a year, from the spring of 1932 to the beginning of 1933. During this period, the banking figures present a classical example of the sequence of events — the rise in Bankers' Deposits at the Bank of England, the rise in the cash reserves and cash ratios of the clearing banks, the rapid rise in discounts, the rather later and slower rise in investments, partly offset by a fall in advances, and the net rise in deposits. Between March 1932 and March 1933 the total of deposits rose by nearly £250 millions, while the ratio of average bank deposits to national income rose from 50 per cent in 1931 to 54 per cent in 1932 and 1933. As a result of this re-inforcement of the natural tendency towards lower interest rates, together with an intensive propaganda campaign and a temporary suspension of new capital issues, some £2000 millions of 5 per cent War Loan was successfully con-verted to a 3½ per cent basis. But thereafter, in a situation in which it may be doubted if the present Chancellor of the Exchequer would have been content to hold his hand at any level above 2 per cent for long-dated securities, the Government of the day was content to follow a very con-servative policy. Although between 1932 and the spring of 1938 the authorities increased their gold holdings by some 90 million ounces, worth, at 1938 prices, well over £600 millions, the greater part of the gain was sterilised in the Exchange Equalisation Account, and the assets of the Bank of England were allowed to rise by only about £170 millions. The greater part of this went to expand the note circulation, in response to the demands of an ex-panding national income, and after the end of 1932 Bankers' Deposits at the Bank of England rose hardly at all. Clearing bank deposits rose less in the five years to 1938 than they had in the preceding twelve months, and it may be doubted if such increase as did occur was more than adequate to provide for the increase in foreign-owned deposits. Long-term interest rates continued to fall slowly until 1935, but the decline was probably no greater than can be ascribed to the natural consequences of the depression, and no effort seems to have been made to check the subsequent rise in rates in 1936–38. The gold purchases of the Exchange Account were mainly financed by long-term loans, with the result that, when gold flowed out in 1934 and 1938 and the Exchange Account took up bills with the proceeds, there were acute bill famines in the market in the springs of 1935 and 1939, to the great discomfort of the banks and the discount market.

The cheap money policy again became important during the war of 1939–45 — the first war on record financed without a rise in interest rates. This was partly because a much larger proportion of the cost was paid for out of taxation than in 1914–18 — over 50 per cent as compared with under 30 per cent — and partly as a result of the help received from overseas in the form of Lend-Lease and the accumulation of sterling balances; but even after allowing for these forms of finance, it is clear that the Government was able to reconcile a position of very high employment with low interest rates only by means of the development of a very elaborate system of controls over the transfer and expenditure of money. It was thus able to prevent a potentially inflationary situation from getting out of hand, and to prevent prices from rising as much as in 1914–18, when the interest rate was so much higher.

The system of controls comprised both financial restrictions on the export and borrowing of capital, and physical controls on the sale and purchase of goods and services, including price controls, rationing, the allocation of materials, the licensing of new construction or repairs, the control of engagements, and the direction of labour. By means of these controls money was robbed of much of its function, and people were prevented from spending more than a part of the money they received as income. They were encouraged to lend the balance back to the Government, but if they preferred to hoard it, it did not really matter, for then the Government could create additional money by borrowing from the banks without causing inflation. On the side of technique, the Government facilitated the business of borrowing from the banks by introducing Treasury Deposit Receipts, which were, to all intents and purposes, compulsory loans from the banks at very low rates of interest and in a form a good deal less liquid than Treasury bills. By these means the Government was able to keep the long-term rate of interest, throughout all but a few months early in the war, at a level well below that of 1937–38, and only slightly above that of 1934–36.

In applying this technique of keeping interest rates low by paying people in money of which they can spend only a part there are two important difficulties. One of these is the danger of evasion, either by breaking the law by buying and selling at levels above the official price — in other words, the problem of the black market — or by extending activities outside its scope. The other is the danger that people will get tired of working to earn money they are unable to spend on buying what they want — that is to say, the problem of incentive. In war-time the urgency of the common danger and the patriotic incentive both to work and to honesty help to keep these dangers in check ; and in war-time the public will put up with many restrictions on their liberty that they will not tolerate in peace-time. With the coming of peace these conditions cease to apply, and the difficulties of reconciling a very low rate of interest both with full employment and with an absence of inflation are greatly increased.

In spite of the greatly increased difficulties, however, the Chancellor of the Exchequer resolutely pursued a policy of still cheaper money. He used two principal methods, the monetary and the psychological. On the monetary side, between January 1946 and January 1947 the deposits of the eleven clearing banks were made to rise by almost exactly £900 millions, from £4729 millions to £5629

millions, or at more than twice the average war-time rate
of expansion. That this expansion was forced on the
country, in excess of the requirements even of the rapidly
expanding national money income, is suggested by the
rise in the ratio of deposits of nine clearing banks to the
national income to over 60 per cent in 1946 and probably
65 per cent in 1947 — or far above the level reached in the
expansion of 1932 under very different conditions of trade
activity.

On the psychological side, the measures taken consisted
mainly of promises (or threats) of a further fall in interest
rates in the near future, thus stampeding speculators,
anxious for quick capital gains, into further purchases of
existing securities. The rise in the price of these was
quickly followed by an issue of new securities carrying
(except for one miscalculation in May 1946) a rate of interest
low enough to consolidate the preceding rise in security
prices. In this way the yield on irredeemable Consols
was brought down from about $2\frac{7}{8}$ per cent in August 1945
to just over $2\frac{1}{2}$ per cent in January 1947. So long as the
Chancellor was prepared to borrow from the banks at
$\frac{1}{2}$ per cent or $\frac{5}{8}$ per cent any money he could not borrow
from the public on the terms he offered, he could continue
to force the pace. But it took a credit expansion of £900
millions to bring the rate down by under $\frac{1}{2}$ per cent, to
$2\frac{1}{2}$ per cent. What degree of further expansion might it
not have required to bring it down from $2\frac{1}{2}$ per cent to
$2\frac{1}{4}$ per cent ?

Meanwhile we must take stock of the gains and disadvantages of this policy. In the first place, it has, of
course, saved the Treasury a certain amount of money for
interest. But the savings on the cost of long-term loans
in the first years of lower interest rates are comparatively
small, unless, as in 1932, there is a conversion operation
of unusual magnitude. It is stated that the saving on
interest on long-term loans in 1945 and 1946 was £6·4

millions gross, or, say, £3 millions after payment of income tax and surtax. If we compare this saving with the profits made from capital appreciation during the year by holders of securities with many years still to run, I think we shall agree that if Dr. Dalton was the rentier's enemy, he was much more the speculator's friend. A second advantage, at least from the point of view of the present Government, is that a permanent excess of demand over supply, held at bay by rationing and price control, is a considerable guarantee against any future outbreak of unemployment due to lack of demand, for any temporary falling-off in demand can be quickly restored by a relaxation of the controls. And a third advantage, again especially from the point of view of the present Government, is that the present system incidentally provides for a much more equal distribution of real income than is easily obtained under a price system ; for the maximum allowable consumption of many commodities is within the reach of most money incomes, and the additional money incomes of the better-off section of the population have only a limited use.

Against these advantages we must set the difficulties caused by the fact that there is too much money in the system and we have the phenomenon of too much money chasing too few goods. The ideal solution would be a large and rapid increase in the supply of consumer goods without a corresponding further increase in money incomes. Unfortunately this solution is rendered impossible by the fact that we must devote a much larger proportion of our available resources than before the war to providing goods for export and to internal capital construction and reconstruction. Alternatively we can continue indefinitely the present system of holding the potential inflation in check by means of controls. But it is becoming increasingly clear that the present controls are inadequate for their task. They can probably continue to prevent a dangerously rapid rise in prices, but now that direction of labour has been almost entirely abandoned they are incapable of directing resources into the industries where they are most wanted. Since prices of nearly everything are held below the point which would equate demand with supply, nearly anything can be sold, and consumers have no longer the power they had under the price system of directing resources into the production of the things they want relatively most by making those industries relatively the most profitable. Thus there is to-day no incentive to produce the things the public want more rather than those they want less — to produce sheets rather than lamp-shades. To rely on appeals to industrialists and workers to produce those things which are most needed rather than those which, in our present system of partial controls, pay them best to produce, is like appealing to the better nature of water to make it run uphill. Indeed, as more and more channels of uncontrolled expenditure are opened up by the pressure of the excess money seeking an outlet we may expect to find the maldistribution of resources becoming worse rather than better.

What are the possible cures for this unfortunate state of affairs ? One remedy would be the imposition of wider and more effective controls. If the Government had the legal powers and the political authority, it could direct resources into those channels which it considered most socially desirable, in the same way as we are still directing young men into the armed forces. This method would require a still larger number of civil servants to run the additional controls, thereby reducing still further the number of workers engaged on actual production, and would create a permanent threat to those personal liberties which this country is supposed traditionally to cherish. It may be doubted whether, except for a limited period of the greatest emergency, the country would tolerate in peace-time the stringency of the restrictions which would be required.

The only other possible remedy appears to be the restoration, at least in part, of the functions of the price system in distributing resources in accordance with the demands of consumers, including, of course, the Government. But to remove or relax the controls while the public has more money than it can be allowed to spend in competition with the Government's reconstruction programme would mean opening the gates to inflation. In this country we cannot hope for such a rapid rise in the supply of goods as occurred in the United States, and even there the withdrawal of controls resulted in an undesirably rapid rise in prices of many commodities. This means that, in preparation for such a relaxation of controls, some means must be found for curtailing the public's excess of purchasing power.

One way of doing this would be to reverse the process of credit expansion — to reduce the assets of the Bank of England, cut down the cash reserves of the clearing banks, compel these banks to sell investments and refuse overdrafts, and so reduce the swollen total of bank deposits. Such a policy would force a sharp rise in rates of interest which, if carried far enough, would compel the postponement of many schemes of capital construction and release resources for an increase in the output of consumer goods. It might very well also lead to a financial crisis, a widespread loss of business confidence, and a severe, if temporary, trade depression. At best it would involve delay in the restoration of the country's capital, and at worst a period of serious unemployment. Nevertheless, if there were no other alternative to the conversion of England into a slave state, it might be better to choose an old-fashioned deflation with all its temporary discomfort.

But it seems possible that there is another way out of our difficulties — unpleasant indeed, but preferable to either of the courses we have so far considered. As has been pointed out, our difficulty at the moment is to find

the necessary resources both to satisfy the public's demand
for consumption goods and to fulfil the Government's programme for reconstruction.   Let us suppose, for argument's
sake, that everyone in this country was suddenly smitten
with a desire to save every penny he possibly could — to
restrict expenditure to the absolutely essential and resolutely
to cut out every non-essential comfort or luxury — and to
lend the money so saved to the Government for rebuilding
the country's depleted capital. We should then see a great
fall in the demand for the products of the less essential
consumption goods industries and a release of the resources
employed therein for employment either in the more
essential consumption goods industries or in the industries
making capital goods or goods for export.   Such a rise in
voluntary savings, despite the heroic efforts of the National
Savings movement, is unfortunately in the highest degree
unlikely. But a very similar result might be obtained if
the Government took more of our money away and saved
it for us, by investing it in the production of the extra
capital goods we need to rebuild the country's productive
capacity.   Of course, at the same time the Government
should also cut its own luxury expenditure, and limit its
own payments to those essential to national safety and recovery, however unpopular some of its cuts might be.   If
by means of increased taxation and reduced expenditure
the Government could achieve a Budget surplus of, say,
£500 millions a year, it would go a long way towards bringing the net incomes of the public into line with the available
supply of consumption goods and simultaneously supply a
large part of the capital needed to finance the country's
reconstruction.   At the same time, by relaxing the pressure
of excess purchasing power, it would permit a substantial
diminution of controls, thus setting free for useful work
those, both in Government employment and in industry,
who now have to administer them.

Any increase in the present level of taxation, or even its

maintenance at its present height, will inevitably raise serious difficulties on the side of incentive. Our present system of progressive direct taxation, which taxes income much more heavily at the margin than in the aggregate, can hardly avoid exercising a discouraging effect on the willingness to undertake extra work, though it is open to argument whether to tax away a large part of the extra earnings of extra work is more discouraging than a strict system of rationing, which prevents a man spending his extra earnings on what he wants. Perhaps something might be done to reduce the disincentive effect of direct taxation by a modification of our present system of P.A.Y.E., but a more hopeful line of approach is through indirect taxation. Where, as is frequently the case, the supply of non-essential goods is inadequate to meet the demand at the existing level of prices, the whole of the existing supply would find buyers even if prices were higher. But it would be undesirable to allow the extra price to be passed on to the producers, for this would encourage them to expand the output of non-essentials. If, however, the extra price were taken by the Government by way of purchase tax, demand would be equated with supply, and the Government would be provided with funds to meet its programme of capital construction. For instance, the fact that a new car can be resold at a price well above its original cost shows that all the available supply of new cars could be sold even if purchase tax on them were considerably heavier. It seems likely that the effect on incentive of heavy indirect taxation is much less than that of heavy progressive direct taxation — a man won't work overtime if half the extra he earns is taken from him in income tax, but he will work to earn money to buy tobacco although three-quarters of what he pays for it goes to the Government.

It seems possible that indirect taxation could also be used directly to influence the distribution of resources into channels the Government considers desirable. If high enough purchase taxes were imposed on the products of industries which are thought to be using more than their due share of resources, the resultant rise in selling prices would ultimately check the demand for the product and compel producers to reduce output, thus releasing factors of production for more urgent work. There may be some cases where there are technical difficulties in taxing the product, especially in certain service industries. For such industries the suggestion is made that it might prove easier to tax, not the product, but the resources employed. Thus a firm might be required to pay to the Treasury a certain proportion of its wage bill. This would be a very difficult tax to evade, and since its main object would not be the raising of revenue but the release of resources for more urgent work, the levying of the tax upon the amount paid for the scarce resources employed would be particularly appropriate. Such a form of taxation might be suitable for the football pools and the betting industry.

To sum up, we have four possible ways in which the present situation may develop — open inflation, increased controls, monetary deflation plus higher interest rates, and a reduction in Government expenditure coupled with increased or maintained indirect taxation, leading to a Budget surplus. In the recent Budget there is some indication that the Government is beginning to move in the direction of the last of these courses. Whether it will move fast enough or far enough remains to be seen.

	Bank of England			Nine Clearing Banks							National Money Income		Bank Deposits as % of National Income		Interest Rate	
	Gold, £ Mn.	Note Circulation, £ Mn.	Bankers' Deposits, £ Mn.	Cash £ Mn.	Cash % of Deposits	Discounts, £ Mn.	T.D.R.s, £ Mn.	Advances, £ Mn.	Investments, £ Mn.	Deposits, £ Mn.	Bowley, £ Mn.	White Paper, £ Mn.	Bowley	White Paper	Short (3 months' Bank Bills (% p.a.))	Long (London & Cambridge Index of Yield on Fixed Interest Securities) (1924=100)
Monthly Averages :																
1932, March	121	357	73	170	10·4	215	—	888	266	1639	…	…	…	…	2·6	97
April	121	356	72	171	10·4	238	—	866	272	1643	…	…	…	…	2·4	96
May	123	357	76	176	10·6	245	—	858	284	1661	…	…	…	…	1·6	92
June	134	358	84	188	10·9	276	—	838	324	1727	…	…	…	…	1·1	92
July	137	367	85	187	10·6	316	—	822	333	1765	…	…	…	…	1·0	83
August	139	368	84	188	10·4	373	—	803	348	1813	…	…	…	…	0·7	84
September	139	361	86	190	10·4	390	—	789	367	1826	…	…	…	…	0·7	83
October	139	360	80	189	10·2	389	—	782	396	1853	…	…	…	…	0·8	79
November	139	360	86	190	10·2	389	—	772	409	1859	…	…	…	…	0·8	82
December	130	370	98	202	10·8	406	—	761	455	1944	…	…	…	…	0·9	82
1933, January	121	357	114	210	10·8	429	—	752	455	1943	…	…	…	…	0·9	82
February	132	356	93	205	10·7	384	—	753	480	1917	…	…	…	…	0·9	81
March	164	363	100	203	10·8	346	—	754	492	1886	…	…	…	…	0·7	82
Yearly Averages :																
1931	142	354	65	179	10·4	254	—	904	285	1723	3450	…	50	…	3·5	107
1932	130	360	81	184	10·5	307	—	830	332	1752	3325	…	54	…	1·9	90
1933	176	371	102	208	10·9	352	—	746	519	1914	3550	…	54	…	0·7	81
1934	191	378	102	208	11·3	288	—	740	543	1842	3700	…	50	…	0·8	76
1935	194	394	98	212	10·8	264	—	755	598	1961	3925	…	50	…	0·6	74
1936	227	432	96	217	10·3	312	—	825	598	2104	4150	…	49	…	0·6	73
1937	320	479	97	224	10·6	276	—	910	607	2172	4350	…	50	…	0·6	78
1938	141	485	104	229	10·9	274	—	930	593	2161	4350	4671	50	46	0·6	79
1939	—	507	103	232	10·7	246	—	943	564	2129	…	5037	…	42	1·2	86
1940	—	574	107	254	10·4	357	—	906	621	2377	…	5980	…	40	1·0	82
1941	—	652	118	293	10·5	220	474	815	837	2818	…	6941	…	41	1·0	77
1942	—	807	131	326	10·5	223	614	758	1006	3104	…	7664	…	41	1·0	74
1943	—	966	148	365	10·5	173	961	711	1072	3484	…	8171	…	43	1·0	75
1944	—	1135	176	415	10·5	164	1338	715	1082	3953	…	8366	…	47	1·0	75
1945	—	1284	207	468	10·5	181	1747	753	1072	4461	…	8340	…	53	0·9	74
1946	—	1358	242	499	10·3	443	1436	847	1251	4846	…	7974	…	61	0·5	72

PLANNING AND THE PRICE SYSTEM[1]

I

THE INSTRUMENTS OF PLANNING

IT is the function of every Government to endeavour to arrange its affairs so that its citizens will co-operate with each other to promote the good of the country as defined by the policy of that particular Government. In its efforts to control the actions of its citizens, a Government can proceed in one of two ways : it can use actual force, or it can place before each citizen such alternatives that he will choose to act in the way the Government would wish. The scope of the use of actual force is very limited. It may be possible to prevent a man from committing an undesirable act by imprisoning or executing him ; but it is rarely possible physically to compel him to perform a desirable action. In the vast majority of cases it is necessary to allow the citizen to choose for himself between alternatives, while weighting those alternatives in such a way as to induce him to choose the course which is in conformity with Government policy.

This weighting of alternatives can be done in three ways. It can be done directly by making some courses of action less desirable by attaching punishments to them. We say, in effect, that a man is free to choose whether he will knock down his neighbour or not, but that in making his choice he must reflect that, if he chooses the assault, he is very probably choosing prison as well.

Secondly, choice can be greatly affected by the climate

[1] Originally published in the *Westminster Bank Review*, August 1947.

of public opinion; and, as has been increasingly realised in recent years, public opinion can be greatly influenced, in favourable circumstances, by Government action. Most citizens obey not only the laws but also many conventions of conduct, because to break them would involve a loss of self-respect and of respect from family and friends. Especially in times of heightened social consciousness, such as during a war, and where the choices to be made are simple, such considerations may well be for many people among the strongest determinants of choice.

But there are many choices in life for the making of which neither the law nor public opinion offers normally a convenient or appropriate guide — the choice of the trade a man shall work in, what kinds of goods and how much of each shall be produced, and how they shall be distributed among consumers. For guidance in answering such questions we normally depend upon the third of the three mechanisms for influencing choice — the price system.

When it is working perfectly, the price system is not only a means of sharing the products of industry in such a way that, at any given distribution of income, consumers derive the largest possible benefit from what is actually produced; it also exercises a continual pressure on everyone to produce those things which the community wants more, rather than those things which it wants less. If a young man insists on earning £3 a week painting pictures instead of £6 a week making boots, the price system not only shows that the community wants his boots twice as much as it wants his pictures, but also charges him £3 for every week that he persists in asserting his own wishes against those of the rest of the world. Under an ideally functioning price system it would be difficult, at least when he was engaged in earning his living, to tell the difference between an egotist and a philanthropist, for the egotist would find that he could serve his own interests only by serving those of the community, while the philanthropist would find that he could serve the ends of the community best by maximising his own income. Such a system would achieve that complete identity of private with social objectives which it is the principal function of Government to promote. If it is said of a country that its inhabitants are honest because they find honesty the best policy, it is less a criticism of their morals than a compliment to their laws and institutions.

A price system which would conform even approximately to this ideal is not a spontaneous or accidental growth. Even the imperfect system as we know it, or knew it before the war, is the result of an age-long process of human trial and error; and it seems overwhelmingly probable that work and thought devoted to restoring it and reducing its remaining imperfections are likely to be more rewarding than if used in trying to extend and improve the infinitely clumsier mechanism of direct control, backed by the threats of legal punishment.

No price system can work satisfactorily without the continual care and support of the State. To begin with, for the price system to work at all a certain framework of law and order is necessary; for only if a man can be punished if he endeavours to obtain what he wants by violence or fraud is there any certainty that he will be prepared to submit himself to the guidance of the market. Next in importance, perhaps, comes the provision of a form of money which can retain public confidence, for without suitable money a price system works with difficulty.

Even when these initial conditions are fulfilled, there are several ways in which the emergent price system needs to be modified by Government action if the objective of making private interests coincident with the public good is to be achieved. Perhaps the most important defect, at least in the public mind, of the price system as we have known it in recent years is its liability to suffer from those major fluctuations in general demand which we call the trade cycle; for these give rise to circumstances in which a man, in taking what appear to him to be reasonable steps to safeguard his own interests, may unwittingly help to spread a rising flood of bankruptcy and panic. Up to a few years ago the chief weapon looked to for combating these fluctuations in demand was the rate of interest. Many economists now think that this weapon needs to be supplemented, if not replaced, by appropriate variations in Government taxation and expenditure, probably undertaken by a number of Governments working in co-operation. The practicability and effectiveness of such policies have not yet been fully tested; but in their development and application there is ample scope for study by those who would welcome an opportunity for extending the functions of the State.

A second difficulty likely to emerge in a free price system is the development of monopolies. So long as an adequate degree of competition exists, a producer can increase his income only by increasing his effort or efficiency, and so making available for the community more or better goods and services. But so soon as he, alone or as a member of a group, is able appreciably to affect the price at which he sells his product by altering the amount of his output, he can increase his income, not by producing more, but by producing less. This means that he can make himself better off by making the rest of the community worse off, and his personal interests therefore diverge from those of society. Since this is exactly the sort of development which Governments, by definition, exist to prevent, it is clear that here is a further subject for State intervention. In some cases it may be sufficient merely to revise or repeal such existing laws as tend to promote monopoly; in others it may be possible to encourage alternative sources of supply, or even for the Government itself to undertake competition; there are

D

cases where it may be necessary to pass new laws, or to re-establish old ones, in order to make illegal certain practices in restraint of trade, or to permit those who have suffered from the effects of monopolies to receive legal redress. The difficulties are many, but there can be little doubt that time devoted to the problems of their solution would be well spent.

A third major criticism frequently made of the price system concerns its effect on the distribution of incomes. Since services are rewarded, and the products of industry paid for, in accordance with their value to the community, it is clear that remunerations must vary very widely. It has long been the practice of Governments, by the relief of destitution, to modify this income distribution in such a way as to mitigate the poverty of those whose services are of little or no value to the community, and in recent years the policy of relieving poverty by the redistribution of incomes has been carried to very considerable lengths. Against such a policy no criticism can be raised on purely economic grounds, provided that two conditions are observed. The first is that it does not substantially reduce the incentive to serve the community either of those from whom income is taken or of those to whom it is given ; otherwise the total size of the national income may be seriously diminished, and the policy may finally result merely in the rich — and even, in the long run, the poor — being made poorer, rather than the poor being made richer. The second condition is that, subject to the reservations to be made hereafter, the additions to the incomes of the beneficiaries are made in money and not in kind ; for otherwise the recipients will be prevented from distributing their total incomes over their various wants in the way which will give them what they consider to be the greatest benefit.

Even with a stable economy, an absence of monopoly, and an optimum distribution of income, action is still needed if a price system is to be made to bring a perfect equation of individual benefit with social advantage. One reason for this is that some acts may involve costs to the community which are not borne by the individual performing them. It does not, of course, give grounds for condemning an action to show that it will involve a loss to some person who is not a party to it ; almost every action, for instance, which has the result of reducing a scarcity, tends to reduce the income of someone who stands to benefit from that scarcity. But some actions clearly inflict a cost on the rest of the community as a whole, and these the Government is justified in restricting or preventing, whether, for example, it be the pollution of a river, the spoiling of a view, or the spreading of an infectious disease, provided that intervention does not entail the sacrifice of a benefit to the community greater than the cost which would have been inflicted.

Another reason for Government intervention is that some demands are collective and not individual, and these a system based entirely on individual demands cannot adequately satisfy. The most important of these collective demands — the requirements for law and order, including national defence — must be satisfied if an orderly price system is to exist at all. Other demands usually included under this heading are for facilities used in common, such as roads and lighthouses, and the list may be considerably extended into more debatable types of demand according to the policy of the Government concerned. Such demands the Government has the power to satisfy without direct charge by making use of its right to levy taxation and to spend the proceeds in what it considers to be the general interest. If, however, the process is carried over into the supply of goods and services which could be adequately supplied in response to individual demands expressed through the price system, the community may lose in two ways. On the one hand, the Government's decisions, like those of any group, have to be taken on broad lines in response to the wishes of the majority, and cannot cater as the market can for individual variations in wants ; and, on the other hand, if a very high proportion of the national income is taken in taxation and spent by the Government, it is difficult to devise forms of taxes which are at the same time fair as between individuals with different incomes and yet do not reduce the incentive to work or to take business risks and thus impair the national income as a whole.

It is very largely this difficulty of imposing extremely heavy taxation without destroying the incentives to work and enterprise which makes it necessary in a major war to put less reliance on the price incentive and more on legal compulsion and on the appeal to patriotism.   Instead, therefore, of the Government collecting, by taxation, all the money it needs to spend, it is obliged to find some of it by creating and spending money which the recipients are not allowed to spend freely.   Other reasons for partially suspending the operation of the price system during a war are that the violent changes in the direction of demand due to the war would otherwise bring immense windfall profits to people who had done nothing to earn them ; and that the pressures exerted by the normal price system on the dis- tribution of labour and other resources are both too gradual and too permanent for securing the violent but essentially temporary adjustments rendered necessary by war.   But the very reasons that make the price system unsuitable in war make it desirable in peace, when the attributes of gradualness and permanence are of the greatest advantage.

There remains one further problem.   Even if we assume that, by appropriate planning of the price system, we have ensured in times of peace that no citizen can benefit himself without at the same time benefiting the community, does there not remain the possibility that many citizens may be unable to judge what is in their own best interests ?   Must the State not therefore be protected against actions which simultaneously injure their authors and the community ? Certain restrictions on the liberty of the individual to spend his post-tax income as he pleases may well be justified as a means of protecting society from direct dangers — such restrictions, for instance, as those on the purchase of fire-arms and poisons. Further, the provisions of free or subsidised goods and services to children — education, school meals, etc. — may be justified on the pleas that the children are not yet old enough to decide for themselves, and, more questionably, that the State is a better judge of what is good for them than their parents are. But to supplement the incomes of the poor by the provision free or at subsidised prices of goods and services, instead of giving them the equivalent additions to their incomes in cash and allowing them to spend it on what they want most, is to treat the poorer citizens of the country as children, not yet responsible for their own choice. It may well be that no human being is fit to be regarded as completely adult. But the personnel of Governments and Government departments are also human beings ; and for some to claim that they are sufficiently adult to decide what is good not only for themselves but for others, while the poorer members of the community are not permitted to decide what is good even for themselves, seems to constitute a degree of intellectual arrogance for which it would be difficult to find moral justification.

II

Planning in Britain To-day

We thus have three types of incentive through which the Government can operate in order to induce its citizens to act together for the common good : the incentive of the law, backed by the sanction of punishment ; the incentive of the social conscience, backed by the pressure of public opinion ; and the incentive of the market, backed by the pressure of the price system. All three are dependent on the care and vigilance of the Government for their success-ful functioning; and perhaps the most important single condition for their combined success is that they should all operate in the same direction. What is to the benefit of society (as envisaged by Government policy) should be at once legal, supported by public opinion, and the most profitable course open to the individual. Much, perhaps most, of the friction and frustration in the present working of the economic system of this country is due to the fact that, while all three types of incentive continue to operate, they have been allowed to get into a position where they are frequently pulling in opposite directions. Profitable transactions, which before the war would have been both legal and generally regarded as socially desirable, are now often contrary to the law, and those taking part in them may be punished by fine or imprisonment; while many of those which are still allowed can be carried out only after long and difficult negotiations, often with several separate and imperfectly co-ordinated Government depart-ments. The difficulty of carrying official policies into effect in the face of this conflict of incentives is increas-ing as war-time powers of legal compulsion, especially the power to direct labour, are abandoned in deference to public opinion. Great efforts are therefore made to in-crease the moral sanctions, and Ministers of the Crown broadcast appeals to the public not to do the work which offers them the highest remuneration but to undertake that which will render the greatest service to the com-munity. In spite of such appeals, it is to be feared that the moral sanctions, which played so essential a part in achieving victory in war, are in peace weakening under pressure of the conflict of incentives, and that much courage and initiative, faced with the blocking both of its war-time and of its normal peace-time outlets, is either running to waste or is finding for itself channels which

are outside the law. If ever the time comes when the incentives both of the market and of public opinion become
united against the law, it is to be feared that there may
ensue a collapse of the authority of the Government in the
economic sphere such as has been seen in so many other
countries.

What is the reason for this self-confessed failure of the
Government so to control the price system that it pulls
with Government policy instead of *against* it ? The main,
and probably the only essential reason, is the condition of
suppressed inflation which developed in this country
during the war, and which still, after nearly two years of
peace, shows little or no sign of diminution. The necessity
for keeping the potential inflation under control makes it
impossible for the Government to allow the price system
to be used as an indication of social priorities, since if, at
existing prices, the population were allowed to spend their
money as they would wish, the volume of demand for
many types of goods would be very greatly in excess of the
supply available for domestic consumption, after meeting
the needs of both the capital construction and export
programmes. The plenitude of money is reconciled with
the shortage of goods at existing prices only by a whole
series of controls over the amount of goods which may be
bought and over the prices at which they may be sold.
But these controls, in the absence of the power to direct
labour, cannot be made effective over the whole economic
field, so that there is a tendency for the shortage of those
goods which can be effectively controlled to be made
permanent. This vicious circle may be illustrated by a
simple example, taken from experience abroad : bread is in
short supply ; it is therefore rationed and its price is controlled. But the effective control does not extend to the
prices of meat and dairy products. It therefore pays farmers
better to feed their wheat to animals than to sell it for bread,
and the shortage of bread is maintained and intensified.

The corresponding process in this country is essentially similar, though more complicated. Because the public gets its necessaries cheaply, it has more money to spare for expenditure on less essential requirements; also, because prices of non-essentials are less effectively controlled than are those of necessaries, resources, especially labour, can easily be attracted into their production. Thus the price system is falsified into making it appear that the public wants, say, more lamp-shades or football pools rather than more clothes, although under a free price system clothes might be the more profitable to produce. This kind of economic waste will tend to increase more and more as the flood of surplus money tends to seep round the ends of the price controls which have been erected to keep it in check. There are only two possible remedies. Either the controls must be greatly strengthened and extended, or the price system must be re-converted into a true indicator of the relative urgencies of the country's needs.

In point of fact there is no real choice. No really large-scale extension of controls is now practicable, both because a revival of labour control would be unacceptable to public opinion, and because the recruitment of the great new Government staffs needed to administer them would still further reduce the already inadequate supply of labour available for production. There remains only the possibility of a restoration of the price system.

To permit the withdrawal of enough of the existing quantitative controls to permit *price* to resume its function as a guide to economic action, it will be necessary to bring the value of goods and services available for sale and the amount of money available for buying them into approximate equality with each other. There are a few people who would rate the loss of output due to the frustration of conflicting incentives so high that they would be prepared to sweep away the controls and trust to the consequent rise in output to restore equilibrium before the initial rise in prices got out of hand. For most people the risk of generating a rising spiral of prices, profits, and wages, leading to open inflation, would forbid so bold a course. There is no doubt, however, that such a removal of controls would be possible without generating inflation if it were accompanied by a sufficiently large reduction in the quantity of money and bank deposits in circulation, initiated by a reduction in the assets and liabilities of the Bank of England. But such a policy would result in a rise in interest rates to levels at least comparable with those reached after the war of 1914–18, when the price of Consols fell to 42 ; it would acutely embarrass the Government's financial arrangements ; and it might easily lead to a major financial crisis and severe, if temporary, unemployment. Further, it would almost certainly achieve the desired balance between demand and supply at existing prices only by compelling the postponement of many of the plans which the Government holds necessary for the rehabilitation of the country's productive efficiency.

If this were the only way in which the deadening effect of conflicting incentives could be removed, it would almost certainly be worth paying even this price for the relief. But there is another possible policy which, while unpleasant enough, seems to be far less objectionable. The ultimate purpose of monetary deflation is to prevent a rise in prices by means of a reduction in purchasing power. But it is also possible to act on purchasing power directly — through taxation. If direct taxation could be increased sufficiently to reduce spendable incomes to the level of the value of the goods and services available, the controls could be removed without inflation. But very high levels of extremely progressive direct taxation, which tax the rewards of extra work much more heavily than income as a whole, have a very adverse effect on output, an effect which might go far towards offsetting the benefits of the removal of the controls. There is, however, another way of achieving the same result. If prices, by a reduction of subsidies and the imposition of additional purchase taxes, were allowed to rise to the point where supply and demand were in equilibrium, there would be additional payments by consumers but no additional receipts by producers, and therefore no risk of a cumulative inflation when the controls were removed. The resulting Budget surplus would enable the Government to finance most of its own capital construction out of current income, and might even enable it to repay some of its existing debt, thus keeping interest rates low and placing resources for capital reconstruction at the service of private industry.

The immediate effect of such a policy would be that, as more money would be needed to pay for essentials, less would be available to spend on non-essentials. As the demand for the latter fell off, resources would be released for the more essential industries, including those engaged on exports and capital construction. As production in the more essential consumer goods industries increased, the tax on their products could be progressively reduced to enable the extra output to be taken up, while the increase in general productivity, both as a result of the release of man-power employed — inside and outside Government service — on working the controls, and of the increase in energy and initiative generated in a free system, would in course of time allow the whole level of taxation to be progressively reduced. If at any time it seemed that demand in the system as a whole was falling short of supply, it might be possible for the Government to check the threatened decline in activity simply by reducing taxation and the size of its Budget surplus ; it is indeed possible to imagine a system kept in equilibrium not by alternating Budget surpluses and deficits, but by varying the size of a continuing Budget surplus.

Such a policy would go far towards solving not merely our internal problems, but also our pressing current anxiety about our adverse balance of international payments. Even though few consumption goods now being imported fall into the non-essential class, it is inevitable that some imported raw materials should, directly or indirectly, be going into less essential uses, and the reduced demand for non-essentials would therefore have some effect on imports. Probably a more important result would be the reduced demand for the home market's share of the products of certain export industries, and the release of resources from less essential production for re-employment on exports. Thus it would be both possible and relatively more profitable for exports to be expanded. It would probably not be going too far to say that our balance of payments problem is in no small degree a by-product of our internal inflation, and would largely disappear with it.

It should be emphasised that such a policy of reductions in subsidies, increased indirect taxation, and Budget surpluses would do nothing to increase the absolute scarcities in this country — rather would it, in course of time, very greatly help to relieve them. The only logical objection to it is that it would tend to redistribute real income in favour of those who have at present a large margin of unspent income, or, more probably, of capital they are prepared to spend. It is certainly true that, to the section of the community which even at subsidised prices can afford only the bare necessities of life, a rise in the price of necessaries, even if only temporary, would mean very real hardship. It is hardly likely, however, that this section is very large, for most wages have risen since before the war by a good deal more than the cost of living. It would therefore be possible to add to the money incomes of the poorest class sufficient to maintain their standard of living at its existing level at a cost to the Exchequer of only a fraction of the saving in subsidies and the yield of the new taxes. An extension of the present children's allowance to the first child (together perhaps with temporary increases

in the general level of the children's allowance, and of old
age and some other pensions) might be a suitable way of
augmenting the incomes of those who would feel the rise
in prices of necessaries most severely.

At the other end of the scale, the fact that the increased
purchase taxes would be progressively reduced, and that
prices could therefore be expected to fall after the initial
rise, might deter people from spending capital, at any rate
on durable goods. It must also be borne in mind that the
Government, rendered largely independent of the capital
market by its Budget surplus, might be prepared to see
some fall in the prices of securities if the owners attempted
to sell them on any substantial scale in order to consume
the proceeds. Such a fall in values would probably constitute a considerable deterrent to capital consumption, for it
is one thing to spend the proceeds of capital appreciation
while interest rates are falling, and quite another to force
sales of securities on a falling market in order to spend
more of an already dwindling capital value. There remains
to be considered the possibility of some form of capital tax
as a deterrent. Such a tax would be difficult to devise so
that it would achieve its object of discouraging capital consumption while being equitable in its operation. But if
some such measure were the political price to be paid for
restoring the price system to its rightful position as the
principal mechanism for bringing private interest into
conformity with public good, it would be a price which
even to those most affected by it would be very well worth
paying.

If the foregoing analysis has any validity, it would
appear that the popular antithesis between planning and
the absence of planning is essentially unreal. The true
choice is not between plan and no plan, but between
planning through the price system and planning against it.
It is contended that a continuation of the present system of
reciprocally conflicting incentives is necessarily wasteful of

effort and destructive of initiative ; and that only by making the effort necessary to overcome the difficulties which hinder us from bringing the price system back into conformity both with the law and with the social conscience, can the country be saved from frustration, poverty, and perhaps disaster.

SAVINGS AND INVESTMENT[1]

In recent discussions about the appropriate level of investment in this country, the case for the view that our investment programmes during the past two years have been excessive is based mainly on two arguments. The first of these is that, by attempting to do more than our available resources permitted, we have both wasted much of our effort and diverted resources away from the exports which we must make if we are to pay our way; and the second is that many of the investments which we have made and are making are of a type which is not essential for national recovery and which could well wait for less difficult times. But these arguments, while containing much truth, fall short of proving that by any absolute standard our investments have been excessive. The resources available for investment are not immutably fixed, but depend in the short run largely, and in the long run wholly, upon the proportion of our total resources which we are prepared to spare from the provision of consumption goods and services. It is not excessive investment alone which causes frustration of effort and checks exports, but an excessive total of investment plus consumption. A large investment programme cannot by itself lead us into serious difficulties unless we fail to match it by correspondingly large savings.

Nor does the fact that our resources available for investment are being distributed among the various needs with less than the optimum of wisdom prove that investment is too large in aggregate; for while many less urgent needs

[1] Originally published in the *Westminster Bank Review*, November 1948.

are no doubt being given an undeserved priority, this is possible merely because more urgent needs are being neglected. The case for a redistribution of our investments is quite separate from the case for curtailing their total amount.

Where then can we look for some objective criterion of the amount of investment we should attempt, provided that we can see our way to accompanying it with a corresponding amount of saving ? I think we can find it in the magnitude of the task which faces us in making good the loss of capital we suffered during the war. Even before the war our rate of national saving, at little over 5 per cent of the national income, was not high, and of this probably well over half was being used during the 1930's to finance the building of new dwelling-houses. Thus the rate at which our industrial equipment was being improved and extended was low, and already in 1939 many firms were less adequately equipped than their competitors abroad. This disadvantage has been greatly increased by our war losses. After allowing for the peace-time value of stores originally created for war purposes, I should put our loss of capital between 1939 and 1945 at not less than £9000 millions at 1948 prices, or perhaps a fifth of the capital we owned in 1939. Of this loss, some £2000 millions was due to unrepaired damage caused by enemy action ; £3000 millions to wear and tear of fixed capital not made good, plus any diminution in stocks of materials and finished goods ; and £4000 millions to the reduction in our foreign assets and the increase in our foreign liabilities. No doubt the bulk of our losses abroad, and some part of our losses at home, while reducing our standard of living, have had no direct effect on our industrial efficiency. But a very large part of our losses at home is due to damage to, or the inadequate maintenance of, our industrial and commercial assets, and, until at least these losses are made good, we shall inevitably be at a great disadvantage in competition with other countries which were able not only to maintain but to increase their capital during the war.

An attempt to estimate how much of our loss of capital we have made good since the war must start from the official estimates of gross capital creation at home made in the White Paper on National Income and Expenditure in 1947 (Cmd. 7371). These estimates are obtained by difference, and are thus exceedingly rough; but they are all that are available, and we must do our best with their assistance. To obtain from them estimates of how much of our capital losses we have really made good we have to make three adjustments. First, we must deduct the cost of making good current wear and tear on fixed assets. In the official estimates of net capital creation, allowance for this cost is based on the amounts allowed for depreciation by the Inland Revenue authorities. These are calculated with reference to the amounts needed to replace the original money cost of the fixed assets concerned, and make no pretence at any close correspondence with the actual cost incurred in making good current wear and tear. In times of rising prices, the depreciation allowances so calculated will fall short of the cost of replacing the fixed assets as they wear out. From the aggregate national point of view (though not necessarily from that of the individual firm) the official allowance is made more adequate by the provision in the 1945 Budget which allows new equipment to be depreciated by 20 per cent in the first year of its life. But, even with this concession, the total allowance of £725 millions in 1946 and £775 millions in 1947 is clearly inadequate. The Economic Survey for 1948 placed the true figure at the end of 1947 at about £900 millions, in which case we cannot put the true cost of making good current wear and tear of fixed assets at less than £800 millions in 1946 and £875 millions in 1947. Some observers would consider these figures to be under-estimates.

The second deduction which we have to make from

gross capital creation is one which does not appear in the official estimates at all, and of which, indeed, the importance seems hitherto to have been largely overlooked. The total of gross capital creation contains the whole of the increase in the values of stocks of goods and of work in progress as shown in the books of business firms — in fact, of what in the United States are termed " inventories ". An increase in the book values of these can be divided into two parts, of which one is due to an increase in quantity and the other to an increase in price of an unchanged quantity. As we are here concerned with estimating how far our physical loss of capital has been made good, we must exclude any part of gross capital creation which does not represent an increase in the physical quantity of capital, and we must therefore exclude any increase in the money value of stocks which merely represents part of the cost of keeping existing stocks physically intact. Unfortunately it is not easy to make any estimate of how much we should deduct from gross capital formation under this head, largely because there seems to be no estimate for any recent year of the magnitude of total British inventories. Any guess made here must therefore be of the roughest kind. But on any reasonable assumptions about rates of turnover, the total value of inventories in this country can hardly have been less than £1000 millions at the end of 1945, £1200 millions at the end of 1946, and £1500 millions at the end of 1947. Now the Board of Trade's index of prices of industrial materials and manufactures rose by about 8 per cent during 1946 and by 15 per cent during 1947. If we apply these price increases to the totals of the inventories held, with appropriate time-lags, we find that the increase in their values due solely to rising prices must have been nearly £100 millions in 1946 and nearly £200 millions in 1947. If we add this cost of maintaining circulating capital intact to the cost of maintaining fixed capital intact, we get total deductions from gross capital creation

E

of £900 millions in 1946 and £1075 millions in 1947.   This gives us an estimate of net capital creation at home.

To obtain an estimate of total net capital creation, both at home and abroad, we now have to make a third deduction.   In addition to our capital at home, we have both assets and liabilities abroad.   Any decrease in our foreign assets, or increase in our foreign liabilities, reduces our total national capital.   The size of the net fall in our capital abroad is measured by our adverse net balance of international payments on income account for the period. In 1946 our adverse balance was £370 millions and in 1947 £630 millions, and these amounts have also to be deducted from our gross capital creation at home.   Thus the total deductions from gross capital creation, which have to be made in order to arrive at estimates of our net total capital creation, amount to £1270 millions for 1946 and £1705 millions for 1947.   These are minimum figures.   Further investigation might put them considerably higher.

We are now in a position to begin to assess our achievements since the war in the way of restoring our lost capital. The gross amounts invested, the deductions which must be made from these to obtain estimates of net investment, and the savings by means of which the net investment was financed, are set out in the table on page 58.   Reference should be made to this throughout the remainder of the article.

Gross capital creation is officially estimated at £1255 millions in 1946 and £2020 millions in 1947, or about 16 per cent and 24 per cent of the national income respectively.   Since the corresponding proportion in 1938 was only just over 16 per cent, these totals could in themselves be regarded as reasonably satisfactory.   Even after making the necessary deductions to obtain estimates of true net capital creation *at home*, the results are still reasonably commensurate with the needs of our situation — £355 millions (or 4½ per cent of the national income) in 1946 and £945 millions (or 11 per cent) in 1947, as compared with £320 millions (or 7 per cent) in 1938. But when we look at the estimates of total net capital creation, *at home and abroad*, we find that the progress made has been almost disastrously small ; for in 1946 the whole of our net increase of capital at home was more than offset by the increase in our foreign liabilities, while in 1947 two-thirds of the larger gain at home was lost abroad. The overall net increase in the national capital for the two years together was thus only £300 millions, or one-thirtieth of our war-time losses. In the light of these figures, it seems difficult to maintain the view that the country's investments in these years were in total too great for the needs of our position. If we have relied too much on help from abroad, the blame must surely lie, not with the amount of our investments, but with our unwillingness or inability to save enough towards financing them out of our own resources.

[TABLE

SAVINGS AND INVESTMENT IN THE UNITED KINGDOM

	1938		1946		1947		Plans for 1948	
	£ Mn.	% of National Income	£ Mn.	% of National Income	£ Mn.	% of National Income	£ Mn.	% of National Income
INVESTMENT								
Gross capital creation at home	770	16·4	1255	15·9	2020	23·8	1900	20·6
Less current wear and tear on fixed assets	450	9·6	800	10·1	875	10·3	925	10·0
Apparent net capital creation at home	320	6·8	455	5·8	1145	13·5	975	10·6
Less rise in value of circulating assets due to increased prices	..	..	100	1·3	200	2·4	200 (?)	2·2
True net capital creation at home	320	6·8	355	4·5	945	11·1	775	8·4
Less adverse balance of payments on income account	70	1·5	370	4·7	630	7·4	250	2·7
NET NATIONAL INVESTMENT AT HOME AND ABROAD	250	5·3	-15	-0·2	315	3·7	525	5·7
SAVINGS								
Savings of Public Authorities	-164	-3·5	-1050	-13·3	-550	-6·5	300	3·2
Business savings	170	3·6	175	2·2	170	2·0	200	2·2
Personal savings	244	5·2	860	10·9	695	8·2	(25)	(0·3)
TOTAL NATIONAL SAVINGS	250	5·3	-15	-0·2	315	3·7	525	5·7

Let us now turn to an examination of the causes of this inadequate rate of national savings. The sources of savings may be classified under three headings. First, there are the savings, positive or negative, of the public authorities, including the Central Government, the local authorities, and the social security funds. The calculation of what, from the national point of view, can be counted as the genuine savings of the Central Government is rendered difficult by the way its accounts are conventionally presented. To get a true picture we must deduct from the published figures of revenue, not only the semi-fictitious items which represent merely the cancellation of old debts, but also all Government income which is not derived from the current incomes of the taxpayers. Any payments made to the Government out of the payer's capital are really being made out of someone else's current savings. Thus, for instance, when the executors of a deceased estate realise securities in order to pay death duties, the securities they sell may be bought by someone who is investing his own or (like the life insurance offices) someone else's current savings. If the buyer is merely reinvesting the proceeds of securities he has previously sold, then these in turn may have been paid for out of current savings. Thus, whether at first or second or tenth hand, it is somebody's current savings which come into the possession of the executors and are by them paid over to the Government; and if the Government spends them as income, it is spending someone's savings and preventing them from being available for the finance of capital construction. We must therefore deduct from the published figures of Government revenue not only most of Miscellaneous Receipts and Surplus Receipts from Trading, but also nearly the whole of Death Duties and of the new Special Contribution, a large part of Stamp Duties, the whole of the proceeds of the sale of Surplus War Stores, and, to be logical, all taxes paid out of net reductions in Tax Reserves and those paid on that part of apparent business profits which is due merely to the under-depreciation of fixed assets or the increase in the price of circulating assets.[1] On the other hand, we can also deduct from current expenditure certain items which represent permanent additions to the country's assets or reductions in its liabilities.

The second source of savings consists of the additions to the free reserves of business concerns. The estimates for these for 1946 and 1947, as given in the table, are a good deal smaller than those made in the National Income White Paper — £175 millions as against £260 millions in 1946, and £170 millions as against £320 millions in 1947. The reason for these differences is that we have already increased the White Paper's allowance for the depreciation of fixed assets from £725 millions to £800 millions in 1946, and from £775 millions to £875 millions in 1947, and have made entirely new allowances of £100 millions in 1946 and £200 millions in 1947 for the money cost of maintaining circulating assets physically intact. Thus the estimates of business profits have been reduced, as compared with those of the White Paper, by £175 millions in 1946 and by £300 millions in 1947. But of the fictitious profits thus eliminated the Government has taken approximately half in income tax and profits tax. We have therefore deducted only £85 millions in 1946 and £150 millions in 1947 from the White Paper's estimates of business saving. The remainder has been allowed for in the estimates of Government saving.

The third source of savings, personal savings, is a residual item, and amounts to whatever part of net capital

---

[1] For a full discussion of the principles involved and the methods used see " The Budget and the National Income, 1948–49 ", by R. C. Tress (*London and Cambridge Economic Service Bulletin*, May 1948). I have followed Mr. Tress's methods entirely, except that I have deducted payments out of tax reserves from Government savings instead of from private savings, have used higher figures for depreciation allowances on fixed assets, and have allowed for the effects of price increases on the value of circulating assets.

creation, at home and abroad, is not covered by Government savings plus business savings. From one point of view it can be regarded as a residual item in fact as well as in method of estimation, for if at any time the total of net capital creation is expanded without a corresponding expansion in other forms of saving, it is personal saving which is forced to expand to fill the gap. This forced saving is brought about by the inflationary pressure induced by the attempt to invest more than the country is saving. If the inflation is an open one, the diversion of resources to producing capital goods and the consequent shortage of consumer goods causes prices to rise, and any consumer whose money income rises more slowly than prices is deprived of part of his purchasing power and compelled to reduce his consumption. In a controlled inflation, on the other hand, although the supply of consumption goods is inadequate to meet the demand, their prices are not allowed to rise, and consumers, finding themselves unable to buy some of the goods they want at any price, are thus compelled, against their wills, to save part of their incomes.

This is the reason why personal savings (before payment of death duties, etc.) continued to constitute a much larger proportion of national income in 1946 and 1947 than they had done in 1938, in spite of the fact that, without the inflationary pressure, people would almost certainly have saved a smaller proportion of their incomes than before the war. There are several reasons why people should wish to save less now than in former decades. There has been a great redistribution of real incomes, after tax, in favour of the lower income groups, thus reducing the ability of the higher income groups to save; the assistance given to the lower income groups has largely taken the form of providing various forms of social security, thus reducing their incentive to save as much as before as a reserve against contingencies; the under-maintenance during the war of personal stocks of durable consumer goods makes their replenishment often a first charge on such savings as are made; and many people still have war-time savings in liquid form which they are tempted to spend as much-wanted goods become available. Thus the whole tendency of developments since 1938 has been to reduce the natural tendency to save.

This phenomenon of forced saving through inflation, open or controlled, is a commonplace of all wars and post-war booms. It occurred during and after the War of 1914–18. But what differentiates the experience of 1946–47 from that of 1919–20 is that, whereas in the earlier period the bulk of the forced saving was made available for the re-equipment of industry, in 1946 and 1947 it was almost wholly absorbed in financing the continued Government deficits. The true deficits of the public authorities, adjusted in the way described above, I should put at about £1050 millions in 1946 and about £550 millions in 1947, thus absorbing more than the whole of the £175 millions of business saving and the £860 millions of personal saving in 1946, and leaving a margin of only £315 millions over the £170 millions of business saving and £695 millions of personal saving in 1947. It is to this continued high level of capital consumption by the Government that our inability to finance our capital reconstruction out of our own resources, and our need to borrow so heavily abroad, must be mainly attributed.

It was, of course, theoretically possible that with sufficiently comprehensive and efficient controls on consumption the Government might have been able to generate sufficient forced saving to finance both the capital creation programme and its own capital consumption. But with the end of the war some controls, especially those over the distribution of labour, had to be relaxed, and the remainder proved to be inadequate for the control of the use of resources released from fighting the war. The result was that too large a proportion of these resources was diverted to satisfying consumption demands, especially for the less essential goods and services over which the control was least effective, and too small a proportion was made available for the export and capital goods industries. Consequently, the level of personal saving, high as it was, was inadequate to meet the double burden of financing both Government dis-saving and the capital creation programme, and a wide gap opened up between net national saving and the planned level of investment. Some part of this gap was no doubt closed by the frustration of investment plans, though this too often resulted merely in the tying-up of resources in uncompleted and temporarily useless projects. The remainder was filled by the foreign borrowing necessitated by the inadequate rate of expansion of exports.

By the third quarter of 1947 it had become apparent that the policy of forced saving through the compulsion of a controlled inflation had broken down, and that if the gap in the balance of payments was to be closed new methods would have to be adopted. Apart from some not very important attempts to strengthen the controls, these measures took the form of a cut in the programme for capital creation, and the conversion of the Budget deficit into a genuine Budget surplus. The first measure proposed to reduce gross capital creation from £2020 millions in 1947 to £1900 millions in 1948. As even the official estimates must have put the allowance for the depreciation of fixed assets at £50 millions more in 1948 than in 1947, this fall of £120 millions in gross capital creation implies a fall of at least £170 millions in net capital creation. The second and more important measure was the emergency Budget of November 1947. This made a really dramatic change, masked though it was by the conventional method of presenting the Government's accounts. The change, which appears to have begun very suddenly at the end of 1947, converted a true Budget deficit of something like £550 millions in the calendar year 1947 to an estimated true surplus of about £300 millions for the calendar year 1948. There was thus on balance to be an increase in Government saving of something like £850 millions, or nearly 10 per cent of the national income.

As against these changes, it was possible to anticipate a fall of about £380 millions in the adverse balance of payments on income account, so that the total planned net investment, at home and abroad, rose by only £210 millions (£380 millions minus £170 millions), from £315 millions in 1947 to £525 millions in 1948. Thus the demands on private saving were planned to fall by £640 millions (£850 millions minus £210 millions). On the assumption that business savings were maintained, or more probably increased as a result of the policy of dividend limitation, the whole of this reduction would fall upon personal savings, which could therefore be reduced almost to nothing without bringing total saving below the level of planned investment.

Now a very substantial fall in personal saving could in any case have been expected. As has been pointed out above, the very high personal savings of 1946 and 1947 were due to the existence of an inflationary pressure which, in combination with the controls on other outlets for expenditure, forced many people to save more than they really wanted to. As soon as the inflationary pressure is reduced in order to prevent money being forced into undesired channels of expenditure, we must expect that some of it will also cease to be forced into saving, and that the effects of the reduced natural propensity to save will become apparent. But was it to be expected that personal saving would really fall almost to nothing ? There are some forms of personal saving which will always rank in priority high among the demands for essential goods. For instance, most modern life assurance policies contain a very large element of saving, and the annual increase in the life funds of the insurance offices is now probably of the order of

£100 millions. Again, the regular payments on the mortgage loans of building societies include a progressively
increasing element of capital repayment and therefore of
saving; I should put this at present at not less than £50
millions a year, in addition to any savings invested in the
shares or deposits of these societies. In addition, there are
savings in contributory pension schemes, and no doubt
many other examples of contractual saving which continue
almost independently of other demands on income, as well
as the large voluntary savings which, partly as a result of
the efforts of the National Savings movement, continue to
be made by many people. If it were indeed true that net
personal savings, before the payment of death duties,
stamp duties on the transfer of property, and the special
contribution, had in fact sunk to zero, it would imply a
truly enormous consumption of capital by the non-saving
members of the community. All things considered, it
seems unlikely that personal savings will in fact fall from
nearly £700 millions in 1947 almost to nothing in 1948;
and it seems likely that the Government's plans, as
embodied in the Budget estimates and in the reduced
programme for capital construction, were based on the
assumption of considerably smaller personal savings than
were in fact likely to be made. A more probable estimate
would have been for a drop in personal savings of perhaps
£400 millions to about £300 millions, a figure representing
a little over 3 per cent of the national income, as compared
with over 5 per cent in 1938.

What was likely to be the effect of this excess of planned
savings over planned investment ? Since actual savings
and investment must be equal, any excess of personal saving
over the estimate would have to be compensated either by
a fall in other forms of saving or by an increase in investment. It is the pressures to bring about such compensating
adjustments which constitute the disinflationary effects of
such an excess of planned saving.

The impact effect of disinflation by means of a Budget surplus comes in a very different place in the economy from that of a disinflation caused by a restriction of credit and a rise in interest rates. Instead of an initial fall in the demand for production goods, we should expect an initial fall in the demand for the less essential types of consumption goods and services. This would at first lead to an increase in investment, owing to the accumulation of unsold stocks, first of finished goods and later of semi-finished goods and raw materials. If this process went far enough, output would be reduced, first in consumption goods industries and later in production goods industries, and unemployment would begin to rise. In present conditions it is unlikely that any great degree of unemployment would develop in production goods industries, for the demand for investment goods is at present being held down by controls at far below its natural level, and it is difficult to envisage so severe a fall in business confidence as to reduce the demand for investment goods below the level now imposed by the controls. Indeed, while profits in some consumer goods industries would fall, profits in capital goods industries would probably tend to improve as a result of the availability of resources released from the consumption goods industries. Any rise in unemployment would therefore be gradual, and would probably not proceed very far before the balance between savings and investment was restored, partly by an expansion of exports and partly by an increase in investment.

Even so, it could have been expected that there would be, at least temporarily, a quite perceptible rise in unemployment, for a proportion of the people released from producing consumption goods would be difficult to re-employ at once either in capital goods industries or on exports. Many observers expected to see quite a substantial rise in unemployment during this year as a result of the combination of a reduced investment programme and the conversion of a large Budget deficit into a surplus. Yet, in fact, up to September, the rise in unemployment was very slight — from 262,000 in September 1947 to 321,000 in September 1948. The figure remains far below what used to be regarded as the minimum attainable in periods of " full employment ", and can be explained only by the maintenance of a large excess demand for labour. What is the reason why the effect of the disinflation, which should have resulted from the excess of planned savings over planned investment, has been so slight ?

The explanation, so far at least, does not seem to lie in any failure of the Government to achieve its planned surplus. It is true that up to the end of September Government expenditure seems to have been slightly above estimate, but this has been offset by a similar increase in the items of genuine revenue with which we are here concerned, so that, whatever may happen later as a result of rearmament, for the first three quarters of the calendar year Government savings seem to have been very close to estimate.

Nor does it seem likely that the minor relaxations that have been made in the controls on personal consumption have had any very marked effect in reducing personal saving below the level it would otherwise have reached. When personal net saving is low, it is less likely that a relaxation of controls will bring more than a very temporary expansion of total consumption expenditure than when saving is high, and more likely that an increase of expenditure on decontrolled goods will be accompanied by a decrease of expenditure on something else. Indeed it is possible that, if all consumption controls were now removed and prices left free to adjust themselves to changes in demand, the general rise in prices might be quite small, though there would be very large changes in the relative prices of different types of goods and services.

A third possible cause for the slightness of the disinflation would have been a fall below the estimate in the

adverse balance of payments on income account. Unfortunately, all the evidence to date shows that it is very
doubtful if our adverse balance for the year can be kept
within the £250 millions originally estimated. If in fact
the adverse balance proves to have exceeded the estimate,
the effect of the change would be to reinforce the tendency
towards disinflation.

There remain only two possible explanations of the
way the savings-investment Budget has been balanced — a
rise in net investment at home or a fall in business savings.
It seems probable that both have occurred. The relaxations
which have already been made in the restrictions on investment in certain types of fixed capital, especially houses,
have probably had some effect. More important may have
been the rise in the volume of stocks. An initial increase
in these is the usual effect of the first impact of reduced
consumption demand, but in normal times this stage is
quickly followed by smaller orders and reduced production.
To-day, however, stocks of many types of finished goods
and components have been extraordinarily low, and many
producers and traders have no doubt welcomed the opportunity to restore them more nearly to normal. Further,
the recent experience of delays to production caused by
the lack of particular items has no doubt encouraged many
firms to increase their stocks to well above the normal level
as an insurance against future shortages. Thus the time-lag
between reduced demand for consumption goods and reduced production has been unusually long. On the whole
this is probably not to be regretted, for while some excessive
stocks may constitute a waste of capital, in general the
increase has served to reduce the risks of those breaks in
production due to shortages of particular components which
are so wasteful of labour and other resources.

As a result of these developments it is very possible
that net capital creation during 1948 has been larger than
anticipated in the original plans. But the increase in the

money figure of gross capital creation is likely to have been a good deal larger still. During the later months of 1947 and the early months of 1948 prices of industrial materials and manufactures were rising with unprecedented rapidity. According to the Board of Trade's index, the rise from December 1946 to June 1947 was 5 per cent; from June to December 1947 it was 9 per cent; and from December 1947 to June 1948 it was 11 per cent. If we allow for the effects of this rise in prices, we can hardly put the cost of making good wear and tear on fixed capital during 1948 at less than £1000 millions, while the amount of extra money-capital needed to maintain inventories intact is put at not less than £160 millions for the first six months of the year alone. Thus during the first half of the year practically the whole of apparent business savings must have been absorbed merely in maintaining physical capital intact, leaving little or nothing with which to finance extensions or improvements. It is no wonder that all available personal savings have been gladly absorbed and that the signs of excess savings have been so small.

Prospects for the near future are conflicting. During 1949 we shall presumably exhaust the proceeds of the sale of the Argentine railways and must expect a considerable reduction in our receipts under the European Recovery Programme. After providing for the necessary repayments of sterling balances and for other exports of capital, we shall have very little foreign aid left with which to cover an adverse balance of payments on current account. Thus we shall have to finance practically the whole of our capital creation at home out of our own resources. At the same time it seems almost certain that the demands of rearmament will bring a substantial increase in Government expenditure and make it much more difficult to provide for an adequate Budget surplus.

On the other hand, it seems likely that a considerable part of the process of replenishing physical stocks has now been completed, and that less capital will be required for this purpose in the future. Further, we have the fact that since June prices of industrial materials and manufactures have ceased to rise and have even fallen slightly. The longer this check to the price rise can be maintained, the less will become the gap between the original and replacement costs of inventories, and the smaller will become the additional amounts of capital that producers and traders will have to tie up in order to maintain their physical quantity intact. If stability of prices could be maintained throughout 1949, the reduction in the absorption of savings required merely to keep circulating capital physically intact would amount to at least £200 millions a year as compared with the first half of 1948, and this would largely compensate for the cessation in the net inflow of capital from abroad. Indeed, it would be true to say that in the first half of 1948 the very rise in prices which made it necessary for us to borrow abroad also made it necessary for us to tie up an almost equivalent amount in financing the rising costs of our circulating assets, so that a cessation of the price rise would enable us to finance an unchanged quantity of net investment without foreign aid. Whether in fact the demands of rearmament will or will not exert a greater upward pressure on world prices than the increase in output from restored farms and mines will exert downwards it is not yet possible to say. All that can be said is that this country's interests are greatly concerned, not only with its terms of trade, but with the course of world prices in general.

Even given stability in world prices, the long-run problem which this country faces in providing for the finance of an adequate volume of home investment is very great indeed. By 1952 we shall be obliged to dispense with foreign aid altogether, while continuing to make an appreciable export of capital in repayment of debt and for the finance of necessary colonial development. This means that we shall have to convert an adverse balance of payments on current account of at least £250 millions in 1948 to a favourable balance of perhaps £100 millions or £150 millions in 1952. If we are to maintain our present rate of net capital creation at home, this will mean a further increase in savings of some £400 millions a year. We may hope that a substantial part of this may be provided by the release of business savings from being absorbed in financing the replacement of stocks at continually rising prices, and perhaps we may also hope that, as the more urgent replacements of personally-owned durable consumption goods are made, private savings may show some increase. But if we are to maintain a net rate of capital creation capable of making good our war-time losses within a reasonable period, we must probably look to Government saving to provide an even larger share than now of the necessary finance. This does not necessarily mean that the country as a whole will be saving more than it would in the absence of any Government intervention, for the low level of personal saving is largely due to the redistribution of incomes which it is Government policy to bring about. What it does mean is that, since a large part of the taxes paid by the rich comes out of what would otherwise have been saved, the Government, if it wishes only to redistribute consumption and not to reduce the aggregate level of national saving, must pass on to the poor only a part of what it collects from the rich, and must itself perform the saving which the rich would otherwise have done. The perpetuation of such a system, under which the Government provides perhaps 40 per cent or more of the savings of the country, will of course raise many new problems. Unless Government expenditure can be drastically curtailed, it will mean the indefinite continuation of very high rates of taxation. Every effort should therefore be made to minimise their adverse effects on incentives to work and enterprise. One measure, which it is hoped will soon be less urgent as regards circulating assets, but will in any case remain

F

important for fixed assets for many years to come, is a change in the method of calculating business profits for purposes of taxation. If business profits were calculated only after making the necessary provision for keeping both fixed and circulating assets *physically* intact, and if businesses were induced to use the same methods in making up their own accounts, a far smaller proportion of apparent business profits would be absorbed in merely maintaining capital intact, a larger proportion would be available for extensions and improvements, and the Government's conventional Budget surplus could safely be correspondingly reduced.

Another problem which will need to be solved is that of securing the investment of Government savings in the most urgent forms of capital investment. A large Budget surplus will provide a standing temptation for a Government to invest too much in its own capital projects, including those of nationalised industries, and to leave too little for private industry. In the rather unlikely event of its resisting this temptation, the Government would have no difficulty in making its savings available for private industry by paying off its own debts. Most people and institutions are holding a far higher proportion of their investments in the form of Government Securities than before the war, and would welcome an opportunity to increase the proportion of industrial securities.

How long it will remain necessary for us to budget for so large an annual surplus it is impossible to say. But it seems likely that we are entering on a long period in which conditions will be the exact opposite of those which ruled in the 1930's. It will be a period when investment requirements will be high and private savings inadequate, so that the system can be kept in equilibrium only by means of large and persistent Budget surpluses, though no doubt it will be found desirable to vary these in size from time to time to meet changing circumstances. It is to be hoped that we shall be able to adjust our ideas to conform with this new situation, even though it will mean that all classes will have to throw off many prejudices derived from the very different conditions of the decade before the war.

THE ECONOMICS OF RENT
RESTRICTION [1]

In view of the important part rent restriction now plays
in the economic systems of many countries, it is remarkable how little attention its economic aspects have attracted.
Apart from the brief though admirable discussion in
Mr. Roy Harrod's *Are These Hardships Necessary?* there is
very little reference to the subject in recent British economic
literature. It is quite understandable that politicians
should have avoided the subject, for the emotions it arouses
are too deep and too widespread to allow it to be discussed
in public with both frankness and safety; but it is a little
surprising that British economists, in the security of their
studies, should have shown so little inclination to follow
up the many interesting questions which the subject
raises.

In the following article, after an outline of the history of
rent restriction and a glance at the legal difficulties of its
enforcement, I approach the subject mainly from two
points of view: the inequity of its results as between
individual tenants and individual landlords, and even
more as between those with houses and those without;
and its economic effects in discouraging the adequate
maintenance of house property and in reducing the
mobility of labour. I shall put forward suggestions for
changes in the law which would, in my opinion, constitute
a great improvement on the existing system from both
points of view, however unlikely it may be that any Party
would find it politically expedient to adopt them.

[1] Originally published in *Lloyds Bank Review*, April 1950

The history of rent restriction in England begins very nearly thirty-five years ago, with the passage of the Increase of Rent and Mortgage Interest (War Restrictions) Act in December 1915. This Act made it generally illegal for landlords of unfurnished houses, or parts of houses let as separate dwellings, of which either the rent charged in August 1914 or the net rateable value did not exceed £35 in London or £26 elsewhere, to charge rents higher than those charged in August 1914, except in so far as improvements had been made or the rates increased. It also prohibited the ejectment of a tenant from a controlled house, except for non-payment of rent or other closely defined cause, or the calling-in of mortgages on rent-restricted property or the raising of interest rates on them. The general principles of this Act have been maintained in all subsequent legislation.

After the 1914–18 War some concessions were made to help the landlord to meet the greatly increased cost of maintenance and repair. In 1919 increases of 10 per cent, and in 1920 of 40 per cent, were permitted in the 1914 " standard rent ", provided that the premises were kept " in a reasonable state of repair ". On the other hand, the scope of the Act was extended in 1919 to cover all houses of which neither the standard rent nor the net rateable value exceeded £70 in London and £52 elsewhere, and in 1920 to £105 in London and £78 elsewhere. Thus all except the largest houses were made subject to control. At the same time, the protection of the Act was extended, not only to the "statutory tenant", but also to his widow or any relative who had been resident in his house for six months or more at the time of his death, though these in turn could not pass on their rights to yet another generation.

In 1923, after the short but violent depression which ended the post-war boom, the first steps were taken towards the withdrawal of rent control. Under the Act of that year, any house of which the landlord obtained vacant possession, or of which the sitting tenant accepted a lease of two years or more, became automatically decontrolled. When, ten years later, the results of the 1923 Act were reviewed, it was considered that, whereas the release of the larger houses had been proceeding too slowly, that of the smaller houses had been too fast. Under the Act of 1933, therefore, controlled houses were divided into three groups. Those of which both the recoverable rent (standard rent plus permitted increase) and the net rateable value were above £45 in London and £35 elsewhere were decontrolled immediately; those below these values, but with a net rateable value of £20 in London and £13 elsewhere, continued to become decontrolled as they fell vacant; and those with still lower rateable values ceased to be decontrollable. In 1938 the second of these groups was in turn subdivided. The upper section, consisting of houses with net rateable values above £35 in London and £20 elsewhere, was decontrolled at once, while the lower section became permanently controlled.

Thus in August 1939 all pre-1914 houses with net rateable values above £35 in London and £20 elsewhere had been excluded from control, together with a substantial though unknown number of smaller houses. The number of these decontrolled houses was estimated by the Ridley Committee in 1945 at 4·5 millions. Also outside the control were some 4·5 million houses built since 1919, of which some 3 millions were in private ownership and were mainly owner-occupied and 1·5 millions were owned by local authorities. Thus out of a total of about 13 million houses and flats, only about 4 millions, all with net rateable values not exceeding £35 in London and £20 elsewhere and almost entirely owned by private landlords, were still subject to control. The recoverable rents of these houses were usually from 20 per cent to 30 per cent lower than the uncontrolled rents of similar houses.

On September 1st, 1939, all dwelling-houses not

subject to the old control and with net rateable values of not more than £100 in London and £75 elsewhere were made subject to a new control, with standard rents fixed at the rents which were being paid on the date of the Act, or, if not let on that day, at the last previous rent paid. All new houses, or those never let before, were to have as their standard rents whatever was charged at their first *bona fide* unfurnished letting. This Act is still in force, though it has been supplemented by the Furnished Houses (Rent Control) Act of 1946, which established Rent Tribunals to review rents of furnished accommodation, and by the Landlord and Tenant (Rent Control) Act of 1949, which gave to these same tribunals power to fix the rents of unfurnished houses let for the first time. The recommendation of the Ridley Committee, that Rent Tribunals should have the power to adjust in either direction anomalies in the existing standard rents of controlled houses, has never been adopted. No attempt has so far been made to control the prices at which houses may be sold.

The results of this long series of Rent Restriction Acts cannot be regarded with satisfaction from any point of view. It has long been realised that they have serious legal difficulties. Apart altogether from the question of evasion, and even after the immense case-law developed by thirty years of litigation, the legal position in any particular case is often still obscure. What exactly is part of a house let as a separate dwelling? Just how many acres of land must go with a house to make it a farm and therefore outside the scope of the Acts? Just how much furniture is needed to constitute a furnished house? Does a man automatically convert his office into a dwelling-house by keeping a camp-bed in it, and if not, how frequently must he sleep there to bring it within the Acts? Would an owner, with an invalid wife and three young children, who wishes to obtain occupation of his own house, suffer more hardship if his request were refused than the tenant, with only one child but a bedridden mother-in-law, would suffer if it were granted? These are a very small sample of the thousands of cases decided yearly in the courts. Apart from such questions, it is often a matter of great difficulty to discover what is the standard rent of any particular house, especially if it has been owner-occupied for any considerable time. If a house was last let in 1815, then the rent paid at the time of the battle of Waterloo is the standard rent to-day.

If the Rent Restriction Acts are a lawyer's nightmare, they offend at least as much against the ordinary standards of equity. Of three identical houses in the same road, one may be let at ten shillings a week under the old control, the second at fifteen under the new control, while the rent of the third, let for the first time since the war, may be twenty-five shillings or more. There is no guarantee that the poorest tenant rents the cheapest house, or that the poorest landlord owns the dearest one. Indeed, the landlord of the cheapest house may well be poorer than his tenant, for before 1914 small house property was a favourite medium for the investment of small savings.

But the inequity of the present system as between tenant and tenant, or between tenant and landlord, fades into insignificance as compared with the inequity as between those who are lucky enough to have rent-restricted houses and those who have no houses at all. It is an economic truism that the fixing of maximum prices without the imposition of rationing normally results in part of the demand at the fixed price going unsatisfied. Even if the maximum rents fixed were completely consistent as between themselves, this difficulty would remain. Since 1939 money earnings and most prices have approximately doubled; controlled rents (apart from increases in rates) have not risen at all. Thus in real terms the rents of some 8½ millions out of the 13 million pre-war

houses have been approximately halved. Is it to be won-
dered that the demand for houses to let at controlled rents
is enormously in excess of the supply ? Is it surprising
that rent-restricted houses are used less economically
than they would have been if rents had risen in proportion
with other prices and incomes, and that an unsatisfied
demand is squeezed out, to be concentrated on the other
sectors of the market — local authorities' houses, furnished accommodation, and houses available for purchase
with vacant possession ?

Of the sectors not covered by the Rent Restriction
Acts, rents of local authorities' pre-war houses, though
frequently higher than before the war, are in general held
at a level far below that necessary to equate supply and
demand ; while rents of their new houses, though higher
than those of their older ones, even allowing for improved
amenities, are held by subsidies at a level far below their
current market values. Thus a great unsatisfied demand
is concentrated on the two remaining sectors, pushing
prices there far above what they would have been if prices
in all sectors had been allowed to find their market level.
Sometimes tenants of furnished rooms (often in rent-
restricted houses) will venture to bring cases of unusually
high rents to the notice of the Rent Tribunals set up under
the Furnished Houses Act, even though the tribunals
cannot give security of tenure for more than a few months
at a time. But such controls, even if successful, cannot
provide accommodation where it does not exist ; and even
if they could be universally enforced, their only result
would be to reduce the supply and expand the demand for
furnished rooms until there remained, for those left over
who were unable to provide the deposit on a purchased
house, the choice only between the hospitality of relatives
and the hardly warmer welcome of a public institution.

There remains only one sector of the market where no
attempt has yet been made to control prices — the market

in houses for sale. In spite of the fact that the demand here is limited to those able to provide at least the minimum deposit, prices for houses with vacant possession, especially for the smaller houses, have been forced up to a level far above that of most other prices. It is difficult to generalise the increase in house prices since 1939, but perhaps it would not be far from the truth to say that in many parts of the country small houses are costing from three to four times, and larger houses from two to three times, what they would have cost before the war. Only for the largest houses, unsuitable for conversion into commercial premises and requiring more service to run than is within the power of most post-tax incomes to command, is the rise in prices not abnormal. The rise in the price of small houses cannot, however, be taken as an indication of the rise in rents which would ensue if rent restriction were withdrawn; for much of it is due to the concentration upon the only completely free sector of the market of the excess demand created by the artificially low rents ruling in at least two of the other sectors. The repeal of rent restriction would almost certainly be followed by a sharp drop in the prices of at least the smaller houses offered for sale with vacant possession.

The economic aspects of rent restriction reveal disadvantages at least comparable with those of its legal and equitable aspects. They are mainly two — the impairment of the landlords' ability and incentive to maintain premises in good condition, and the impediments which the Acts place in the way of the mobility of labour.

As regards the first of these, it is common ground that the cost of maintaining and repairing houses has risen very greatly since before the war, probably more than twice everywhere, and in some areas three times or more. At these prices, many landlords are unable to pay for adequate repairs out of the controlled rents and leave themselves any income at all, while others, especially owners of older property unsuitable for owner-occupancy, find that it pays them better to collect what income they can until their property becomes actually uninhabitable than to spend money on repairs which will never yield a reasonable return on the expenditure. The probability that property will be treated in this way is increased by the tendency of the better landlords, faced with the choice between running their property at a loss and allowing it to decay, to sell it for what it will fetch to those who are less scrupulous in their methods of management. Thus much property is being allowed to degenerate into slums, or at best maintained at a level much below that which is economically desirable and which it would have paid landlords to achieve if rents had been allowed to find their market level. For the ultimate results of this policy we have only to look across the English Channel, where the degree of inflation has been greater than here and the gap between controlled rents and those which would enable property to be kept in good repair is even wider.

The second of the economic disadvantages of rent restriction, at least in the short run, is probably even more serious than the first. Rent restriction involves what is in effect a tax on the landlord and a subsidy to the tenant. But it is a subsidy which the tenant receives only so long as he stays in his existing house. Should he leave it for any reason, he is deprived, not only of his subsidy, but also of his right to rent another house even at the full market price. If he happens to live in a council house it may be possible for him, by arrangement with the local authority, to exchange houses with someone else in the same district, or even to be allotted a new house on surrendering his old one. But if he lives in a privately-owned house, or if he wishes to move outside his district, his chance of renting another within a reasonable time is small unless he either has access to some special favour or is prepared to break the law by offering some consideration in addition to the controlled rent. Otherwise he will have to make do with furnished lodgings until first he qualifies to be regarded as a resident and then his name has slowly climbed to the top of the local authority's housing list. It is little wonder that the much-needed increase in the mobility of labour is so difficult to achieve.

If, however, a tenant inhabits a privately-owned house suitable for owner-occupancy, there are ways in which he may be able to retain at least part of the benefit of his rent subsidy after leaving his present house. So long as he remains a statutory tenant, the selling value of his present house is probably a good many hundred pounds less than it would be if the landlord were able to offer it with vacant possession. It may sometimes be possible for the tenant to obtain a share of this margin between the " sitting tenant " and the " vacant possession " values of his house, either by agreeing to leave in exchange for a cash payment, or by buying his house for something more than its " sitting tenant " value and subsequently re-selling it for its full market value with vacant possession. How much of the margin he will be able to secure for himself, and how much he will have to leave for his landlord, will depend on their relative bargaining powers; the tenant will no doubt do his best to conceal his desire to leave until the bargain has been completed. If in either of these ways he can make a substantial profit, he can use this to pay part of the purchase price of a house in the district to which he wishes to move, borrowing the remainder from a building society or other source.

It should be noted that every time this sort of trans- action occurs a house is permanently transferred from the letting market to the selling market. The same is true whenever a house falls vacant on the death of a tenant; for it will usually pay the landlord to sell it to an owner- occupier rather than re-let it at the controlled rent. Thus, despite the delay due to the right of a resident wife or relative to succeed to the tenancy for one further lifetime, it seems probable that the indefinite continuation of the present system will result in the gradual withdrawal from the letting market of all privately-owned houses suitable for owner-occupancy. The demand for houses to let will therefore become increasingly concentrated on the new houses built by public authorities. The satisfaction of this demand, at subsidised rents, would require not only a long-continued diversion to housing of resources urgently needed in other fields, but also a continually mounting annual charge on the Exchequer and local governments for subsidies. This cost, for pre-war and post-war houses, is already in the neighbourhood of £40 millions a year (in addition to the subsidies on temporary houses) and is rising by something like £5 millions a year.

While, however, it is easy enough to see the defects, legal, social, and economic, of the system of rent restriction into which the country has been allowed to drift, it is much less easy to suggest an acceptable remedy. The mere repeal of the existing Acts, though a solution of the economic difficulties and in the long run likely to prove highly beneficial to the country as a whole, would in the short run frustrate many justifiable expectations, and bring about a sudden redistribution of incomes which the electorate would certainly not desire nor the individuals affected in many cases deserve. While some of the land-lords who would benefit from repeal have no doubt suffered unjustly as compared with receivers of income from other types of property, there are others, such as the recent purchasers of rent-restricted property at the " sitting tenant " price, who would make large windfall profits; and on the other side, while many tenants could no doubt afford to pay higher rents without real difficulty, others, especially those with children or living on small pensions, would suffer the most serious hardship. Simple repeal would therefore give rise to so many hard cases and obvious injustices that it would offend against the principles of equity almost as much as do the existing Acts, and against the public sense of equity probably far more.

Various suggestions have been made which, while maintaining the Rent Restriction Acts in force, would mitigate some part of their ill effects. The Ridley Committee Report of 1945 (Cmd. 6621), among recommendations for minor improvements in the working of the system, made three suggestions on points of substance. The first of these was that the various Acts should be consolidated and their legal anomalies cleared up; the second was that Rent Tribunals should be set up to overhaul the whole system of standard rents and remove their inconsistencies with each other; and the third was that after three years a committee should be appointed to report on the cost of house repairs, with a view to a possible increase in the level of permitted rents. None of these recommendations touches the central problems, and, apart from the power given to Rent Tribunals to review post-1939 rentals, none has been acted upon.

The recommendations of a report published in November 1949 by P.E.P. come rather nearer to dealing with the real difficulties. The report looks, not too hopefully, to the Local Government Act of 1948, with its programme for reassessing rateable values on a consistent basis throughout the country by 1953, to provide a means of carrying out the Ridley Committee's recommendation for the elimination of inconsistencies between restricted rents; and it urges some relief to landlords, by means of increased rents and/or special tax allowances, to provide the means of carrying out repairs. This last recommendation would do something to prevent large stretches of low-rented premises from degenerating into slums, while the first would help to remove the inequity as between one tenant of a controlled house and another. But neither would do anything towards solving the problem either of the inequity between those with houses and those without or of the immobility of labour.

Various suggestions have been made to deal with the problem of immobility. It might, for instance, be possible to make people more mobile by giving to anyone who surrendered the tenancy of a house priority for a new tenancy, whether in his own district or elsewhere. Such a measure, however, would encounter insuperable political difficulties; for to give a new-comer in the district priority over existing inhabitants, some of whom had waited perhaps for years, would reveal far too plainly the injustice of the present system towards those who are not lucky enough to have a house. No solution which does not make a serious attempt to deal with this injustice either has or ought to have any chance of acceptance.

A similar objection can be made to the otherwise most valuable suggestions made by Mr. Roy Harrod in his book *Are These Hardships Necessary?* Mr. Harrod suggests that the Acts should be repealed and rents be allowed to rise to their full market level, but that for a period of ten years the landlord should be taxed the whole of the increase and the proceeds handed back to the tenant, who would receive them whether he stayed in that house or not. At the end of the ten years " some readjustment of wages or taxes could be made, so as to avoid any transfer of income from the poor to the rich that the abolition of the old system might entail ". This scheme would clearly have great advantages over the present system. So long as the tenant stayed in his existing house, his extra rent would be exactly equalled by his extra income, and he would be neither better nor worse off than before. But he would now have the choice between spending the whole of his new allow-ance on the increased rent and moving to a cheaper house, thus freeing part of his new allowance for spending on other things. Further, since rents of other houses would be at their full market level, he would be able to find another house, at a rent, no doubt, higher than its previous controlled level, but lower than the new rent of his existing house. The tenants most likely to move in this way would probably be elderly people, who are at present both enabled by the low rents they are paying and compelled by the difficulty of finding other accommodation to stay on in a house too large for them now that their children have grown up and left home; but no doubt there are many other people who would find that they preferred to spend some part of their increased money incomes in other ways and would move to smaller and cheaper premises. Thus the demand for house-room, now artificially stimulated by the reduction in real rents, would fall to a normal market level, and the unfortunates who compose the surplus demand, now squeezed out of the market, would be able to get a house. No existing tenant would be worse off if he stayed, and since any move he made would be voluntary, he would move only if he thought that he was thereby making himself better off.

While Mr. Harrod's scheme would do much to remedy the disadvantages of the present system, and would largely solve the problem of mobility, it has three serious deficiencies. The first of these is that it does nothing, for at least ten years, to make the landlord better able to provide for the increased cost of repairs; for the heavy tax would be just as efficient a promoter of slums as the present restriction on rents. Secondly, it perpetuates the random distribution of the subsidy between tenants, regardless of their means, so that a tenant with a larger income or smaller responsibilities might well receive a larger grant than one poorer or more burdened.

Most serious of all is the difficulty that, while the injustice to the man without a house would in fact be somewhat reduced by making it possible for him to get one at the full market rent, Mr. Harrod's scheme would make the remaining inequity explicit and therefore less acceptable to public opinion than the even greater inequity implicit in the existing system. We have only to think of the feelings of a man who is on the point of getting a house, for which perhaps he has been waiting for years, at a controlled or subsidised rent and who suddenly learns that its rent has risen by fifty or a hundred per cent. He will receive no compensation for the rise in rent of a house he has never inhabited, while his next-door neighbour, who got his house perhaps a month ago, will receive an allowance which is not only sufficient to cover the rise in his present rent but which he will retain in full if he moves into a cheaper house. The resentment against treatment so obviously unfair would certainly prevent Mr. Harrod's scheme from being put into force as it stands.

Any scheme, to be logically defensible, must endeavour to deal with the difficulties which Mr. Harrod's scheme ignores, as well as with those which it resolves. Landlords must be given a sufficient share of the increases in rent to enable them to maintain their premises in repair, and the benefits of the amounts collected in tax must be shared, not only by existing tenants, but also by those who are without permanent accommodation.

To meet these points would involve two substantial departures from Mr. Harrod's scheme. In the first place, the landlord, instead of passing on the whole of the additional tax collected, would be allowed to retain, say, 25 per cent of the addition as provision for repairs, provided that the premises were in fact kept in a condition satisfactory to the local authorities. The second difference would be that, instead of using the proceeds of the tax to subsidise only existing tenants, the Treasury would use part of it to supplement incomes in accordance with need, by increasing children's allowances, old age and other pensions, and so forth, and the remainder to reduce the general level of taxation. They would thus increase all net incomes, but especially those of people least able to pay the increased

G

rents. It might very well happen that the incomes of people with large families of children would be increased by more than the increase in the rents of their existing houses, so that they would be able to afford to move into the larger houses vacated by people without families now finding it advantageous to move into smaller ones.

There is one further measure that would be needed to make this suggested scheme complete. Since all members of the population would benefit, in greater or less degree, from the increased allowances and reduced taxation, to impose the landlords' tax only on the owners of rented houses would mean subsidising owner-occupiers at the expense of tenants. Owner-occupiers would therefore also have to be made liable for landlords' tax on their own houses to provide the means of financing the benefits which they, as a class, would receive from higher allowances and lower taxes. One of the major practical difficulties of the scheme would be to assess the tax on owner-occupiers in such a way that it would be both fair as between different owner-occupiers and would yield an amount sufficient to finance the benefits which they collectively would enjoy. This task of assessment would be considerably eased after 1953, on the completion of the reassessment, on a more consistent basis, of rateable values throughout the country.

The amount of revenue which the Treasury might expect to receive from the landlords' tax cannot be estimated with any degree of accuracy. It is, however, possible to make a guess at the order of magnitude involved. If rents of controlled houses were allowed to rise to levels which effectively equated supply and demand, the average increase per privately-owned house let at controlled rents would hardly be less than 10s. per week. On $8\frac{1}{2}$ million houses this would yield about £220 millions a year, of which £55 millions would remain with the landlord and £165 millions be passed on to the Treasury. If owner-occupiers paid a corresponding tax at the same average rate of

7s. 6d. a week, this, on 3 million houses, would yield a further £60 millions a year.

The saving on subsidies on local authorities' houses would also be substantial. It is true that, even at full market rates, post-war temporary houses would have to be let at rents which would not cover more than a fraction of their present subsidies, which (on the basis of a ten-year life) amount to some £21 millions a year on 157,000 houses, or about £2 : 10s. per house per week. The same might well be true, to a smaller degree, for the post-war permanent houses built by local authorities, on which the present subsidies are about £23 millions on less than 700,000 houses, or about 13s. per house per week. On the other hand, the raising to the full market level of rents on the nearly 1½ millions of pre-war council houses would certainly yield more than the present subsidies of £17 millions, or about 4s. 9d. per house per week. Further, the local authorities would save the whole of the increase in rents and not merely 75 per cent of it. While therefore the rents of local authorities' houses, which are now on the whole higher than those of privately-owned houses, would rise less if they were let at full market price, the net gain to the authorities might be of about the same magnitude, or about 7s. 6d. per house per week, except perhaps where the class of tenants permitted to occupy certain houses was narrowly restricted, as in some slum-clearance schemes. On the 2¼ millions of local authorities' houses, this saving on subsidies would yield about £45 millions a year out of the present £61 millions. How this saving was shared between central and local governments would not be of great importance, for the only question would be whether the benefit was passed back to the public in reduced rates or reduced taxes. If, however, we assume that the local authorities retained sufficient to free them altogether of their share of the subsidies — perhaps £20 millions — this might leave something like £25 millions a year as the gain to the central government. Thus the total yield to the central government from landlords' tax and subsidy savings might be something like £250 millions a year. If it were considered expedient to continue to build local authorities' houses in the present quantities at costs which could not be covered by full market rents, the remaining cost of subsidies, estimated at about £16 millions a year, would begin to rise again, but only at the rate of some £2 millions a year as compared with the present rate of increase of about £5 millions a year.

The proposals here put forward seem on the whole to conform fairly well to the three criteria enunciated above — administrative convenience, equity as between persons and classes, and economic desirability. To calculate the tax payable on a rented house, only two factors would need to be known — the rent paid on the date on which the new regulations came into force and the rent paid in the current year. The whole of the elaborate legal framework of the existing Rent Restriction Acts would fall away.

Tax on owner-occupied houses would presumably have to be based on rateable values. Until the results of the new valuations under the Local Government Act of 1948 were available, this would lead to some inequities as between one owner-occupier and another, but these would presumably be temporary. Landlords would continue to be treated more harshly than owners of other types of property, though less harshly than at present. In due course the tax would no doubt come to be regarded as most unjust and high in order of priority for reduction whenever the budgetary situation permitted. Pressure for its reduction would be all the more effective because the tax would also be paid by owner-occupiers, though these, unlike the landlords, would, as a class, be receiving commensurate benefits in other ways. For existing tenants as a whole the aggregate cost of increased rents would be greater than the aggregate benefits received, both as a result of the deduction to meet the increased cost of repairs and because the remaining benefits would have to be shared with those without houses; but the benefits would be distributed in such a way as to prevent cases of serious hardship, while some, especially those with large families, might be better off. Those without houses would receive a double relief of the injustice they are now suffering: they would be able to find houses to let, and their increased allowances and lower taxes would give them help towards paying the full market rents.

The economic advantages of the change would include not only the restoration of mobility but also an increase in the supply of the sizes of houses and flats most in demand. As people in houses too large for them tried to economise by moving into smaller premises, rents of the larger houses would fall relatively to those of the smaller ones. This would not only make it easier for people with large families to occupy the larger premises, but would make it more profitable to convert the larger houses, with relatively lower rents and therefore relatively lower landlords' taxes, into maisonettes or flats for small families. Thus the number of dwellings available for letting would be increased at a fraction of the cost of building new houses. The tax on such converted premises would continue to be paid at the rate appropriate to the whole house before conversion.

Whether such a scheme, however logically satisfactory, would ever be acceptable to the electorate of this country, or whether, even if accepted, it would meet with sufficient co-operation from tenants and landlords to render it workable, is open to considerable doubt. A large number, perhaps a majority, of tenants would be called upon to surrender in favour of other groups in the community some part of the rent subsidy they now in effect enjoy, and it may well be that the habit of regarding money rents as fixed whatever the fall in the purchasing power of money is too ingrained to be altered by a change in the law, however desirable in the interests of the community as a whole. It is not unlikely that, even if such a measure could be passed into law, many landlords would be deterred by fears of trouble from raising their rents, at any rate to existing tenants. In this case, the Treasury would receive less revenue and would be able to pass on smaller benefits to taxpayers. Thus tenants paying full market rents would receive less than appropriate compensation, especially as the failure of some rents to rise would raise the market rents of the remainder; owner-occupiers would suffer a similar injustice. Mobility would also be less than fully restored, for those with complaisant landlords would be reluctant to move. No doubt in course of time rents would gradually become adjusted to their new level, but the injustice suffered in the meantime might well discredit the whole scheme. To meet this danger it might be necessary to compel landlords to raise their rents by assessing them on the basis of estimated market rents, but this would be an undesirable complication.

If the abolition of rent restriction could be made to coincide with a general reduction in taxation, its path could be made much easier. An additional £100 millions or so would enable allowances to landlords for repairs and to those without houses to be given without reducing allowances to existing tenants as a class below the level required to meet the whole of their increases in rent. In this case it might be expedient to return to an adaptation of Mr. Harrod's scheme. It is true that this would perpetuate the inevitably inequitable distribution of the rent subsidies now received by tenants. It is also true that difficulties would arise in fixing the rent grants given to persons without houses; for if the grant were to be determined by the increase over the standard rent of the first house subsequently occupied, it would create a fictitiously expanded demand for the houses with the largest increases, which would drive their rents still higher. After a decent interval the new tenant could move to cheaper premises, taking his inflated grant with him, and leave the house free for the temporary occupation of a similar tenant. Allowances to those without houses would therefore have to be determined on some other basis, either in relation to need or on some kind of flat rate. Nevertheless, in spite of these objections, such a scheme would represent so great an improvement on the present system that if its chances of acceptance were better than those of a theoretically more perfect scheme it would be foolish to let them slip.

If neither of the schemes suggested is regarded as politically practicable, the simplest alternative would be to return to the methods of the Act of 1923. These would include some immediate increase in rent for landlords who kept their premises in adequate repair, and the release from control of any premises which fell vacant. As a statutory tenancy can be inherited only once, it then should not take more than two generations to rid ourselves of the disastrous incubus of the Rent Restriction Acts.

BANKING POLICY AND THE BALANCE OF INTERNATIONAL PAYMENTS[1]

THE following observations are based largely on the writer's personal experience in South Africa during a period when that country was undergoing violent fluctuations in her balance of international payments. This experience has led to the belief that, in such a country as South Africa, the process of adjusting an adverse balance of payments differs appreciably from that in such a country as Great Britain. It should be emphasised that attention is here concentrated upon the process of adjustment, and that little or no attempt is made to touch upon its effects. The discussion is mainly concerned with quite short-term problems, and supplements rather than amends the work on long-term problems, such as the effects of given changes upon commodity or factor terms of trade, to which the attention of investigators has hitherto been largely devoted. The time scale used here must be measured in months, or even weeks, rather than in years. Nevertheless, it is hoped that the suggestions here advanced may provide some addition to the equipment of those who are investigating the more important long-term problems; while on the immediately practical side it is hoped to develop this method of approach in such a way as to facilitate the making, in certain conditions and for certain geographical areas, of rather more reliable short-term forecasts of business prospects.

[1] Originally published in *Economica*, November 1936.

94

I

Strictly speaking, every receipts and payments account, whether it be the account of a single individual or firm, or the collective account of many individuals and firms, invariably balances ; for every pound that has been paid out has been obtained from somewhere. Nevertheless, it is in accordance with the normal use of terms to say of a man whose money reserves have become depleted during the course of a year that his money payments have exceeded his money receipts — that he has, if we care to use the term, " an adverse balance of payments ". This adverse balance is, of course, not necessarily inconsistent with an excess of income over expenditure for the same year and with an improving financial position, for the decrease in his money reserves may be equal to only a part of the debts he has paid off or of the new investments he has made during the year. At the same time, it will, generally speaking, indicate some reductions in the liquidity of his position, of which one possible cause may have been an excess of expenditure over income.

In a country where the great bulk of the money reserves of the inhabitants is kept in the form of bank deposits, any excess of an individual's money payments over money receipts is likely to be reflected mainly in a change in the size of his bank balance, for the total of the cheques he draws during the period exceeds that of the deposits which he makes, and his credit balance is thereby reduced or converted into a debit balance, or his debit balance is increased.

What is true of one individual is equally true of a group of individuals inhabiting any given district. If during any period the aggregate amount of the cheques they have drawn exceeds the aggregate value of the amounts they have deposited, it would be possible to say that, as a group, their money payments have exceeded their money receipts, and that collectively they have " an adverse balance of payments ". If the group consists of all the customers of a local bank, this excess of payments will be reflected in this bank's accounts by a fall in its total deposits and/or a rise in its total advances. Any disturbance of the equilibrium of the balance of payments of any given district is thus, in a cheque-using community, primarily a banking phenomenon. The purpose of this article is to discuss, under various conditions, the reactions of the banks to this change in their position, and the effects of such reactions.

It is at once obvious that very different amounts of attention are given to the question of the balance of payments in different geographical areas. No one, for instance, seems to take any interest in the balance of payments of Devonshire, while, on the other hand, a good deal of interest is taken in the balance of payments of the United Kingdom or Australia. Why is it that the inter-regional balance of payments is regarded as important in one case and unimportant in the other ?

The first difference seems to be that the banks in Devonshire are merely branches of large banks whose activities extend over a much wider area. Any excess of withdrawals from Devonshire branches will therefore probably be balanced by an excess of deposits in other branches of the same banks. The only case where this does not hold good is when there is an excess of withdrawals from the system as a whole, due either to an increase in the public's holdings of currency or to a net transfer of funds to outside the system altogether. Apart from this, the chief effect of Devonshire's adverse balance is an increase in the indebtedness of Devonshire branches to other branches of the same banks, or a decrease in the indebtedness of other branches to Devonshire branches. Since banks, generally speaking, have no objection to any

amount of inter-branch indebtedness, provided that their
total figures for all branches are unaltered and that all
advances made are sound, they need take no action to
check this process. Indeed, it is well known that certain
areas, especially residential areas, habitually lend large
amounts to industrial areas through the medium of the
banks.

If, however, the banks in Devonshire, instead of being
branches of large banks, had been independent banks, or
even if some of them had been doing a more important
share of the banking business of Devonshire than of the
rest of the country, Devonshire's adverse balance of payments would have been reflected in a change in inter-bank
indebtedness and not merely in inter-branch indebtedness.
Such inter-bank debts, whether in the form of deposits,
advances, or re-discounts, would hardly be likely to be
allowed to rise to anything like the level customary for
inter-branch debts, and unless the movement in due course
came to an end of its own accord (for reasons which will
be discussed later) the Devonshire banks would sooner or
later be obliged to take steps to adjust the position.

The time within which such measures would be thought
necessary would probably be greatly shortened if there
were also present a second difference which usually exists
between national and other regional areas — the difference
of currencies. The importance of this difference depends
mainly on the degree of possibility of any substantial altera-
tion of the rates of exchange; but if there is even a fairly
remote chance of exchange fluctuations, no bank can see
with equanimity any large margin between its assets and
liabilities in each separate currency. This consideration
precludes any considerable amount of inter-bank indebtedness not balanced by other assets or liabilities in the same
currencies. It would even preclude the existence of large
debts between branches of the same bank operating in two
separate currency areas.

The third important difference between national and other geographical areas is the existence of different political controls. This factor is of importance rather for its influence on the type of action likely to be taken to restore the balance of international payments than for determining whether or no some sort of action needs to be taken. If there is a separate Government, there is a considerable probability that the action taken to restore equilibrium will be of a non-banking character, and that one or more of the familiar expedients of exchange depreciation or devaluation, restrictions of imports or exchanges, repudiation of foreign debts, and so forth, will be resorted to in order to evade the necessity for banking action. In this article the effects of such measures are not discussed.

II

The immediate effect on the banks in any country of the development of an adverse balance of payments is that there takes place a fall in their local deposits or a rise in their local advances, or both. This rise in local assets (other than cash) and/or fall in local liabilities have their counterpart in a depletion of the banking system's reserves of gold and/or of external liquid assets, or, less commonly, in a rise in external liabilities. To the banks, therefore, the problem presents itself as a need of restoring the customary ratio of cash and foreign exchange reserves to deposits, or, which is another way of viewing the same thing, of reducing local assets (other than cash) to their customary ratio to local liabilities. If they are forced to take action, this is, therefore, in the direction of reducing the total of local advances and/or security holdings.

The exact methods used to attain this end will depend partly on local custom and organisation, partly on the form in which the adverse balance is reflected in the bank statements, and partly on the urgency of the necessary adjustment. The best way of ensuring that the reduced volume of advances was available to those who needed them most would be for the banks to raise interest rates equally on all advances, new and old, until the repayments of loans by old borrowers and the reduced demands of new sufficed to reduce the total of advances and to restore equilibrium by the means and after the delays which will be discussed later.

In some countries, however, a general rise in interest rates usually plays only a part, often a minor one, in bringing about this adjustment. Instead, advances are arbitrarily refused or reduced to particular classes of borrowers, and especially to the whole class of new borrowers. Where the movement is reflected mainly in an increased demand for advances, the restriction of new advances may be sufficient in itself. Where the movement takes the form of a fall in deposits, an actual reduction in advances may be necessary. Even in this case, since a proportion of the advances will normally be paid off each week in the normal course of business, a rigorous restriction of new advances will cause the total of advances to fall steadily. Only in extreme cases, where the total of deposits is falling rapidly, will it be necessary to call up existing advances before their normal date of expiration, or to insist on reductions when they come to be renewed. In this case, when the banks' need to adjust their position is urgent, the advances called up are likely to be those which can be repaid in a hurry, that is to say, the safest and best secured, which in normal times the banks would be best pleased to continue. These measures are tantamount to very large discriminating increases in the rate of interest, for some of those who are refused advances will be obliged to attempt to borrow elsewhere at high rates, while advances not called up continue to pay the old rates.

It may be that, in order to avoid calling up advances, the banks will realise securities. Such action will have a similar effect of depressing security prices, raising long-term interest rates, and probably causing an increased demand for bank advances which must be refused.   At the same time, by reducing the market value of securities deposited as cover for existing advances, it will cause the banks to reduce certain overdraft limits.   Thus the effect is again that of a rise in bank interest rates, either discriminating or general.   In any case, the effect of the banks' reactions to the adverse balance of payments is a rise in interest rates outside the banks.

Hitherto the case considered has been that of a banking system without a central bank.   The inclusion of the latter complicates but does not fundamentally alter the position. Instead of the commercial banks holding the whole of the system's reserves of gold and foreign exchange themselves, they hold their cash reserves in the form mainly of notes of, and balances with, the central bank, which in turn holds much of the whole system's reserves of gold and foreign exchange.   When an adverse balance develops, it first causes a fall in the public's deposits with, or a rise in their advances from, the commercial banks, and at the same time either a fall in these banks' own reserves of gold or foreign exchange, or a fall in their holdings of the notes or balances of the central bank, accompanied by a fall in the central bank's holdings of gold or foreign exchange. If the whole system wishes to return to its old ratios, both the central and the commercial banks must reduce their local non-cash assets until the position is restored.   If, however, the central bank so desires, it can *increase* its local non-cash assets by purchases of local bills or securities at existing prices from the Government, the commercial banks, or their customers, thus restoring the commercial banks' balances with the central bank, removing the pressure on the commercial banks, and preventing any tendency for interest rates to rise in order to restore equilibrium.   In this case, unless the movement soon comes to an end of its own accord, the central bank's reserves will be increasingly depleted until it may become too late to restore equilibrium by banking measures.

III

In discussing the need for, and the effects of, a rise in interest rates in order to maintain a particular existing exchange standard, it is necessary to take into account three main questions. First, has the balance of payments a tendency to return to equilibrium of its own accord without a rise in interest rates, or will it, if present interest rates are maintained, tend to get progressively further and further out of equilibrium? Secondly, if there is a tendency to return to equilibrium, either spontaneously or in consequence of a given rise in interest rates, how long will it take for the movement away from equilibrium to be reversed and the position restored? And thirdly, are the banks' reserves of gold and foreign exchange large enough to fill the gap in the interval, and if not, how much must interest rates be raised in order to effect adjustment before they are too seriously depleted? No precise answer can, of course, ever be given in advance to these questions; nevertheless, it is possible to enumerate certain factors, the consideration of which may enable estimates to be less erroneous than they might have been.

Broadly speaking, an adverse balance of payments tends to adjust itself spontaneously (without a rise in interest rates) when it is due to causes which at the same time cause local business to become less profitable. For instance, if there occurs the failure of an important export crop uncompensated by a rise in the world price, the impact effect will be that exporters, in order to meet maturing liabilities and to maintain their customary standard of living, will draw upon their bank accounts, thus decreasing their credit balances or increasing their overdrafts.[1] If the fall in their incomes is moderate and expected to be purely temporary, exporters may wish to maintain their existing standards of living and scales of production, and will therefore continue to draw from their bank accounts more than they deposit. But if the fall is large and likely to be prolonged, sooner or later they will either see the necessity of curtailing expenditure to correspond, or will be compelled to curtail it owing to the depletion of their bank deposits or overdraft facilities. The exhaustion of unused overdraft facilities may be accelerated by reductions of overdraft limits by the banks in consequence of the deteriorating financial position of the customers concerned.

IV

Assuming a tendency towards adjustment, the period taken for it to become fully effective will depend on how rapidly reduced receipts by exporters are reflected in reduced payments by them, and how rapidly these in turn are reflected in reduced payments to foreigners. If the amount by which exporters' expenditure is reduced would have been, for instance, spent wholly on imported goods, the demand for these will fall off at once, importers will

[1] During the period during which expenditures of exporters are maintained despite lower incomes, the total of cheques drawn each week on local banks will be maintained while the amounts deposited are reduced, thus reducing the banks' reserves. The position is slightly more complicated where, as is not unlikely in the example under consideration, deposits fall in comparison with the corresponding month of the previous season rather than with the previous month. In this case the banks will look, not only at their current position, but at their probable position after the exporting season is over and the period of seasonal import surpluses has to be faced. The inadequate replenishment of their reserves of foreign exchange during the exporting season may render them unable to finance the former volume of imports during the remainder of the year, and may compel them then to raise interest rates more sharply, in order to adjust the position, than if the fall in imports had started earlier, while the absolute amount of their foreign reserves was still rising. In other words, banks must use seasonally adjusted figures for the purpose of determining policy.

reduce their new orders, and as soon as existing orders have been filled, imports will decline. Thus the fall in the banks' local liabilities or the rise in their local assets will be checked, and the concomitant fall in their foreign reserves will cease or their expansion be stimulated.

If, on the other hand, the exporters' economies are made partly or wholly on locally-produced goods or services, adjustment will be a more prolonged process. Other local residents will now be faced with a reduction in their money receipts, and will be able to maintain their expenditures only by reducing their deposits with the banks or increasing their overdrafts. This excess expenditure in turn must come to an end sooner or later, and economies made, again on payments either for local or for imported goods and services. If the latter, adjustment is achieved; if the former, a new set of customers of the local banks tend to decrease deposits and increase overdrafts until they in turn have to economise. This process must continue until the original reduction in exports is reflected in an adequate [1] reduction in the local demand for imports. The length of the process will depend partly on the number of stages needed, which in turn will depend on the distribution of economies between local goods and imports at each stage, and partly on the length of the delay at each stage before reduced receipts are reflected in reduced payments. The first of these questions will be considered in a later section. With regard to the second, the delay at each stage, in the absence of a change in rates of interest, will depend chiefly on the expectations held about the future. If people are optimistic, they will delay curtailing expenditure as long

[1] What will be regarded as an " adequate " reduction in imports will depend upon the attitude which the banks take towards the size of their reserves of gold or foreign exchange. If they are content merely to check their depletion, monthly imports need be reduced only by as much as monthly exports. If, however, they wish to restore their reserves, imports must for a time be reduced more than exports, and only be permitted to recover to their equilibrium level as the banks' reserves approach their former size.

H

as possible; if they are pessimistic, they will react much
more quickly, or may even reduce their expenditure in
anticipation of a future fall in receipts. The more optimistic the atmosphere, the slower will be the adjustment.
It is, however, probable that the atmosphere will become
progressively less optimistic as the process of adjustment
continues, and that the later stages of adjustment will be
accomplished more quickly than the earlier ones.

Let us now take an opposite case, where the causes of
the adverse balance also bring about, not reduced, but
increased profitability of business. Let us suppose, for
instance, that increased optimism, or perhaps Government
loans for public works or armaments, brings about the
release of idle balances and a general increase in demand,
resulting in an increase in imports, and perhaps a decrease
in exports due to the diversion of goods from export to
the home consumer. In this case there is no spontaneous
tendency towards equilibrium, but rather a progressive
disequilibrium. Business is more profitable, business men
are more credit-worthy, the demand for advances expands
at existing rates of interest, not merely temporarily for
purposes of distress borrowing, but progressively to finance
an increase of business at probably rising prices.[1] Unless
some extraneous event occurs, such as a long-term loan
from abroad (often the natural solution of the problem),
or an internal loss of confidence, due perhaps to an un-
balanced Budget and fears of higher taxation, advances will
continue to rise until the banks' reserves are entirely depleted. To check the movement, they must raise interest
rates to a level which will check the further expansion of
advances, or even, if they need to replenish their foreign
reserves, to one which will induce their repayment. When
this occurs, the progress of events will be exactly similar

---

[1] It may be noted that in such conditions the effect on the banks' local
accounts is rather to cause a rise in advances than a fall in deposits. It is
quite probable that deposits will increase, though more slowly than advances.

to that described in the previous section, except that since the movement starts in an atmosphere of general optimism, adjustment will probably be very slow in its early stages. It is therefore all the more important that it should be started before the banks' reserves have become seriously depleted.

It is possible to imagine an intermediate case where the adverse balance of payments is accompanied by no effect at all on internal conditions. If, for instance, owners of bank balances which would in any case have remained idle elect to transfer them to other banks abroad, all that happens is that the banks' local deposits and their reserves are equally depleted. The profitability of local business is in no way directly affected, and if the banks have ample reserves they may choose to take no action, for the supply of truly idle balances is limited, and if the transfer of balances is carried beyond that limit, local payments are reduced and a depression ensues, which will ultimately tend to correct the position. If, on the other hand, the banks have reason to believe that their reserves will become dangerously depleted, they must raise interest rates in order to restore equilibrium by checking imports.

V

It is now possible to turn to the discussion of the factors which affect the distribution of any reduction in expenditure between imported and locally-produced goods and services, and thus in turn help to determine the length of the time-lag between a fall in incomes and a fall in imports. It is clear that one of the most important of these is the relation which exists between the demand for the type of goods imported and the demand for the type produced locally. In a country importing mainly such goods as durable producers' goods and finished consumers' goods of the better qualities — goods for which the demand

changes more than in proportion to changes in expenditure
— a fall in expenditure will be reflected largely in a reduced
demand for imports; it is even possible that there may be
a diversion of demand from the more expensive types of
goods imported to the cheaper and rougher types made
locally, so that the demand for some sorts of locally-made
goods may actually expand and the profits of their producers be increased. In this type of country the adjustment of the balance of payments through a reduction in
imports will be both rapid and effected with comparatively
little difficulty or disturbance. There seems to be practically no limit in countries of this type to the amount of
adjustment which can be brought about by means of a
restriction of bank credit.

With the opposite type of country the position is very
different. In a country which imports mainly such things
as basic foodstuffs and raw materials, perhaps together
with the cheaper types of finished goods, the first impact
of reduced expenditure is felt mainly upon the demand for
local products, while the demand for certain types of
cheap imported goods, other than raw materials, may even
increase. Local producers in turn reduce their demand
mainly for local goods and services, and the depression in
internal markets may continue to spread for a considerable
time without seriously diminishing the demand for imports.
Thus, apart perhaps from the limited effects of a reduction
in stocks, there will be no rapid and direct adjustment of
the balance of payments. The adjustment will be slow
and probably painful, and when it ultimately comes, will
take one of two forms. Either the effect of the reduced
internal demand will be to reduce factor prices and costs
of production, in which case adjustment will come through
a fall in the local price level, leading to an expansion of
exports and to a transfer of demand from some imported
goods to the now cheaper local products; or, if factor
or other prices are monopolistically or compulsorily main-

tained, production will decrease and the demand for raw materials will fall off, while the intensified fall in incomes due to unemployment will decrease the demand for imported foodstuffs and for even the cheapest types of consumers' goods.

Between the two extreme types described above there are, of course, numerous countries in intermediate positions; in fact, it is unlikely that any country stands exactly at either extreme. Nevertheless it seems probable that the countries of the world can mostly be assigned to one or other of two rough groups — those in which the proportion of expenditure at the margin devoted to imports is large and those in which it is small. To adapt a phrase of Mr. Keynes, we may describe the former group of countries as having a high Marginal Propensity to Import and the latter a low one (to save space, these will in future be referred to as countries having respectively a high or low M.P.I.).[1]

In attempting to estimate the M.P.I. of any particular country, two methods of approach suggest themselves. A detailed comparison of the goods and services produced locally with those imported might be expected to give at least some *prima facie* indication of its M.P.I. This could, in some countries at least, be confirmed by a study of the sequence of recent fluctuations in its balance of payments, banking statistics, interest rates, and imports, though the

[1] An alternative phrase, which would have the advantage of fitting in with similar conceptions in other fields, would be " an elastic (or inelastic) Expenditure Demand for Imports ". This phrase, however, seems to imply a greater precision of definition than is warranted. It might be justifiable to speak of the Expenditure Demand for Imports of a particular individual, or even of a more or less homogeneous group under specified conditions over a specified period of time. But for a country in general over an indeterminate period of time the demand for imports might vary, not only with the total expenditure of the population, but according to the precise groups or classes whose expenditure changed, the sources of the funds expended (whether from earnings, hoards, or loans), and the period of time taken into consideration. It has therefore been thought wiser to use the vaguer phrase, which indicates a rough general tendency rather than a precise relationship.

results would in all cases have to be interpreted in the light of other local and foreign developments, such as changes in tariffs, etc. Further, it would have to be remembered that the M.P.I. of a country might change greatly with changes in the volume of expenditure. In most high M.P.I. countries the M.P.I. would probably alter directly with expenditure, and in low M.P.I. countries inversely, especially if changes in expenditure were accompanied by changes in the employment of factors. In addition, the whole relationship would naturally alter gradually over a long period of years with changes in the types of goods and services produced and imported. In spite, however, of the obvious difficulties in the application of the conception of the M.P.I. to actual conditions, it is believed that the differences between the extreme representatives of each type of country are so great that distinctions could be drawn which would hold good in almost all conditions and over periods of many years. In existing circumstances, it seems probable that advanced " industrial " countries, such as Great Britain, would be found to have a relatively low M.P.I., and the " raw material " countries, such as South Africa or New Zealand, a relatively high one.

VI

Before proceeding to draw further conclusions from the arguments already advanced, it will be necessary to introduce two further considerations. The first of these is the form in which an adverse balance of international payments is reflected in the banking figures. Hitherto it has been assumed that the immediate effect of an adverse balance is shown in a fall in the banks' reserves of gold and foreign exchange. While this has always been true for most countries, and is now more nearly true of all countries than formerly, it is not true of all countries at all times. Certain countries, generally of the low M.P.I. type, have been, and to some extent still are, international banking centres, where foreign banks are prepared to keep deposits which they regard as the equivalent of cash. For such countries, therefore, the immediate effect of an adverse balance may be seen, not in a depletion of the banks' reserves, but in an increase in the total of deposits held with them by foreign banks.

This expansion of foreign banks' deposits may arise in one of three ways. Firstly, the banks of countries which are not financial centres and which themselves have favourable balances may be prepared to keep the additional reserves thus obtained in the form of bank deposits in the centre concerned. Secondly, quite a small rise in interest rates may be sufficient to induce such banks to transfer their reserves from other financial centres; and thirdly, one effect of the adverse balance may be to cause interest rates in foreign financial centres to fall, thus inducing the transference of funds to the centre in question, even though interest rates are not raised there.

Where the effects on the banks' position of an adverse balance of payments takes this form, it is obvious that the pressure on the banking system to restore equilibrium by restricting credit is much less. If the foreign banks' balances are kept with commercial banks, there is no direct incentive to contract credit, except in so far as the fear that foreign balances are more likely than the balances of local residents to be withdrawn in cash may induce the banks to attempt to increase their cash ratios. Nevertheless, there will still be some tendency towards adjustment from the monetary side, apart from any tendency which may exist owing to a direct decrease in the profitability in local business. Even where the adverse balance is accompanied at first by a trade improvement, the passage of balances formerly owned by local depositors into the hands of foreign banks will first tend to offset the idle balances released by the expectations of improvement, and ultimately reduce the volume of deposits in active circulation.

This reduction of effective deposits must in turn lead to reduced purchases of commodities or services, either directly or in consequence of a rise in interest rates due to a shortage of funds available for investment. The process of adjustment will then follow the lines indicated in an earlier section.[1]

It should be emphasised, however, that while the ultimate effect of an accumulation of bank deposits in the ownership of foreign banks is similar to that of the withdrawal of cash from the banks, the pressure towards adjustment will be far more gradual in the former case; for active deposits will then be reduced only by the actual amount of the adverse balance, while a depletion of the banks' cash reserves will (if existing ratios are maintained) compel a reduction in deposits by an amount equal to many times the adverse balance.

Even if the foreign balances are kept with the central bank, the effects on the commercial banks will probably be less severe than if the central bank's own cash reserves were depleted to the extent of the adverse balance. For in the former case the commercial banks' cash reserves will be depleted (even if the central bank does not offset the movement by open market operations) only by the amount of the adverse balance, while in the latter case the central bank, if it is to maintain its existing ratios, must reduce its deposits, including bankers' deposits, by a multiple of its loss of cash.

The deflationary effects of an accumulation of foreign banks' assets in any centre will be mitigated, but not entirely removed, if these assets are held, not in the form of bank deposits, but of investments; though in this case the movement should probably be regarded as an adjustment of the balance of payments by means of loans from

---

[1] This assumes, of course, that the banks do not allow deposits to expand so as to offset the growing amount held idle in the hands of foreign banks; since their cash reserves are assumed to be unchanged, any such expansion of deposits would presumably be strictly limited, even at higher interest rates.

abroad rather than as the effect of an adverse balance. If foreign banks were prepared to invest their funds in the same way as local residents, the effect of such an adjustment of an adverse balance would probably be similar to that of an ordinary increase in saving. In fact, however, foreign banks will almost certainly wish to keep these assets in a very liquid form. They will therefore part with their bank balances only if they can obtain suitable short-term invest-ments in exchange for them. Unless the supply of short-term investments increases, or unless existing owners of short-term securities are prepared to invest the proceeds in long-dated securities or loans, the balances thus released by the foreign banks will remain idle in the hands of their new owners ; or, if it is the local banks which fail to secure their usual supply of short-term securities, the balances will simply disappear. The final effect of the whole trans-action, including the original adverse balance, will be a fall in short-term interest rates, and a fall in the demand for commodities, either directly or in consequence of the rise in long-term interest rates, which will occur in conse-quence of the transfer of resources from long- to short-term investments. Since, however, some addition to the supply of short-term securities and some transfer of funds to longer-term securities may be expected, this tendency towards adjustment is likely to be less marked than that which follows the accumulation of bank balances in the ownership of foreign banks.[1]

An offsetting of an adverse balance by an increase in the short-term local assets owned by foreigners other than banks will probably have a very similar local effect to that of an increase of local assets in the hands of foreign banks, though its effects abroad will be very different.

There is also the possibility of a more permanent

[1] If the whole of the increase in foreign-owned funds were invested in additional Government short-term loans, which in turn were expended, *e.g.* on unemployment relief or Government works, there would be no tendency at all towards adjustment so long as the process could be maintained.

adjustment of an adverse balance of payments in a low
M.P.I. country, which is also a financial centre, by means
of a reduction in the volume of its new long-term loans to
foreign countries, and the gradual repayment of old loans.
Where there is only one centre lending abroad on a large
scale, or where there are several lending centres, if each
supplies capital mainly to its own particular areas, it would
probably take a substantial rise in interest rates to check
foreign borrowing.   Further, the curtailment of foreign
loans by any one country, whether by high interest rates
or other means, would reduce the total amount of international lending, cause difficulties in borrowing countries,
and probably have the effect of reducing the volume of
international trade, including the exports of the country
which had curtailed its loans.   In a world, however, in
which there were a number of financial centres of comparable importance, competing with each other for the
supply of capital to all parts of the world, it would take
only a small rise in interest rates in any one centre to
divert borrowers, both of new funds and for conversion
purposes, to other centres.   If the same causes which had
induced a rise in interest rates in one centre brought about
a fall in others, there would need to be no net reduction
in the total of new long-term international lending and no
adverse repercussions in borrowing countries or on international trade.   Such a system would be very different
from any which the world has yet seen ; but it is at least
possible that developments in this direction may ultimately
help to solve the difficulties of the adjustment of the
balance of payments in low M.P.I. countries.

VII

The other important factor, which needs to be taken
into consideration in determining the effect on a particular
country of its development of an adverse balance of pay-

ments, is the effect of its repercussions on other countries. By definition, if one country develops an adverse balance of payments, some other country or countries must simultaneously develop a favourable balance (this does not, of course, imply anything whatever concerning the balance of direct payments between the countries concerned). The reactions of a country developing a favourable balance of payments are, in general, the obverse of the reactions to an unfavourable balance, described above. They will be determined partly by the direct effects on the profitability of business, and partly by the indirect effects *via* a fall in the local rate of interest. It should be noted, however, that while a favourable balance resulting from local developments may well be accompanied by a fall in local incomes, a favourable balance resulting from developments abroad will usually be accompanied by a rise.

This direct effect on incomes will be reinforced by the effect on interest rates. The normal effect of a favourable balance is to increase the banks' reserves of gold and foreign exchange, and at the same time to increase the ratio of their local deposits to local advances. If the country concerned is a financial centre, the effect may take the alternative form of transferring to local residents local balances and short-term assets hitherto held by foreign banks. In either case there is a tendency for money available for investment to become more plentiful and for interest rates to fall, though the effect will be more marked in the former case than in the latter.[1] After a longer or shorter delay, depending partly upon the direct effects of the favourable balance

[1] There is one apparent exception to this which it is worth pausing to examine. If a flight from a foreign currency results in an increase in local deposits held by foreigners other than banks, and a simultaneous decrease in local deposits held by foreign banks, the movement will appear to the foreign banks as an adverse balance of payments. To the local banks, however, the position will not have altered ; the total of foreign-held deposits has not changed, nor has their ability to make loans been increased. There will therefore be no tendency for the local rate of interest to fall. It is doubtful, however, whether such a movement can be rightly described as entering

and partly upon the pre-existing state of business psycho-
logy, the fall in interest rates will tend to be followed by
increased business activity and rising expenditures. The
connection is, however, much less positive than between
rising interest rates and falling expenditures ; for interest
rates can, if necessary, be raised to whatever level is necessary to restore the position, if necessary to infinity by a
complete refusal to grant or renew loans. But they cannot
be lowered beyond zero, if as far.

The development of an adverse balance of payments
by one country will usually be followed, especially in times
of fairly active trade, by a rise, after a longer or shorter
time, of expenditures in one or more other countries which
at the same time develop favourable balances. Whether
this rise in expenditures elsewhere will help quickly to
restore the balance of payments of the country with the
adverse balance will depend on two further considerations :
firstly, upon the extent to which an increase in expenditures in the countries with favourable balances is reflected
in their imports (*i.e.* upon their M.P.I.), and secondly, upon
the time-lag, if any, before these increased imports are fully
reflected in increased exports from the country with the
adverse balance.

VIII

In the light of the foregoing discussion, it seems clear
that it is only in high M.P.I. countries that the consequences
of an attempt to adjust an adverse balance of payments by
means of a restriction of bank credit and a rise in interest

into the balance of international payments. The transaction is not one
which directly concerns the local banks at all, and may be regarded as a
private arrangement between the foreign banks and their customers. It is
exactly analogous to the withdrawal of gold by foreign depositors from their
own banks for purposes of hoarding, and will have the same effect of causing
a rise in interest rates in their own countries without producing a fall elsewhere. It will in due course bring about a rise in interest rates in other
countries also, as the banks draw gold from abroad or obtain new foreign
balances from their former owners.

rates can be predicted with any confidence. In high
M.P.I. countries, unless local business prospects are so
favourable that expenditures are maintained in the face
of a rate of interest high enough to draw sufficient long-
term investments from abroad, the balance of payments
will be adjusted mainly by a reduction in imports. There
need be no fall in local prices or wages, no expansion
in exports, and comparatively little increase in unemployment. The whole process of adjustment can be
carried through rapidly, at the cost, indeed, of inconvenience to those who have to reduce their expenditures,
but without any serious check to local business activity.
The time taken to complete the adjustment and the
severity of the credit restriction required will depend
upon the size of the adverse balance, upon whether expenditures are spontaneously tending to fall or to rise, and
upon the adequacy of the banks' reserves of gold or foreign
exchange.

For low M.P.I. countries, on the other hand, confident
forecasts can be made only in cases where developments
are merely the obverse of developments in high M.P.I.
countries. To take an extreme hypothetical example, if
every low M.P.I. country had an adverse balance of payments, and every high M.P.I. country a favourable one, it
would be fairly safe to prophesy that, in the absence of
Government intervention, adjustment would take place by
means of an expansion of exports from low to high M.P.I.
countries, even without any restriction of credit in low
M.P.I. countries (this is not to say, of course, that such
restriction of credit would be unwise from the long-run
point of view; for in its absence there might well occur
an excessive expansion of credit in the world as a whole,
leading ultimately to a serious reaction). The time-lag in
the adjustment would depend partly on whether the banks
in the high M.P.I. countries wished to replenish their reserves of gold or foreign exchange before relaxing credit

conditions, and partly upon whether incomes and expenditures in high M.P.I. countries were already expanding. If the adverse balance of the low M.P.I. countries had been due to an increase in their imports or in their loans to foreign countries, the adjustment would be likely to be rapid.

So extreme a case as this is hardly likely to occur in fact; but it is possible that an approximation to it exists at the present moment, when in at least three important countries — Great Britain, the United States, and France — all of which have probably a fairly low M.P.I., imports have recently been rising fairly sharply, while exports have been rising more slowly in Great Britain and U.S.A., and falling in France. There is some probability that in this case the adjustment will take the form of an expansion of exports from low M.P.I. countries (though not necessarily from all of them). This probability seems to be increased by the fact that in certain other countries whose M.P.I. is probably in normal conditions also fairly low, quotas and exchange restrictions have made the value of imports more or less directly dependent upon the value of exports, so that the foreign trade of these countries reacts in some respects as if their M.P.I. was high.

Where the probable repercussions of developments abroad are so small or delayed as to be negligible, no definite forecast can be made of the results of an attempt to restore equilibrium in the balance of payments of a low M.P.I. country by means of credit restriction. If the country concerned is an international financial centre, adjustment may be brought about by a diversion of long-term borrowing, or more temporarily by an inflow of foreign short-term funds, which, however, may merely mitigate, but not entirely remove, the effects of a rise in interest rates upon internal business activity. In the absence of adjustments through the capital markets, equilibrium can be restored only by a fall in local incomes, either as a direct result of the causes producing the adverse balance of payments or in consequence of a restriction of bank credit, leading in turn either to a fall in internal prices and costs, and to an expansion of exports, probably accompanied by some contraction of imports, or, if the internal cost structure is rigid, to a contraction of imports due to unemployment.

FORECASTING FOREIGN TRADE [1]

Lest the title of this paper should be misunderstood, it must be stated immediately that its subject is not the forecasting of foreign trade in general, but the forecasting, for comparatively short times ahead, of imports of particular countries under particular circumstances. Nevertheless it is hoped that by limiting the goal it will become possible to indicate a technique which may prove of direct practical use to exporters and firms manufacturing for export. For, since these have to practise market forecasting whether they wish it or no in the ordinary course of their business, anything which enables them to make their forecasts even slightly more accurate is so much to the good.

It is of course only at intervals that the difficulties of business forecasting arise. For considerable periods of time, sometimes for years on end, all that is necessary is to anticipate the continuance of the existing trend of economic developments. Unfortunately, every now and then there comes a sharp change in the trend, which sometimes catches nearly everyone unawares. It is this change in trend, and especially the change in trend from business activity to business depression, which forecasters are always attempting to foretell, and which, before the beginning of the recent depression, some at least, especially in the United States, believed that they had perfected a system for foretelling. Of the coming of the recent depression, however, they were not forewarned by the indices upon which they had relied, and to-day few, if any, of them are

---

[1] Originally published in *Some Modern Business Problems* (Longmans, 1937).

prepared to commit themselves as definitely as they were wont to do in the past.

While, however, business forecasters are to-day far less confident than they were a few years ago, it would be a pity to go to the other extreme and abandon all hopes and attempts to anticipate changes in economic trends, and a good deal of quiet investigation is going on into the causes of the fluctuations in business activity which are commonly called the trade cycle.

These investigations may be divided into two types : the most usual and the most important are those which deal with fluctuations of activity arising spontaneously within a country — fluctuations which would occur even in an isolated system. The study of these has made great strides during the last few years and it is possible that one day it will have developed to a point where it will have an important practical application. But these questions lie outside the scope of this paper. The fluctuations in business activity which are considered here are those which arise, not from within a country, but from without — fluctuations which in turn are reflected in the demand of these countries for imported goods and in the export trades of other countries. It is here that their interest for the business man of this country lies, for by the use of the methods outlined here it should sometimes be possible to foretell by at least several months changes in the demand for imports of certain types of countries.

I

FORECASTING THE PURCHASES OF AN INDIVIDUAL

Perhaps the easiest way to approach the subject will be to take a simple case of a single individual. Let us suppose there is, shall we say, a farmer whose suppliers are anxious to discover how his total purchases are likely to compare in the near future with those of the recent past. If they have figures for all his sales and purchases as they take place month by month, and if they find from these that the value of his payments has recently been considerably exceeding the value of his receipts, there is some presumption that sooner or later, unless he can increase his sales, he will be compelled to decrease his purchases. How long the delay will be between the development of what we may call his adverse balance of payments and a reduction in his purchases will, however, depend on a number of considerations. Thus, if he himself thinks that the " adverse balance " will be temporary, and he has substantial reserves of cash or credit, it is possible that for a time he will reduce his purchases little, if at all, meanwhile drawing on his reserves in the expectation of replenishing them later. Thus a farmer, even though his receipts are concentrated mainly into one or two months, may be able to maintain his purchases fairly constant throughout the year, drawing temporarily on his reserves and replenishing them at harvest time. If, however, he has not an adequate reserve, he may be compelled to postpone some of his less urgent purchases until just after the harvest, so that his purchases, as well as his sales, will show a seasonal fluctuation.

Further, if he has considerable reserves, he may be able to ignore a more prolonged fall in receipts due to an exceptional cause, such as an unusual crop failure, and to maintain his expenditure as usual, in the belief that his income will in due course be restored to normal, and that he will be able to rebuild his reserves later on.

Even if his " adverse balance " is due to a permanent fall in his income, or to the absence of an increase which he had confidently expected and in anticipation of which he had allowed his expenditure to expand, there is likely to be some delay before he adjusts his expenditure to his changed circumstances. The lag will be determined partly by the time it takes him to make up his mind that the changed conditions are permanent, partly by the fixity of his future commitments, and partly by the size of his reserves. If he takes a hopeful view of the future and his reserves are large, he may go on for a very long time before cutting his expenses. If, on the other hand, his reserves are limited, even if he takes a hopeful view of the future, he *must* reduce his expenditure as they approach exhaustion. The longer he delays making any given reduction, the more sudden it must be when at last it is forced upon him. Thus, to forecast a reduction in his expenditure with any degree of accuracy it is necessary to know, not only the size of his " adverse balance ", but also what is the size of his reserve of cash and credit. Where reserves are large, for a long time his expenditure will depend on the view that he himself takes of the future, and any forecast regarding the date at which his reduction of expenditure will begin will therefore be unreliable. Where his reserves are small, forecasts can be made with considerable confidence.

Forecasts of an *increase* in expenditure will in both cases be rather unreliable; for whereas a *decrease* in expenditure can be forced upon a poor man, whether he *increases* his expenditure as his receipts increase will depend on his own wishes. Nevertheless, even here there will probably be a closer correlation between the receipts and expenditure of a poor man than of a rich one. A poor man is likely to spend more, fairly soon after his receipts increase; a rich man may prefer to replenish his reserves or increase his savings.

Forecasts could be extended still further into the future if information were available upon which could be based an estimate of the probable future changes in our farmer's receipts. If, for instance, his coming crop is going to be a failure, or its value is likely to be reduced by a fall in price, it may be possible to judge several months before the harvest by about how much a poor farmer's purchases during the following year are likely to be reduced.

The particulars of our farmer's receipts and payments might be obtained in one or two ways. It might be possible for his suppliers and customers to aggregate the figures of his receipts and payments directly. A simpler way, if it were a possible one, would be to consult his bank pass-book, which would show not only the amounts of his payments and receipts but also the size of his remaining balance. This information and perhaps some knowledge of the probable amounts of his receipts in the near future, based upon information concerning the condition of his crops, would undoubtedly enable his suppliers to form a better idea of the likelihood of his having to buy less from them during the following months. Forecasts of an increase in his purchases would be less reliable, for, though an excess of receipts over expenditure and a rising bank balance might show an increase in his ability to buy, it would not be absolutely certain that he would in fact make use of this ability.

II

FORECASTING THE PURCHASES OF A VILLAGE

The technique outlined above for estimating the future purchases of an individual is equally applicable to forecasting the purchases of a group. If, for instance, we know the collective receipts and payments of a whole village, it may be possible, especially if the inhabitants of the village do not have many outside assets and if their cash reserves are relatively small, to forecast a decrease or, less certainly, an increase in their purchases from outside. There is, however, one additional point that may arise in the case of the village and not of the individual. If all the villagers bank at the local bank, and this is an independent institution and not a branch of a larger bank, the changes in the collective receipts and payments of the village will be reflected in the village bank's own position; for when, say, the local innkeeper draws a cheque in favour of a brewer in a distant town, who does not bank at the village bank, two things happen: first, the innkeeper's account at the village bank will be decreased, or his overdraft increased; and second, the bank will have to pay over, in cash, a corresponding amount to the bank in which the brewer deposits it. Thus the village bank's deposits will fall or its advances will rise and at the same time its cash reserves will be depleted. If the payments of the village as a whole to outside are equal to its receipts from outside, then deposits with the village bank will equal the withdrawals and its cash reserves will not be affected; but any excess of payments over receipts will be reflected in an excess of withdrawals over deposits, and the bank's cash reserve will decline; while, if the village as a whole has an excess of receipts from outside over payments, deposits with the village bank will exceed withdrawals and the bank's cash reserve will rise. Thus, by watching changes in the accounts of the village bank we shall be able to ascertain changes in the relation between the receipts and payments of the village as a whole. An adverse balance of payments for the village is reflected in a rise in the bank's advances or a fall in its deposits, or both — together with a fall in its cash reserves; while a favourable balance of payments will be reflected in a fall in advances or a rise in deposits, or both, and in a rise in its cash reserves.

Whether a fall in the bank's cash reserves is accompanied by a fall in deposits or a rise in advances, and a rise in its reserves by a rise in deposits or a fall in advances, will depend largely upon the state of feeling in the village regarding business prospects. In a closed system, a worsening of business expectations usually results in a decreased willingness to lend and borrow, and in a fall both in bank advances and bank deposits, while improving expectations lead to a rise in both advances and deposits. In an open system, where a considerable proportion of payments is made to, and of receipts derived from, persons outside the system, a large adverse balance of payments accompanied by unfavourable business expectations is likely to result mainly in a heavy fall in deposits, while advances rise only slightly, or even fall to some extent. This situation indicates a probable sharp fall in purchases from outside in the near future. An adverse balance accompanied by favourable business expectations, on the other hand, is more likely to be accompanied by a rise in advances, while deposits fall only slightly or even rise a little. In this case, the check to purchases from outside, though still ultimately probable in a poor community, is likely to be more delayed, though possibly more violent when at last it comes, as the bank's reserves will by then have been more severely depleted. Similarly, a favourable balance of payments accompanied by unfavourable business expectations is likely to be reflected in a fall in advances, while deposits rise only slightly, or even fall slightly. In this case a recovery in imports, though ultimately likely, will probably be delayed. Finally, the most promising situation, a favourable balance of payments accompanied by favourable business prospects, is likely to be reflected in rising deposits, while advances fall only slightly or even rise. This conjuncture indicates a strong probability that imports will increase substantially in the near future.

The means by which the local bank would proceed to deal with the situation created by a fall in its cash reserves would probably be something as follows : as the bank found its cash reserves falling it would endeavour to replenish them by asking its debtors to repay it a part of what they owed. Unless they could borrow from outside the village, they could do this quickly only by borrowing from their neighbours ; but this would help the bank relatively little, because it would be paid back, not in cash, but in its own deposits, so that the fall in advances would be accompanied by a fall in deposits and not by a rise in cash. But in the long run, not only those who had been compelled to repay advances, but perhaps also those who had been tempted by the offer of higher interest rates to lend to their friends, would begin to spend less, and, in so far as this reduced expenditure was reflected in a reduced expenditure on purchases outside the village, the village's balance of payments would be adjusted by cutting down payments and the decline in the bank's cash reserves checked or reversed.

Similarly, if the bank's cash reserves are increasing it will be willing to lend more freely, possibly at reduced interest rates, and sooner or later this monetary ease will tend to be reflected in increased expenditures, partly on goods purchased outside the village.

How much changes in expenditure would affect purchases of goods from outside would depend on the types of goods produced locally and bought from elsewhere. If a village produced most of its own necessaries of life, while buying its comforts and luxuries from outside, then the result of a reduction of expenditure would be seen mostly in a fall in its demand for imports. In this case a restriction of advances by the bank would have a rapid effect in reducing purchases from outside, and changes in the bank's accounts would provide a good guide to future changes in imports. But if, as is rather unlikely, it produced its own comforts and luxuries but imported its necessaries, then any reduction of expenditure would fall mainly on the sales of local products. Less of these would be sold in the village and their price would tend to fall, and more of them would be sold to outsiders. In this case, the effect of a restriction of credit would be seen rather in a rise of exports from the village than in a fall in its imports. In this case, changes in the balance of payments and in the bank's accounts would provide a much less reliable guide to changes in the village's future imports. If in addition the bank had very large cash reserves, or the villagers large liquid assets outside the village, changes in its balance of payments and in the bank's accounts would give hardly any indication upon which a forecast of imports could be based.

III

FORECASTING THE IMPORTS OF COUNTRIES

When, therefore, we come to apply this technique for forecasting changes in imports to those groups for which balance of payments and banking figures are sometimes available, that is to say, to countries, we shall find that it cannot well be applied to countries which are major financial centres and which have very large gold reserves or large liquid resources or credits available abroad, just as it could not be well applied to the farmer with large cash reserves. Further, it is less reliable when applied to countries where a decrease in expenditure will mean mainly a reduced demand for local goods and where the decline in imports will therefore be small. These two objections frequently apply to the same country, and generally speaking render the technique unreliable for forecasting the imports of what we may term advanced industrial countries, such as this country, the United States, and France.

Further, it cannot be applied to countries which receive payments for a large proportion of their exports in currencies of countries with rigorous exchange restrictions. For the possession of large balances in such currencies does not enable their owners to purchase additional imports in world markets. This consideration probably hinders the application of this technique under present conditions to many countries in Central and Eastern Europe.

Lastly, of course, it is impossible to apply it to countries in which, though otherwise suitable, sufficiently prompt or adequate figures of their foreign trade and of the position of their banks are not published.

IV

STATISTICS NEEDED FOR FORECASTING

The full figures which are needed are as follows :

(1) Totals of imports and exports. These are regularly published monthly by most countries, and fairly up-to-date total figures can be obtained from the League of Nations *Monthly Bulletin of Statistics*.

(2) Estimates of other receipts from and payments to abroad, on income account, the so-called " invisible " imports and exports. Under this head are included such items as interest and dividend payments, tourists' expenditure, payments or receipts on account of shipping, insurance and banking, other services, and gifts made or received, such as remittances by immigrants. The League of Nations in its annual memorandum on " Balances of Payments " gives such figures for over thirty countries. Unfortunately the League Statistics are generally a year and often more in arrear, and for only a few countries are balance of payments figures obtainable earlier from other sources ; but many of the items constitute fixed charges and change comparatively slowly, and for the others, such as dividends paid to overseas shareholders and tourists' expenditure, there is usually a certain amount of information available upon which estimates can be based, which can be corrected when the official figures are available.

(3) Estimates of capital movements. These are usually given in the League's memorandum on " Balances of Payments ". For more up-to-date figures, statistics of new public issues of capital and of repayments of publicly held securities are relatively easy to obtain or compile. Other

capital movements, and especially short-term capital movements, can be estimated only by comparing the apparent balance of payments with the changes in the banking system's reserves of gold and foreign exchange. If, for instance, an apparent ADVERSE balance is accompanied by a RISE in the banks' reserves, it is probable that there has been an inflow of capital from abroad, and vice versa.

(4) With regard to the banking statistics, all, or almost all, the reserves of the banking system are sometimes held by the central bank. In that case, provided that the bank's returns distinguish foreign from local assets, the returns of the central bank are all that are necessary for the purpose of checking the estimates of the balance of payments, and for observing what further margin exists for meeting an adverse balance. Since in such a case the commercial banks probably operate entirely within the country, figures of their total deposits, advances, investments, and so forth, are adequate material for estimating the probable course of internal demand. Where, however, the commercial banks do business in a number of different countries, and themselves hold part of the country's reserves of gold and foreign exchange, then their statements, to be of any use, must separate local assets and liabilities from those elsewhere. If local assets and liabilities are given, changes in reserves of foreign exchange can be approximately determined by observing changes in the margin between local assets, other than gold, and local liabilities. For if local assets, other than gold, rise relatively to local liabilities, it is evident that there has been a fall in gold, or in foreign assets relatively to foreign liabilities; in other words, the stock of gold or the margin of foreign assets is reduced.

Weekly figures of many foreign central banks are published in the daily or weekly press, as well as in the official publications of the countries concerned. Complete figures of commercial banks are usually published only half-yearly, or sometimes quarterly; but summary figures of advances and deposits are sometimes published monthly. The League of Nations *Monthly Bulletin of Statistics* publishes up-to-date monthly figures of the " Gold and certain Silver and Foreign Assets Reserves ", of note circulations, and of deposits with the commercial banks, for over thirty countries. It should be emphasised that, for forecasting purposes, promptitude is far more important than completeness. For even such incomplete figures as those of monthly imports and exports and the banking figures given in the *Monthly Bulletin of Statistics* may enable a rough estimate of the actual position to be made; while admirably complete figures, published after a long delay, or at long intervals, merely enable one to see how well one could have forecast developments if one had only had the figures in time. In general, the best method is to make as good estimates as possible on the basis of the up-to-date figures available, revising them, and one's methods of estimating, in the light of the more complete figures as they become available.

There is one more consideration which may, in some cases, reduce the value of the internal banking figures of advances and deposits as a guide to changes in imports. If the Government is unwilling to allow an adverse balance of payments to be adjusted by means of a restriction of bank credit, with its ensuing check to internal business activity, it may prefer to effect an adjustment, at least temporarily, by direct restrictions on imports by means of tariffs, quotas, exchange restrictions, etc., or it may resort to currency depreciation. In any of these cases, it may be possible for a rise in imports to be checked and to be succeeded by a fall without any restriction of bank credit. If the authority which holds the principal gold and foreign exchange reserves of a country, whether it be a government, a central bank, or the commercial banks, allows its reserves to fall seriously without taking steps to check the fall by restricting credit, there is usually good ground for expecting that the adjustment of the balance of payments will ultimately be attempted by direct restriction of imports or by currency depreciation.

V

South Africa. Balance of Payments

In proceeding to describe in greater detail the use of the technique outlined above, it is proposed to use as an illustration the overseas country with which the writer is personally best acquainted — the Union of South Africa.[1] The country where this technique of forecasting is best known and has been most frequently applied is, of course, Australia, where much work has been done on the subject, by, among others, Professor Copland and Dr. Roland Wilson, and at the end of this paper there is presented a chart for Australia, based partly on their work, for comparison with the charts prepared for South Africa.

Of these, Chart 1 shows an estimate of South African receipts from and payments to the rest of the world from the beginning of 1926 to the end of 1936. The amounts are throughout in South African pounds. The upper figure on this chart indicates the various items which go to make up the total of South African receipts from abroad. The thin solid line represents what South Africa receives on account of her most important product — gold. And here there arises a small technical difficulty which it is worth while to clear up right away.

In most countries imports and exports of gold are excluded from the normal trade figures, for the reason that they usually represent transactions which do not enter into the balance of payments of the country. If the central

---

[1] Early in 1930 the writer constructed for South Africa a chart somewhat similar to Chart 6 described below. This chart has since been regularly continued in the *Monthly Review* of the Standard Bank of South Africa, Ltd.

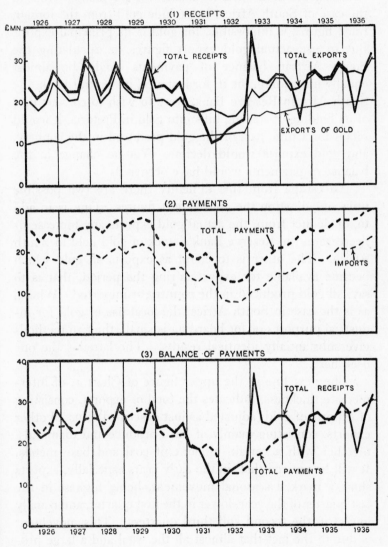

CHART I

INTERNATIONAL RECEIPTS AND PAYMENTS OF THE
UNION OF SOUTH AFRICA (QUARTERLY)

(1) RECEIPTS

(2) PAYMENTS

(3) BALANCE OF PAYMENTS

bank, for instance, is adding to its gold holdings, those additions may represent a surplus of national receipts from abroad over payments to abroad, and are the visible embodiment of a favourable balance of payments. But in the case of South Africa, to exclude gold from the foreign trade figures is impossible, for gold is its principal export. But to use actual gold export figures in calculating the South African balance of payments might be almost equally misleading, for if, for instance, its central bank, the South African Reserve Bank, were to wish to convert part of its holding of sterling bills into gold in Pretoria, it would retain for a time part of the gold produced in the country, and gold exports would decline. Yet no change in the balance of payments would have occurred.

To escape from this difficulty there are two possible ways of adjusting the gold export figures. One is to add to, or deduct from, the actual gold exports any increase or decrease in the Reserve Bank's stock of gold held in South Africa. The other is to count as exports all gold which became available for export during the period, that is to say, all gold produced in the country or imported. Where, as is the case in South Africa, the local use of gold for industrial purposes or for hoarding is small, the two methods give substantially identical results. The latter is the one used here.

The next line in the upper figure of Chart 1, of intermediate thickness, indicates the total of exports, consisting of exports of gold (adjusted as just described) plus all other exports, consisting mainly of farm produce and diamonds, together with a certain amount of coal and base metals. It will be noticed that, in the early years especially, exports show a marked seasonal movement, being highest in the last quarter of the year, lower in the first quarter, and usually lowest in the second and third quarters. This movement is due to the fact that almost all the wool and a large proportion of other farming exports are shipped in the last and first quarters, while exports of farm produce in the second and third quarters are relatively small. The smaller seasonal movement since 1929 is due to the lower values of farming exports.

The heavy solid line in the upper figure of Chart 1, in addition to exports, takes account of capital movements. Up till 1931 these almost invariably took the form of an import of capital into South Africa — involving the selling to South African banks of sterling in exchange for South African currency. It thus formed an addition to South African cash receipts. Since 1931 in several periods capital has on balance been exported. In these periods the heavy line which represents the total of the receipts side of the South African balance of payments falls below the line which represents exports only.

Turning now to the side of the account representing payments made abroad by South Africans, shown on Chart 1 in the middle figure, the thin broken line represents quarterly imports, including imports of gold, which have been allowed for in adjusting the figures of gold exports. The heavy broken line represents the total of the payments side, including not only imports, but net payments on account of interest, freight, tourists' expenses, and all the other items included in the generally used but rather misleading term of " invisible imports ".

In the bottom figure of Chart 1 the net total of credit items (the heavy solid line) is compared with the net total of debit items (the heavy broken line). The vertical interval between these lines represents the balance of payments for the quarter, " favourable " when the solid line lies above the broken one, *i.e.* when exports exceed imports, and " unfavourable " when the broken line lies above the solid one, *i.e.* when imports exceed exports.

The figures used in constructing this chart have been obtained from official South African sources, except that those of invisible imports and capital movements since 1933 are based on private estimates.

Chart 2 shows the results of Chart 1 in a simplified form. The thin line shows the favourable or adverse

CHART 2

INTERNATIONAL BALANCE OF PAYMENTS OF THE UNION OF SOUTH AFRICA (QUARTERLY AND CUMULATIVE)

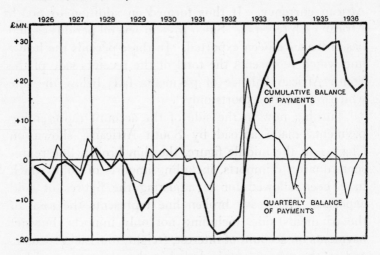

balance for the quarter, and the heavy line the cumulative favourable or adverse balance from the beginning of 1926. This chart shows clearly the cumulative effects of an adverse or favourable balance in several successive quarters.

VI

SOUTH AFRICA. BANKING STATISTICS

With Chart 3 we come to the bank figures. On this chart are shown the principal features of the combined accounts in South Africa of the commercial banks. It is important that only the figures for within the country should be included, for the South African banks operate on an appreciable scale not only in South Africa,

CHART 3

SOUTH AFRICAN COMMERCIAL BANKS

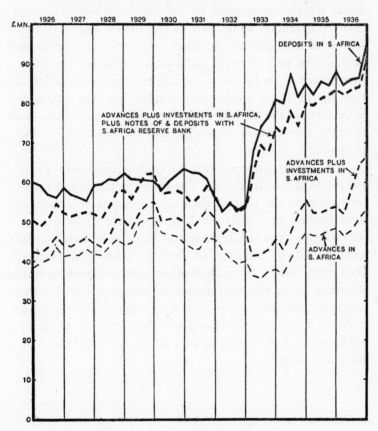

but also in London, East Africa, Rhodesia, Egypt, and other places. The bank figures are published quarterly in the *Union Government Gazette*, and conveniently summarised in the *Standard Bank of South Africa Monthly Review*. Monthly figures of Deposits and Advances

K

only are published in the *Monthly Bulletin of Union Statistics*.

In Chart 3 the heavy solid line indicates the banks' total deposits in South Africa. These roughly represent the amount which is available for lending, investment, and cash reserves in South Africa without drawing upon the assets which are needed to balance liabilities elsewhere. Strictly speaking, some part of the banks' capital and reserves should also be included, since increases in capital or reserves may provide additional funds for lending or investment. As, however, capital and reserves are largely tied up in fixed assets, and further, as they fluctuated little during the period under consideration, it has been thought unnecessary to complicate the diagram by their inclusion.

The broken lines indicate the commercial banks' principal assets in South Africa. The lowest and thinnest broken line indicates the total of their advances and discounts, the next broken line their total of advances, discounts, and investments, and the highest and thickest broken line this total plus their holdings of deposits with, and notes of, the central bank. Since their other assets inside the country fluctuate little, the movements in the gap between their deposits and their total assets, as shown on the chart, indicate fairly well the changes in their reserves of sterling exchange and (if they held any, which for some years they have not) of gold.

VII

SOUTH AFRICA. RELATION BETWEEN BALANCE OF PAYMENTS, BANKING STATISTICS, AND IMPORTS

If we compare the movements in this chart with those in the first two charts we see that up to the middle of 1927, deposits, allowing for seasonal fluctuations due to fluctuations in exports, are falling slightly, while advances are rising slightly. During this period imports are slightly declining. Towards the end of 1927 deposits begin to rise with the rise in exports, while advances fall slightly. This indicates a favourable balance of payments, improving business, and prospects of a maintained rise in imports. By the middle of 1928 advances are rising as rapidly as deposits ; exports have ceased to rise owing to the beginning of the fall in agricultural prices, and the favourable balance has disappeared, but trade is active and imports are likely to continue to rise. In the first half of 1929 exports are stationary, with imports still rising rapidly. Advances continue to rise, while deposits fall slightly — active trade, with an adverse balance of payments. Imports will continue to rise for a time, but the process cannot continue indefinitely. As the year continues and the banks' reserves continue to fall, they attempt to check the rise in advances by refusals of credit and a rise in interest rates, but without avail. Meanwhile the fall in prices has now reduced the value of farming exports, and the opening of the export season in September brings them little relief. In September, therefore, the commercial banks were obliged to seek to replenish their reserves by presenting bills for re-discount to the Reserve Bank, thereby endeavouring to obtain additional cash in South Africa with which they could buy from the Reserve Bank some part of its reserves of sterling. We must therefore at this stage introduce the figures of the Reserve Bank.

The South African Reserve Bank was only created after the 1914–18 War. Its functions were to manage the note issue, and to act as bankers to the Government and to the commercial banks. The commercial banks were obliged by law to keep minimum balances with it equal to 3 per cent of their fixed deposits plus 10 per cent of their demand deposits. Until 1929 the commercial banks rarely, if ever, availed themselves of their right of re-discounting trade bills with the Reserve Bank. The assets the Reserve Bank might hold were then limited to gold, certain types of trade bills, and to British and South African Government Treasury bills, and since the banks would not re-discount trade bills and the South African Government's issues of Treasury bills were small and irregular, the bulk of the Reserve Bank's assets consisted of gold and British Government Treasury bills, these together forming its reserves of gold and foreign exchange. In Chart 4 is shown the fluctuations of its holdings of these two items. The gold (the thin line) is valued at cost in South African pounds because, after 1932, while it is valued in the bank's returns at its old parity, it is paid for at market price, and the difference is included in the returns under the heading of " other liabilities ". The sterling bills are valued at their worth in South African pounds at the current rate of exchange.

In Chart 5 these reserves of the South African Reserve Bank are added to the estimated foreign reserves of the commercial banks (the thin solid line). This gives an estimate (the heavy solid line) of the reserves of gold and foreign exchange reserves of the banking system as a whole. There is also inserted a line (broken) showing the commercial banks' total reserves, including their holding of Reserve Bank notes and balances; for while changes in these do not affect the total reserves of the whole banking system (since while they are assets of the commercial banks they are liabilities of the Reserve Bank), they do reflect the extent to which the effect of an adverse balance reduces the reserves of the Reserve Bank or those of the commercial banks.

From these charts it is clear that in 1929 the commercial banks bore the brunt of the effects of the adverse balance, that is, the bulk of the decline took place in their sterling reserves; in fact, the Reserve Bank, when approached for re-discounts, discouraged them by a sharp rise in its re-discount rate. The result was that the commercial banks

CHART 4

BANK RESERVES

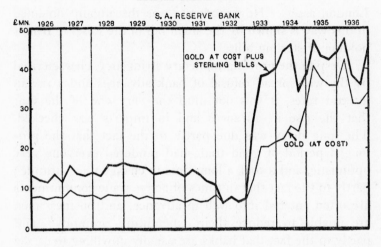

S. A. RESERVE BANK

GOLD AT COST PLUS STERLING BILLS

GOLD (AT COST)

CHART 5

BANK RESERVES

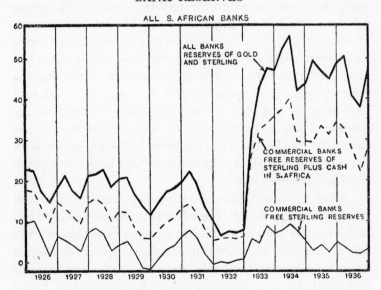

ALL S. AFRICAN BANKS

ALL BANKS RESERVES OF GOLD AND STERLING

COMMERCIAL BANKS FREE RESERVES OF STERLING PLUS CASH IN S.AFRICA

COMMERCIAL BANKS FREE STERLING RESERVES

were able to replenish their London reserves only to a small extent by buying from the Reserve Bank part of its London assets. How moderate was the amount obtained in this way is shown by the small fall in the Reserve Bank's holding of sterling bills.

Despite the growing monetary stringency, characterised by the widespread refusal of bank advances and a rise in interest rates, it was not until the very end of the year that the rise in advances and in imports was checked. The long delay was due partly to the fact that the prolonged period of good trade had rendered everyone very optimistic, and it took a long time to change their attitude ; partly to the fact that in times of active trade commitments are often entered into well in advance, and business men are unable to reduce their expenditure promptly ; and partly to the fact that banks are usually unwilling to cancel overdraft limits within less than the period originally granted. Thus, even if new advances are refused, and limits renewed at a lower level, the fact that everyone is using his existing overdraft facilities more fully causes advances to rise for a time.

Nevertheless, to anyone who in June 1929 was trying to forecast trade movements on the basis of the figures as shown on these charts, it should have been clear that the country was over-importing, and that unless the value of exports recovered (which was most unlikely in view of the continued fall in prices) imports would soon have to be reduced. If they had at that time had such information before them, British exporters would have been saved much trouble and some loss.

After the acute financial stringency had at last caused imports to begin to fall, the fall was rapid, and as a revival of borrowing from abroad offset to some extent the further fall in exports, the favourable balance which developed began to replenish the banks' reserves. The first stage of this, while credit is still restricted, shows itself in a heavy fall in advances, accompanied by a smaller fall in deposits.

When, however, the recovery in the banks' reserves had gone far enough by the second quarter of 1930 to ease their position, we get a slower fall in advances accompanied by a rise in deposits. We also get the usual symptom of easy money in a time of depression in a rise in the banks' South African investments, which previously had remained fairly constant at a low figure. It is, however, difficult to draw an exact line between advances and investments, for most of the investments seem to have been in short-dated Government Securities, hardly distinguishable from advances to the Government. By the early part of 1931 the credit position had become quite easy, and since the fall in exports had almost come to an end it seemed likely that imports would presently recover. The commencement of a recovery in advances seemed to bear this out, and indeed, in the third quarter of the year, there was a perceptible rise in imports. Unfortunately, shortly before the end of this quarter the departure of Britain from the gold standard and the ensuing flight from the South African pound entirely changed the outlook. On this occasion the Reserve Bank took a much larger share of the burden of supplying the abnormal demand for sterling, and by the end of the first quarter of 1932 its holding of sterling bills was completely exhausted. In spite of this, the heavy withdrawal of deposits for transfer overseas depleted the commercial banks' reserves also very seriously, and an extremely drastic restriction of credit ensued, even more drastic than that of 1929–30, which after a time-lag of about six months brought about a new very heavy fall in imports to a level far below that for which South Africa could have afforded to pay, out of the proceeds of her exports, if the flight from the currency had not occurred.

By the middle of 1932 the fall in imports had been sufficient to check a further decline in the banks' reserves, and thereafter, with the help of another Government loan

raised in London, some replenishment took place. Rates
of interest were reduced, and it seemed likely that imports
would soon recover to a more normal level.   Just before

CHART 6

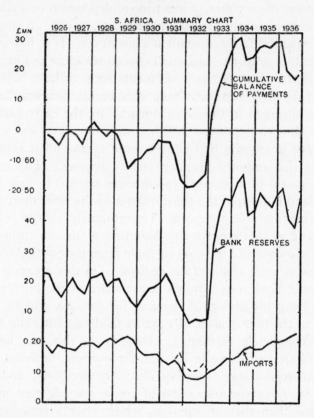

the end of the year, however, a renewed flight from the
currency caused the abandonment of the gold standard,
and immediately a terrific inflow took place of all the funds
which had previously been exported.   The result was an
immense rise in the Reserve Bank's holdings of gold and
sterling and in the commercial banks' deposits with the
Reserve Bank, and the return of the commercial banks'

own reserves of sterling to a comfortable level. At first this resulted in a rise in deposits accompanied by a fall in advances, but later advances rose parallel with deposits, an indication of trade activity. Meanwhile imports have

CHART 7

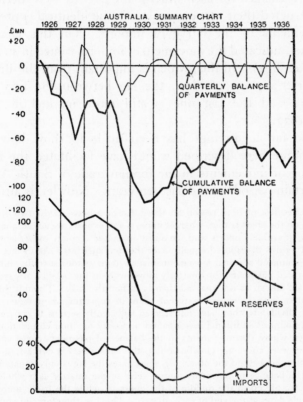

been rising rapidly, and at present the country's balance of payments on income account is approximately in equilibrium — that is to say, receipts and expenditure are nearly equal.

The charts used above are perhaps too complicated for presentation, for instance, to a board of directors. A summary chart has, therefore, been prepared (Chart 6) which shows on one sheet the cumulative balance of payments (the top line), the movements in the reserves of the banking system (middle line), and the movement in imports (bottom line). This chart shows clearly how movements in the first two curves (which are to a large extent a check on each other; for if both were perfectly constructed their movements would be identical [1]) precede movements in the curve of imports. On this chart is further indicated the movement of imports valued in sterling (broken line). In this, which is important from the British exporter's point of view, the lag between the first two curves and the last one is still more marked in 1932 and 1933.

So far an attempt has been made to show how the technique here described would have facilitated the forecasting of movements in the foreign trade of South Africa at certain periods of the past ten years. Now let us attempt

---

[1] The most obvious reason for the differences between the two lines as shown on the chart is that, whereas imports and exports are actual quarterly figures, invisible imports and, in most instances, capital movements are annual figures distributed equally over the four quarters. As in fact there is a pronounced seasonal movement in such items as tourist traffic, interest, and divided payments, the quarterly movements in the balance of payments curve are shown as less marked than is in fact the case. Though the discrepancies have increased in recent years in consequence of larger gold-mining dividends, they have not seemed sufficiently serious to warrant the large amount of additional investigation necessary for their elimination.

Even where the movements in the balance of payments curve and the bank reserves curve are closely similar, the bank reserves curve frequently appears to lag behind the other. In some cases the lag is only apparent, for since the balance of payments figures refer to the quarter as a whole, the points are placed in the middle of the quarters, while the bank figures are for single dates at the end of each quarter. There is, therefore, an apparent lag of about six weeks.

Where the lag is greater than this, it may be due to the following cause : not all exports and imports are represented by bills and not all bills are discounted with the banks. Where goods are shipped between branches of the same firm, or sent on consignment, or where bills are sent for collection, several weeks or even months may elapse before the imports or exports are reflected in transactions affecting the banks. Meanwhile, the imports or exports may be regarded as being financed by short-term credits by foreign or local exporters. Thus some part of a change in the total of imports or exports may not be reflected in the bank figures until the following quarter.

to make a forecast on the basis of the present information.

The present position of South Africa is one which does not make reliable forecasting easy. It will be remembered that at the beginning of this paper it was pointed out that if an individual is possessed of large liquid reserves, the size of his expenditure, at least for a long time, depends largely on his own inclinations. The enormous reserves of gold and sterling held by the South African Reserve Bank now put South Africa in a similar position. It is a position of some danger. A private individual, coming suddenly into the possession of a large amount of ready cash, can easily get into the habit of greatly over-spending his income, only to be pulled up with a jerk when his capital is at last exhausted. In exactly the same way, a country with very large bank reserves of gold and foreign exchange could continue for some time to have a heavy adverse balance of payments, but would have to curtail imports sharply when the reserves had been reduced again to normal.

In the case of a country, the decision as to what policy is to be pursued rests largely in the hands of the banks. They have enough cash to be able greatly to increase their loans if they wish. But if they do, imports will increase, their cash reserves will be depleted, and ulti- mately they may be compelled to cease making new loans or even to call in some of the loans they have already made. This is what happened last time the South African banks were in a position comparable to that which exists to-day. Owing to the high price of exports, South Africa had a very favourable balance of payments in 1919. The banks accumulated abnormally large reserves of sterling and in consequence lent very freely in South Africa. As a result, in 1920 South African imports went up very sharply, and since prices of exports fell, there developed a very large adverse balance, which reduced the banks' reserves of sterling to below normal and forced them in 1921 to restrict credit in South Africa. In the ensuing crisis, both the banks and many of their customers suffered heavy losses.

At the present time the banks seem to be pursuing a much more cautious policy. Advances in South Africa have certainly risen, but only slightly above the pre-depression level, which was about two-thirds of that which existed at the end of 1920. Meanwhile the country, through the action of the Government, has been making what is often the best use of surplus cash resources. It has been using them to pay off debts owed in London, with money obtained partly from the Government's share of the profits of the gold mines and partly by borrowing in South Africa. The recent sharp rise in the banks' South African invest-ments seems to be due to this cause. These repayments of foreign debt are doing something to reduce the cash reserves of the banks to a more normal level. At the same time the reduction of interest payments due abroad will tend to decrease the total of " invisible imports ", that is, of payments due abroad, and to set free a larger proportion of the proceeds of South African exports, that is, of the country's receipts in foreign currencies, for buying things abroad.

In view of the cautious policy of the banks and the Government, it does not seem likely that we shall see South African imports rising much faster than her exports, though perhaps a little faster on account of these reduced interest payments. As, however, exports themselves are rising, it would be reasonable to expect to see a steady and continued, but moderate, rise in imports for some time to come. Even if imports were to begin to rise a good deal faster than exports, so that a substantial adverse balance of payments developed, the still very large bank reserves would enable imports to be maintained at this higher level for a long time. In this case they would, of course, ultimately have to be checked, if exports did not catch up, either by bank action in the form of restricting advances or raising interest rates, or by direct restrictions on imports by the Government. Study of the figures of advances and deposits in South Africa, and of the bank reserves in South Africa and overseas, would reveal the course of developments and the probable method of ultimate adjustment.

VIII

RELATION BETWEEN BALANCE OF PAYMENTS, BANK RESERVES, AND IMPORTS IN AUSTRALIA

There happens to be at the present time another country where the position is very different — that is Australia. It may be of interest to illustrate this same forecasting method in its application to the current Australian position. Chart 7, constructed on the same principles as Chart 6, shows the cumulative balance of payments for Australia (top line), an estimate of the gold and sterling reserves of the Australian banking system (middle line), and Australian imports (bottom line). In the case of Australia the question of the size of the banks' reserves of sterling is complicated by the fact that some of their sterling assets, which would normally form part of their reserve, consist of sterling debts owed to the London offices of the banks by the Australian Government; it cannot, therefore, properly be counted as part of Australia's true sterling reserve. In view of this and other difficulties no attempt has been made to construct private estimates of the banking reserves, but Dr. Roland Wilson's yearly estimates as quoted in the League of Nations *Memoranda on the Balance of Payments*, for the years 1928 to 1933, have been taken, and extended forwards and backwards in the light of other available information to 1926 and 1936. Other figures are from the usual official sources, except for the figures for " invisible imports " and capital movements after 1933, which are private estimates.

While the chart shows clearly how much worse was

the impact of the depression on Australia than on South Africa, in consequence, of course, of the greater importance of the South African gold-mining industry, the earlier movements of the curves show very similar characteristics. The lag between the decline in the banks' reserves and in imports in 1929 is even greater, while the subsequent recovery in reserves and imports is much less marked. The chief difference is in the present position. While South Africa seems likely to be able to finance a considerable further expansion in her imports, it seems doubtful if Australia will be able to continue indefinitely even to maintain her present level of imports unless her exports increase. Fortunately the rise in prices of farm produce seems likely to ease her position this year, but her banks' reserves seem to be inadequate to finance even a temporary adverse balance, such as might occur owing to a crop failure, and such an event would only too probably be followed either by a restriction of credit and higher interest rates or by renewed restrictions on imports. In either case imports would decline. As an export market, Australia under present conditions seems to offer less prospect of expansion than South Africa.

How far this technique can be applied to other countries can be ascertained only by further investigation. But wherever even a part of the necessary figures are available, it is believed that their systematic arrangement and analysis on the lines indicated above would well repay the research staff of manufacturing or merchant firms interested in exporting to the countries concerned.

CAUSES OF CHANGES IN GOLD
SUPPLY [1]

UNTIL fifty or sixty years ago there was a good deal to
be said for the view that changes in the output of gold
were due rather to the accidents of the discovery or
exhaustion of gold deposits than to any changes in the
economic data, including costs of production and the price
of gold. Many of the most important discoveries of the
nineteenth century seem undoubtedly to have been made
as the result of pure accident, and accident seems to have
played an important part in the greatest discovery of all,
the Main Reef series of the Rand, though in this case, in
view of the intensity of the search that was being conducted,
it is doubtful if accident accelerated the discovery by more
than a few months. Nor did many of the original discoveries do much to remove uncertainty. The local richness of many of the alluvial discoveries caused almost as
much over-estimation of the profitability of further work
in the vicinity as the strangeness of the Rand formation
caused its importance at first to be under-estimated. The
thousands of miners who flocked to the public alluvial
diggings of California and Australia in the fifties of the last
century probably earned, on the average, a good deal less
than if they had stayed at home. For instance, Del Mar
(*History of the Precious Metals*, p. 264) estimates that on
the Californian diggings in the year 1856 the value of the
gold produced per miner was under £74, a sum quite

[1] Paper delivered at the International Conference of Economic Services
at Pontigny, France, on September 3rd, 1938, and originally published in
Economica, November 1938.

insufficient for their support in that place. Clearly, under conditions of production by a multitude of small entrepreneurs, each of whom has preferred an unknown chance of substantial wealth to the greater certainty of a modest livelihood, it is impossible to establish any reasonably approximate correlation between the value of gold produced and the value of the opportunities forgone.

During the last third of the nineteenth century, however, the conditions of gold-mining began to change, and there can be little doubt that the major changes that have taken place in the output of gold since about 1890 have been due mainly to changes in costs of production or of the price of gold. This great change in conditions has been due largely to the fact that for many years the whole trend of development has been to reduce the uncertainties of gold-mining. Some uncertainty, of course, still exists. The old adage that a miner cannot see beyond the end of his pick has not yet lost all its truth, and surprises, pleasant or unpleasant, can still occur. But it is clear that the great increases which have taken place in the knowledge of particular gold formations and of geology in general, and the immense technical improvements in methods of prospecting, of testing likely areas, of developing new mines, and of managing old ones, have eliminated many uncertainties and have converted others into measurable risks. At the same time the bulk of the world's gold has come to be produced by large, and much of it by very large, technical units, which within themselves can pool many risks and convert them into more or less calculable costs. Further, the development of mining finance companies, each interested in many different mining companies, has enabled the risks, especially of new developments, to be spread still more widely than would be possible within the individual technical units.

This reduction in the element of risk does not mean, of course, that the size and distribution of the natural deposits of gold-bearing ore are unimportant factors. Since the known and accessible deposits are limited in extent, there will necessarily be a tendency always present for output to decline unless new discoveries or lower costs intervene to check or reverse the process, while it is conceivable that the whole position might at any moment be changed by the purely accidental discovery of large and hitherto unsuspected deposits of rich ore. What is true, however, is that the power of economic forces to accelerate or delay the exhaustion of existing deposits, and to promote or discourage the discovery of new ones, is now so great that changes in the output of gold are now much less " accidental " and much more " induced " than they were half a century ago. To-day, indeed, there is no reason to assume that the output of gold is less sensitive to changes in costs than is the output of other commodities. It is therefore possible to consider the principal causes of such changes in costs, and the conditions which determine the manner and extent of the response which output makes to them.

During the past fifty years many of the more accessible reserves of gold ore have been worked out, and during the same period there has been a great increase in the general level of prices and wages. Nevertheless, the cost to-day of mining and milling a ton of ore is much lower than it was fifty years ago, and in many areas as low, or almost as low, as it was thirty years ago. If we look for the underlying cause of this achievement we shall find it mainly in the growth that has taken place in technical knowledge.

It is true that in the early part of the period much of the fall in costs in many areas was undoubtedly due to the application of increased amounts of already known forms of equipment, and above all to improved transport facilities, which gradually brought the exceedingly high price levels which formerly ruled in the vicinity of many gold mines more closely into accord with those in other

L

parts of the world. Nevertheless, but for the various technical inventions that have been made during this period, costs of gold production in many mining areas would be several times higher than they are to-day, and the output of gold only a fraction of what it is. Probably the most important of these was the introduction in the 1890's of the cyanide process of extracting gold from refractory ore, by means of which the percentage of extraction was raised from 60 or 70 to well over 95. The effect of this increase, of the order of 50 per cent, in the amount of gold extractable from each ton of certain types of ore, was twofold. In the first place, it increased the output of gold directly, and apart from any increase in the scale of operations, by increasing the quantity of gold obtained from the existing tonnage of ore milled; and in the second place, it made it payable to mine ore of a lower gold content, and thus added to the known or potential ore reserves any ore lying between the old and the new limits of payability.

Of the three causes of changes in mining costs hitherto mentioned, two — discoveries of new supplies of ore and improved methods of production — necessarily tend to reduce costs of production, and one — the exhaustion of the more accessible of the known ore deposits — to raise them. To these must now be added a cause which may work in either direction — changes in the supply schedules (to the gold-mining industry) of the factors required. The direction of these changes is largely influenced by the general movement of world prices, though prices of the collection of goods and services purchased by a gold mine may at times move very differently from those of the collections which are used to calculate wholesale or retail price index numbers. Until about 1909 it seems that the upward tendency of world prices which had begun in the 1890's either had little effect on gold-mining costs or was offset by other factors. From 1910 until the beginning of the war there was a slight rise in costs, especially in

Australia, where its effect was to accelerate the decline in the output of gold which had begun in 1905 in consequence of the progressive exhaustion of the richest deposits. The rise in prices during, and especially just after, the war brought a very sharp rise in gold-mining costs. In Australia, for instance, costs per ton of ore milled nearly doubled between 1910 and 1921, while in South Africa they rose by about 40 per cent. The smaller increase in South Africa was partly because the general rise in whole-sale and retail prices between 1910 and 1920 was less in South Africa than in Australia, and partly because of the conditions, peculiar to South Africa, governing the price of unskilled and semi-skilled labour. In South Africa all mine employees except those in charge of machinery and explosives, or in positions of authority, are natives. The average native money wage is less than one-tenth of the average wage for Europeans, so that, as the ratio of native to white employees is in the neighbourhood of ten to one, the total native wage bill is rather lower than the total white wage bill, though it should be added that the natives receive food and shelter in addition. It is to this supply of cheap native labour, together with the very large local supply of very cheap coal, that the exceptionally low costs of mining in the Transvaal are principally due. Native wages are not only low, as compared with those paid to European workers, but are also much more stable. The whole work of recruiting natives is controlled by the Transvaal Chamber of Mines through two subsidiary organisations, and the labour available is apportioned among the various mines. Native wages are centrally determined, and the mines do not compete against each other for labour.

This fixation of wages has had the effect of reducing the amplitude of fluctuations in their level. For instance, between 1913 and 1921, whereas average white wages and the cost of stores each rose by about 50 per cent, average native wages rose by only about 15 per cent, and the rise in total working costs per ton was only a little over 40 per cent. On the other hand, one result of this control of native wages is that the mines frequently complain that they cannot obtain as much native labour as they would like to employ at the wages fixed, and that, in consequence, they have been unable to work at full capacity. This tends to cause some rise in other costs per ton of ore milled, though not as great a total rise as if native wages had been determined by competition. One effect of the fixation of native wages is, therefore, that a lower grade of ore can be milled profitably than if wages had been free to move, but that the tonnage of ore milled is smaller than if the mines were free to attract more labour by raising wages. Thus the amount of ore worth milling is increased, but the number of tons milled a year, and probably also the average grade of ore milled, are reduced. The annual output of gold is therefore lower, but the lives of the mines are more than proportionately lengthened.

In the short period, the supply of native labour to the gold mines fluctuates with the demands of alternative occupations open to them, including farming in their own reserves. Good farming seasons, high prices for farm produce, increased activity in the diamond, coal, or base metal mines, all tend to keep labour from the gold mines, while crop failures and lower prices tend to improve the labour supply. It is through this indirect effect of price changes that the South African gold mines most rapidly feel the benefits of a fall in the prices of other commodities, for white wages are difficult to reduce, and most mine stores are bought on long contracts and reflect price changes only slowly.

As a result partly of the control of native wage rates, partly of the reduction of white wages after the strike of 1922, and partly of the continual improvements in mining technique, gold-mining costs in South Africa had fallen by

1926 to only about 6 per cent above the 1913 level, although wholesale prices were still about 20 per cent above the pre-war level. This may be contrasted with the experience of Australia, where costs of production in 1926 were still something like 40 per cent above the pre-war level. It is to South Africa's remarkable success in reducing costs that the continued rise in her gold output must be attributed at a time when production in most other countries continued to decline, and in Australia, the world's largest producer in 1903, it had become insignificant.

Since the beginning of the depression in 1929 gold producers have benefited in two ways. In the early part of the depression the fall in the prices of other commodities increased the supply of available factors and brought both some fall in costs of production and, in South Africa, an ample supply of native labour. Later, as one producing country after another left the gold standard, the price of gold increased.

Hitherto we have been discussing causes of changes in gold-mining costs. We must now consider both the relationship between changes in costs of production or in the price of gold and change in output. As we have seen, a change in the cost of producing gold may take two forms. It may take the form of a change in the amount or value of the yield of gold from each ton of ore of a given grade, or it may take the form of a change in the cost of mining and milling a ton of ore. The first will lead to an automatic change in the quantity or value of the gold produced, in addition to any indirect effect it may have via an induced change in the quantity or grade of ore milled. The second will affect the output of gold only through its influence on the quantity or grade of ore milled. It is to this indirect effect that we must now give our attention.

The relationship between the size of a given deposit of ore and the amount of that ore which is milled in any one year is exceedingly complicated. Here it is possible to give only a broad outline of the principal considerations involved, in the hope that the conclusions thereby reached will not be so different from those obtained by more refined methods as to be seriously misleading.

In most types of production we have to consider the problem of the optimum rate of application of variable factors, including raw materials, to certain fixed equipment of which the useful life does not greatly vary with the intensity of utilisation. In other words, the proportion of marginal cost which consists of user cost is relatively small, and even substantial differences in estimates of user cost would have very little effect on total marginal cost and on the rate of output. In the case of a mine, however, the position is the exact opposite. There is a given stock of raw material of which the rate of output, and therefore the length of life, is almost infinitely variable according to the amount of fixed capital and other resources which are applied to its exploitation. In this case, every ton of ore extracted means a ton less to be extracted at some future date ; and if the deposit is a valuable one, which is expected to show a large profit over costs of extraction, the greater proportion of marginal cost may be the user cost of the deposit. In this case the simplest method of approach to the problem of the optimum rate of output seems to be to attempt to ascertain the scale of output at which the dis-counted present value of total future receipts during the whole life of the deposit shows the greatest margin over the discounted present value of all costs to be incurred.

Let us attempt an examination of this question by taking the case of a virgin mine for which we have to decide the scale of capital equipment, rate of annual output, and life, which give us the largest present value of the future profit. To begin with, we shall make certain initial simplifying assumptions, and shall then observe the effects of their progressive removal. Let us assume, therefore, that we are studying the exploitation of an undeveloped ore deposit of given size, the contents of which are completely homogeneous, equally accessible, and exactly known. Let us further assume constant costs and a constant price of the product. On these assumptions, at any positive rate of interest it will pay to work out the deposit in the shortest period that is physically possible. If we carry our assumption of constant costs to absurd extremes, it will be most profitable to work it out instantaneously. At a zero rate of interest, on the other hand, any rate of output is as good as any other, and the problem is indeterminate.

Let us now abandon our assumption of constant costs, and assume that costs per unit of output (since the ore is at present assumed to be of constant grade, output can be calculated equally well in terms of tons of ore or ounces of gold) are free to change with the rate of output. These costs may be divided into two main categories. Of these, one is working costs — costs of labour and of non-durable or non-specific equipment which must be incurred more or less evenly through time. It is not unreasonable to assume that working costs per unit of output will vary with the rate of output, for reasons which are common to all types of enterprise. Up to a point the increased specialisation rendered possible by increasing the scale of output will cause average working costs per unit produced to fall as the rate of annual output rises. Beyond a certain point the application of additional factors to a given mine will cause diminishing returns to set in, and average costs will begin to rise again. In some cases, where the mine itself is very large, diseconomies of large scale may begin to appear after a certain point, due to the increasing costs of central control. Further, where the supply of factors of production to this particular mine is not perfectly elastic, the price per unit of factors will rise and with it the average cost per unit of output. We may summarise these conclusions by saying that working costs will fall for a time as annual output increases and sooner or later begin to rise again. It is possible that there is a range of output over which working costs are constant, but it is at least equally possible that there is a single rate of output at which they are at their lowest point. Since on our present

DIAGRAM 1

UNDISCOUNTED AGGREGATE WORKING PROFITS AND INITIAL COSTS

(As a Function of Annual Output)

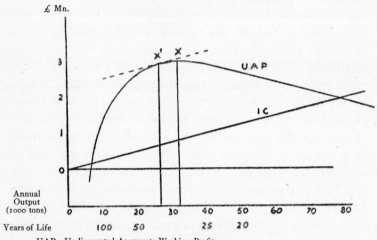

£ Mn.

Annual Output (1000 tons)

Years of Life

UAP = Undiscounted Aggregate Working Profits.
IC = Initial Costs.
X = Point of maximum profit with no initial costs and a zero rate of interest.
X¹ = Point of maximum profit with initial costs IC and a zero rate of interest.

assumptions the quantity of gold to be produced from the mine is given, the point of lowest average working cost per ounce produced is also the point of lowest aggregate working cost for the whole output of the mine, and since the price of gold is also given, it is the point of highest average and aggregate working profit.

In the absence of any costs other than working costs and in the presence of a zero rate of interest, the most profitable life of the mine would be that at which un-discounted aggregate working profit (curve UAP in Diagram 1) was at its maximum (x). In most mines, however, there will be a second type of cost — the irregularly occurring cost of durable and specific equipment. A large part of this equipment cost, under our present assumptions, will be incurred at the very beginning of the life of the mine and before any gold is produced, and if we assume for the sake of simplicity that the whole of it is incurred at the beginning, the assumption may not be very unreal. It will further simplify exposition if we assume that the initial expenditure on durable and specific equipment (of which in the case of deep-level mines the most important item will be the mine shafts) will be directly proportionate to the designed rate of annual output, though this assumption is in no way essential to the argument. In this case, as the absolute horizontal scale is in terms of annual output, the curve of initial costs (IC in Diagram 1) will take the form of a straight line sloping upwards and to the right from the origin. At a zero rate of interest, the most profitable output rate of the mine will be that at which the undiscounted aggregate working profit most exceeds initial costs. In Diagram 1 this point will be where the curve UAP is parallel to the line IC. We shall find that this new optimum point (x^1) will lie to the left of the highest point of the UAP curve (x), and will move further to the left the steeper is the slope of IC up to the point where IC becomes tangential to the UAP curve and the development of the mine ceases to be profitable. Thus the greater the cost of initial equipment per unit of annual output, the smaller will be the most profitable rate of annual output and the longer the optimum life of the mine. This is presumably the chief reason why alluvial mining areas, which require relatively little durable and specific equipment per unit of annual output, are usually worked out more rapidly than quartz or banket mines, and why a shallow mine is likely to have a shorter life than a deep one.

We must now abandon our assumption of a zero rate

of interest. What in fact a mine-owner would wish to maximise is not the aggregate net profit of his mine over the whole period of its life, but the discounted present value of the aggregate net profit. This involves the discounting

DIAGRAM 2

UNDISCOUNTED AGGREGATE WORKING PROFITS, DISCOUNTED AGGREGATE WORKING PROFITS, AND INITIAL COSTS

(As a Function of Years of Life of Mine)

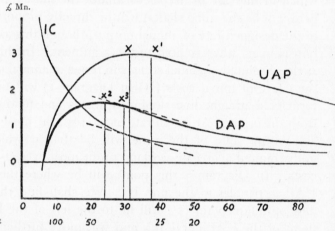

UAP= Undiscounted Aggregate Working Profits.
DAP= Discounted Aggregate Working Profits.
IC= Initial Costs.
X= Point of maximum profit with no initial costs and zero rate of interest.
X¹= Point of maximum profit with initial costs IC and zero rate of interest.
X²= Point of maximum profit with no initial costs and a 5 per cent rate of interest.
X³= Point of maximum profit with initial costs IC and a 5 per cent rate of interest.

back of the working profit to be earned throughout the life of the mine and the deduction from it of the actual initial cost. Since the discounting must be done on an annual basis, it will be convenient to change our absolute horizontal scale from annual output to its reciprocal, years of life of the mine. If we keep the origin as zero, this will involve the reversal of the diagram. The Initial Cost curve now becomes a rectangular hyperbola.

If we now proceed to discount the aggregate working profit at any given rate of interest, we shall obtain a new curve of *discounted* aggregate working profits (DAP). This curve will coincide with the *undiscounted* curve (UAP) when profits are at zero, will fall by an ever-increasing proportion below UAP as the life of the mine is increased, and will again coincide with it when zero profits are again reached. We shall find both that the peak of the DAP curve (x^2) lies to the left of the peak of the UAP curve (x) and that the point (x^3) where it shows the greatest margin over the initial costs curve will also lie to the left of where the UAP curve showed its greatest margin (x^1). Thus the life of the mine will be shorter and the annual output greater with a positive than with a zero rate of interest. We shall also find that the higher the rate of interest the higher will be the optimum annual output and the shorter the life, up to the point where the DAP curve becomes tangential to the IC curve and the development of the mine becomes unprofitable.

This is true even though the expansion in the rate of output involves additional initial expenditure on capital equipment, up to the point where the increase in initial expenditure becomes equal to the increase in the discounted present value of future working profits.

Thus conditions are conceivable in which a rise in interest rates will make profitable increased expenditure on capital equipment. At first sight this seems contrary to the conclusions of the theory of capital. But the contradiction is only apparent, for the ultimate effect of the rise in interest rates is to accelerate the rate at which the ore is consumed, and to shorten the life of the mine. It is very doubtful, moreover, whether even on our assumptions of homogeneity of ore in each mine and the absence of uncertainty, the *total* demand for capital for mine equipment would increase. For a rise in the rate of interest, while increasing the optimum scale of equipment of such

mines as it still pays to develop, will probably prevent
other mines, with smaller potential profitability, from
showing a profit even at the optimum rate of output, and
will therefore destroy their potential demand for capital.
Only if all potential mines have ore so rich that the rise
in interest rates has little effect on the world total of workable ore, is the rise likely to have the effect of increasing
the total demand for gold-mining capital.

The importance of the effects of changes in the market
rate of interest on the rate of gold output is further diminished if we remove our assumption of perfect foresight
concerning the contents of our mine, future costs of
production, and future selling prices. As soon as any
substantial degree of uncertainty is present, the supply of
capital to a given mine ceases to be elastic. The main
reason for this is that, whatever the effect on the *total*
amount of profit earned, the *rate* of possible profit *per
unit of capital employed* falls as the amount of capital
is increased. In order to attract capital to a highly speculative venture it is essential that the *possible* profits should
be very high. The risk is high because the capital must
be expended largely on equipment (including knowledge)
which is specific to the mine in question. Any over-
spending on development and equipment cannot therefore
be rectified, while a mistake in the opposite direction can
usually be rectified by further expenditure. Mines about
whose contents or costs there is considerable uncertainty
are, therefore, started on the smallest possible scale. A
few hundred or thousand pounds are spent on prospecting
an area where gold is only a possibility. When the possibility becomes a probability, more capital can be obtained
and profitably applied to financing development on the
smallest practicable scale. As the probability grows and
uncertainty diminishes, more and more capital can be
added and production increased towards what would be
the optimum if there were perfect knowledge. Thus the

greater the certainty, the greater the annual output and the shorter the life of the mine. This conclusion has particular interest in relation to uncertainties about the future price of gold. The possibility of a fall in the price will certainly discourage investment in gold-mining, prevent present output from increasing as much as it would otherwise have done, and lengthen the lives of the mines.

It is interesting to note that where it is technically essential, as in most deep-level mines, to begin the development of a new mine (or of a new area of an existing mine) by means of a large initial capital investment, development is likely to be delayed until uncertainty has been greatly reduced, perhaps by the gradual extension of contiguous mining areas.

The elasticity of the supply of capital to speculative mines is not, of course, constant, and there are times when it increases so greatly that the foregoing considerations cease to have general application. That there are periods when the risks of new development are more gladly borne than at other times in no way differentiates gold-mining from other speculative industries, which are equally characterised by investment fashions or booms. The chief difference between gold-mining and other booms lies in the times of their occurrence. The last two great gold-mining booms, that of 1894–95 and that of 1933–36, have taken place during the early stages of industrial revival after a depression, when risk-bearers have begun to recover their nerve after the preceding crisis, but when there is still an unemployed surplus of fixed assets in most other types of industry. The lower prices of factors (and now the higher price of gold) during the depression have reduced the costs and increased the profits of existing mines, and have encouraged discoveries of new mines and projects for the extension of old ones. The fall in interest rates and the higher profits have combined to raise the prices of shares of established mines to a point where they offer relatively little prospect of further appreciation. It is not surprising that in these circumstances the supply of unemployed risk-bearing tends to flow into the shares of new and developing mines, nor that promoters multiply the supply of shares to meet the demand. Under present conditions, it is probable that quite a large part of the money subscribed will actually be used to develop and equip new gold mines, a proportion of which will ultimately produce gold in substantial quantities.

We can now return to our consideration of what effect changes in costs of production or in the price of gold have on output. Let us for the moment continue our assumption of a homogeneous ore body, so that changes in costs do not affect the size of the stock of ore that can be worked at a profit, and let us at present consider only the effect on the rate at which an unchanged stock of ore is worked.

We shall find that the effect on the optimum life of a mine of a change in working profits will depend on the way it alters the slope of the discounted profits curve. By way of illustration we may consider three of the most probable ways in which working profits may alter:

(1) A rise in working profits by a given number of shillings per ounce (such as might be caused by a rise in the price of gold), representing a rise in the undiscounted profits curve by an equal amount throughout its length. Since the new *undiscounted* curve is parallel to the old one, the new *discounted* curve will approach the old discounted curve as the life of the mine is lengthened. The peak of the new DAP curve will lie slightly to the left of the old one, while the downward slope to the left is less steep and to the right more steep in the new DAP curve than in the old. The point of maximum margin over the initial cost curve (x^3) will therefore move to the left and the optimum life of the mine will be shortened.

(2) A rise in working profits by a given percentage (such as might be caused by an equal proportionate rise in the

price of gold and in working costs). In this case the rise
in the undiscounted profits curve will be at its maximum
when the curve is at its highest point, and will fall to zero
as the curve falls to zero, so that the undiscounted curve will
fall more steeply than before in both directions. The peak
of the discounted curve will be directly above the former
peak, but the new curve will fall more steeply in both
directions than the old one. Its point of maximum margin
above an unchanged initial cost curve will therefore move
to the left and the optimum life of the mine will be
shortened. The effect is identical with that of a fall in
initial costs, working costs and the price of gold being
unchanged. If initial costs as well as working costs rise
proportionately with the price of gold, the optimum life is
unchanged.

(3) A rise in working profits proportionate to the
working costs incurred in earning it (such as might be
caused by a fall in working costs unaccompanied by a
change in initial costs or in the price of gold). In this
case the rise in working profits is least when working
profits are at their maximum, and increases as profits fall
to zero. The undiscounted curve will therefore fall less
steeply in both directions than before. The peak of the
discounted curve will move to the left more than in case
(1), and the new discounted curve will fall less steeply to
the left than the old one. Whether it will fall more or less
steeply to the *right* will depend on the shape of the undiscounted curve and on the rate of interest. Generally
speaking, the optimum life will be shortened unless the
rate of interest is very low or unless costs rise very rapidly
as the rate of annual output falls; it will also probably
be shortened in any case if initial costs are very small.

On the whole it may be said that, except in very exceptional conditions, the effect of a rise in working profits
will be to increase the most profitable rate of annual output
and to shorten the optimum life. A fall in initial costs

will have the same effect.   Conversely, a fall in working profits or a rise in initial costs will tend to lengthen the optimum life.

In the foregoing discussion, it will be remembered that we are considering the optimum scale of output of a mine upon which nothing has yet been spent, and for which we are therefore quite free to decide the optimum expenditure on equipment.   Once a decision has been made and specific capital equipment installed, the expenditure on that equipment becomes irrelevant for purposes of calculation.   All that matters is the present value of the excess of future revenue over future expenditure.   If we find that we have under-estimated the optimum annual output, or if changed conditions make an increase profitable, it is always possible (in the absence of serious indivisibilities) to adjust the position by an increase in specific equipment.   But if we find that we have over-estimated the optimum amount of equipment, we have to consider how to maximise the present value of the excess of future revenue over future working costs only, and the deterrent effect of rising fixed costs per unit of output as output is increased will be absent. We shall, therefore, find it profitable to continue to produce, so long as the equipment lasts, an annual output greater than that which we should have arranged to produce if we had had better foresight, though possibly smaller than the output it was originally intended to produce.

It is this factor of the irrevocability of most of the capital expenditure on gold mines which helps to maintain the level of gold output after an investment boom.   On such an occasion it is only to be expected that many speculative shares will be bought above the price that a rational estimation of the chances and dimensions of future profits would justify, and that many mines will be developed and equipped which with better foresight would either not have been developed at all or would have been developed on a smaller scale.   Nevertheless, many of these will produce gold in an amount and at a cost which, while not such as to render the original investment profitable, will be sufficient to prevent the abandonment of shafts and equipment already in existence. So long as these last, output will remain above the level which it would have reached under conditions of greater foresight. Thus an unfounded expectation of increased future profits — due, perhaps, to the unfulfilled hope of a rise in the price of gold — may have the effect of increasing the output of gold over a period of many years.

We must now turn to the consideration of the effect of a change in costs or in the price of gold on the amount of ore which it will pay to mine. Let us for a moment longer retain our assumption of homogeneous ore, and consider the question of an increase in the available supply of ore of the existing grade without a reduction in the cost of mining existing ore reserves — due, perhaps, to an invention that has rendered possible the mining, under the same conditions as the existing stock, of ore hitherto regarded as inaccessible. In this case, after the delay due to the time taken to add to the capital equipment, it will pay to expand the rate of output. Unless, however, the cost of production per ounce is the same for the new output as for the old, the scale of output will not increase proportionately. If the effect of increased output is to increase costs per unit of gold, annual output will increase less than proportionately to the increase of ore reserves, and the life of the mine will be lengthened; while if costs per unit decrease with increased output, output will increase more than in proportion, and the life of the mine will be shortened. The former possibility seems to be the most likely.

We now have examined, on our simplified assumptions, the two possible ways in which reduced costs or higher prices may increase output — by increasing the rate of working of the existing ore reserves, and by increasing the ore reserves and the scale of working of the whole mine.

M

We must now abandon the assumption of homogeneity of ore, and bring our assumptions more closely into accordance with actual conditions. Let us now assume a mine with a wide range of ore grades, varying from the merest trace of gold to half an ounce or more to the ton. The effect of a change in costs or in the price of gold will now be necessarily twofold. It will alter the cost of working the ore which throughout remains within the limits of payability, and by altering those limits it will alter the amount of ore in the mine that can profitably be worked. Before, however, beginning our consideration of the effect of these changes upon the size of the annual output, it is necessary to make a digression in order to examine the factors which govern the order of working of ore of different grades of richness.

If the order in which the ore is mined makes no difference to costs and to the total profits earned over the whole life of the mine, it is clear that, at a positive rate of interest, the mining company will maximise the present value of its profits by mining the richest ore first. If, as may sometimes happen, costs are *reduced* by mining the richest ore first, this course will be profitable even at a zero rate of interest. But it more frequently happens that to mine the richest ore first, and leave the less payable for future years, may increase the cost of production and possibly lead to the ultimate abandonment of much of the less payable ore. This may well occur, for instance, if small areas of high- and low-grade ore are closely intermixed. The additional costs of selective mining, and of maintaining old stopes with a view to returning later for the extraction of the low-grade ore left behind, may be so high as more than to offset the advantages of concentrating the higher earnings in the earlier years. Nevertheless, it will always pay to sacrifice *some* part of the total profits earned over the whole life of the mine for the sake of increasing the profits in the earlier years. How far selective mining will be a payable

policy will depend on the distribution of ore in each particular mine. Broadly speaking, the larger the more or
less homogeneous blocks of high- and low-grade ore, the
more profitable to the shareholders will a policy of selective
mining be.

Nevertheless, such a policy of " picking the eyes of the
mines " is universally frowned upon by responsible mining
opinion. In so far as this is due to a belief that the consequent rise in costs would render such a policy unprofitable,
this point of view is justified. But there is reason to believe
that the policy of selective mining could profitably be
carried a good deal further than in practice it is. Why then
do the mining authorities so object to it ?

It is difficult to find any clear answer to this question,
but on the whole the objections seem to be based on two
main grounds. Firstly, the practice of selective mining
clearly lends itself to fraud on investors. If the profits
earned in the early years of a mine are greatly above the
level which can be maintained throughout its life, investors
may well be induced to expect the high dividends to continue and pay too much for the shares. This will in turn
impair the investment reputation of gold mines as a whole,
and cause yields of all mines, including those which do
not or cannot practise selective mining, to be capitalised
in the market at a lower level. Closely connected with
this is the argument that shareholders prefer a steady to
a declining income, even though the discounted present
value of the declining income is greater. This latter difficulty does not appear to be insuperable. It is always open
to a mining company to withhold part of the high profits
earned in the early years and re-invest them, either in the
same mine or elsewhere, so as to earn interest or profits
upon them. In this way dividends could be maintained at a
more or less constant level higher than that which is possible under the system of mining proportionately from all
grades of ore, which is tantamount to investing part of the

potential profits without interest in holding back stocks of rich ore.

The other important reason for the dislike of selective mining is that most of those who are responsible for the formation of mining opinion are interested rather in the longevity of the mines than in their profitability to shareholders. For managers, employees, consulting engineers, as well as for those who are dependent on the gold mines for their market, the important thing is that the mines should continue to employ as many factors as possible for as long as possible. Selective mining without a consequent rise in costs would not necessarily shorten the life of the mine, for all payable ore would still be mined, though in a different order. But if the effect of selective mining were to raise costs, the amount of payable ore would be reduced and the life of the mine shortened; while even if costs were not affected by the order of mining, a later rise in costs, due to other causes, would shorten the life of the mine much more if the high-grade ore had already been extracted. This would not involve any additional loss to shareholders (indeed, the expectation of a subsequent independent rise in costs would make selective mining profitable even at a zero rate of interest), but it would mean that the risks of factors becoming prematurely unemployed would be increased — a contingency not to be regarded with equanimity by employees, suppliers, local authorities, or the Government.

Whatever the true reasons, the practice of the mines seems to approximate closely to their stated policy of milling ore of the same average grade as that contained in the mines. This is certainly true, at least, so far as concerns that part of the contents of the mines which has been developed, sampled, and included in the published ore reserves — usually about the equivalent of three or four years' supply to the mill. It is not possible to say as definitely how far it is followed in deciding how much of each of the various grades of ore is to be developed and added to the ore reserves. Where high- and low-grade ores are closely intermixed there is little room for discretion; but where some zones or reefs are believed to consist mainly of high-grade and others mainly of low-grade ore, it is clear that for many years the average grade of the ore added to the known and published reserves may be largely controlled by managerial policy. The fact that, when a mine is approaching the end of its life, the average grade of ore milled usually falls, seems to indicate that some low-grade ore is left after the high-grade ore has been worked out, and that *some* degree of selection is, therefore, practised. In any case, since the contents of undeveloped ore blocks can be estimated only roughly, the policy of mining equal proportions of each grade cannot be followed with any high degree of exactitude.

On the whole, however, it seems that the assumption that mines follow the policy of milling the average grade of ore contained in the mine is sufficiently realistic to permit practical deductions to be drawn from it. This is very convenient for purposes of analysis, since for many purposes a mine can be considered as containing ore of homogeneous grade equal to the average of the various grades it actually contains. The conclusions previously reached in our consideration of a mine with homogeneous ore, therefore, are usually more or less valid, and we can proceed with our examination of the effects on output of a change in costs or in the price of gold.

Owing to the presence in a producing mine of durable and specific equipment, the effects of increased and de-creased working profits are not fully symmetrical. We must therefore consider them separately. Let us first consider the case where working profits have increased. This will mean that some ore, of a lower grade than any at present worked, will come within the margin of payability. The quantity of payable ore in the mine will, therefore, be increased and its average grade reduced. As we assume that the mine's policy is to mill ore of an average grade equal to that of the mine as a whole, the average grade of ore milled will fall, and less gold will be produced per ton of ore milled. On the other hand, the increase in the working profit earned and the increase in the payable ore content of the mine will make it profitable to increase the number of tons of *ore* milled per annum. In the long run, the net effect upon the annual output of gold of the two opposing influences will depend on the grades and proportions of the new and old ore, and upon the elasticities of the supply of labour, capital, and other factors. If the quantity of low-grade ore which is added to the reserves is relatively small, the reduction in average grade will also be small, and unless the supply of factors is very inelastic, the increased rate at which it now becomes profitable to work the existing ore will cause annual output to rise by proportionally more than the gold content of the mine, so that its life will be reduced. Where the quantity of low-grade ore added is substantial this is unlikely, and the annual output of gold, though higher, will probably increase by less than the gold content of the mine, so that the life of the mine will be lengthened. Finally, where the addition of low-grade ore and the reduction in grade are very large, a mine may possibly find it profitable to increase its tonnage of ore milled only by an amount which is insufficient to offset the fall in grade, so that the annual output of gold will fall and the life of the mine will be lengthened more than in proportion to the increase in its gold content. Of the three possibilities, the second seems much the most likely.

The extent to which the effects of an initial fall in costs or rise in the price of gold are perpetuated will depend largely upon the elasticity of the supply of factors, not merely to each mine, but to the industry as a whole in each area. If the supply is inelastic, as the whole industry endeavours to expand its tonnage of ore milled, the cost schedule of each particular mine will rise, some of the new low-grade ore will cease to be payable, and the average grade will rise. If the rise affects working costs more than costs of durable and specific equipment, the fall in capital costs relatively to working costs will tend to increase the rate of output for any given average grade of ore milled; if the rise in working costs goes so far that the average grade milled returns to its former level, the continued lower level of capital costs will make profitable an increased scale of working and a shorter life for the mine. If capital costs rise *pari passu* with working costs until the average grade milled recovers to its former level, the scale of output will not be affected, unless in the meantime the amount of capital equipment has been increased.

The case in which there will most certainly be a permanent fall in the rate of output is where a rise in the price of gold adds a large new tonnage of low-grade ore to the reserves and therefore greatly reduces the average grade of ore milled, and where at the same time the price of a factor in inelastic supply is monopolistically prevented from rising. In this case there will be no rise in costs or in the grade of ore milled; but the shortage of the factor will limit the increase in the output of ore, which will therefore be insufficient to offset the fall in grade.

In the present instance, the rise in the price of gold has coincided with a fall in alternative demands for factors, and, despite the greatly increased demands of the mines, costs have remained low. If, however, the price of gold were raised at a period of full employment, it is possible that the resulting increase in output would, in many areas, be relatively small; while if the prices of factors were prevented from rising, it might actually decrease. Even as it was, the improvement in the demand for diamonds, farm produce, and base minerals in 1936–37 rapidly brought complaints of a shortage of native labour in South

Africa, and it is only now that the effects of the renewed fall in prices are being seen in an improvement in the labour supply.

While the long-run effects of a large and sudden rise in the price of gold or fall in costs are to some extent dependent on circumstances, the short-run effects are still more doubtful. The time taken to reduce the grade of ore milled to the new average of the mine, though appreciable, is in many cases shorter than the time needed for increasing the annual tonnage of ore milled. Broadly speaking, the delay in expanding output will depend on the accessibility of the ore. Where the gold is in alluvial deposits or shallow mines, the time needed for expansion may be quite short. In deep mines, it may well be a matter of years before the rate of output can reach its new optimum, unless there is some excess capacity in the existing fixed equipment. The same considerations apply to the development of new mines or the reopening of old ones. If the ore is near the surface, or if disused fixed equipment has been kept in serviceable condition, the response of increased output to the stimulus of higher profits will be rapid. If deep shafts have to be sunk and deep development carried out, it will be slow. Thus in a deep-mining area, where the existing equipment is already used to capacity, and where the rise in working profits has brought much additional low-grade ore within the limits of payability, the existing amount of fixed equipment will be temporarily used for raising and milling ore of a lower average grade, and output of *gold* will decline. As equipment is expanded and the tonnage of ore milled increases, gold output gradually recovers to its former level and probably ultimately rises well above it. But the intervening period of lower output may last for several years.

There is another factor which may intensify this temporary fall in the output of gold. In an old-established mine there are probably substantial areas of low-grade ore which have been rendered known and accessible by the development and extraction of the higher-grade ore, but which it has hitherto not paid to remove. Some of these low-grade zones have no doubt been irretrievably lost by the collapse of old workings, and so forth, but it is likely that enough will remain to add a larger proportion of low-grade ore to the developed ore reserves than the amount of still undeveloped low-grade ore bears to the rest of the mine. Thus the average grade of the developed ore reserves becomes lower than the average grade of the remainder of the mine. As the average grade milled will approximate to that of the known reserves, it will for a long time be below the average grade of the mine, rising slowly as the existing ore reserves are replaced by new development.

It is largely to the foregoing causes that we must attribute the remarkable difference between South Africa and other gold-producing countries in the years 1932 to 1937. In 1932 the gold production of the world, excluding South Africa and Russia, was about 10·8 million ounces. It thereafter rose rapidly and continuously to 11·4 million ounces in 1933, 13 millions in 1934, 14·3 millions in 1935, 16·4 millions in 1936, and 17·8 millions in 1937. In South Africa, on the other hand, the output of gold *fell* from 11·6 million ounces in 1932, the year at the end of which South Africa left the gold standard, to 11 millions in 1933 and 10·5 millions in 1934, and it was not until 1937 that the output again reached the 1932 level. A glance at the figures shows the cause of this movement. Between 1932 and 1934 the average grade of ore milled on the Witwatersrand fell from 6·3 dwts. per ton to 5 dwts., so that, despite an increase in tons milled from 34·6 millions to 39·4 millions, the output of gold showed a decline of over 1 million ounces. Since 1934 the increase in tons of ore milled to 49·9 millions has more than offset a further decline in the average grade from 5 dwts. to 4·46 dwts., and the output of gold has steadily expanded. It is probable that this expansion will continue. In 1932 there was only one developing mine in South Africa. In 1937 there were twenty developing mines, of which many seem likely in due course to produce gold in substantial quantities. It is true that the number of natives employed on the gold mines has already risen by nearly 50 per cent since 1932, and that it may be difficult to find the further additions to the supply which will be necessary if all the mines, new and old, are to be worked to full capacity. But even if the native supply of labour were to remain in the vicinity of the present total, it is probable that the gradual transfer of workers in new mines from development to production, and the continued introduction of more labour-saving methods, would allow the rise in output to continue. Hitherto the rise in the world's output of gold has been entirely due to expansion outside South Africa. Henceforth it is likely to be increasingly due to rising South African output, which may well be still expanding when output in other countries, with deposits at once more rapidly developed and more rapidly exhausted, has already begun to fall.

A further point which is well illustrated by the recent history of South Africa is the difference in the results of a rapid and of a gradual change. Between 1928 and 1932 average costs per ton of ore milled on the Witwatersrand fell gradually from 19s. 9d. to 19s., though the decline in effective costs, in the form of a more plentiful supply of native labour, was a good deal greater. The average grade of ore milled fell from 6·5 dwts. to 6·3 dwts., but owing to the slowness of the change the tonnage of ore milled had time to rise from 30 million tons to 34·6 million tons, so that the output of gold increased from 9·9 million to 11 million ounces.

The best historical instance of a movement in the reverse direction — of a rapid rise in costs and a fall in working profits — occurred during and after the 1914–18

War. For South Africa the best years to take are 1915–19, for the higher costs of 1920 and 1921 were more than offset by the higher price of gold, and the fall in the price of gold from 1921 to 1924 was offset by lower prices and wages. In 1915 the Witwatersrand mines milled 28·3 million tons of ore of an average grade of 6·2 dwts. at an average cost of 17s. 5d. per ounce, and produced 8·8 million ounces of gold. By 1919 the average cost had risen to 22s. 11d. per ton, and the tons milled had fallen to 24 millions, or by 15 per cent, but the average grade had been raised to 6·7 dwts. and the output of gold was only 700,000 ounces, or 8 per cent lower at 8·1 million ounces. In the case of a still sharper rise in costs, or of a sudden fall in the price of gold, it is quite possible that the rise in the average grade of ore milled might temporarily more than offset the reduction in tonnage, so that for a time the output of gold might conceivably rise. This would be most likely in the case of a mine where there were both a large amount of durable and specific equipment and zones of high-grade ore which could be mined selectively without much additional increase of costs. In such a case, the output of gold would remain higher so long as the durable equipment and the supplies of high-grade ore lasted. On the other hand, mines with little specific equipment would probably reduce their scale of output fairly rapidly, while mines with little ore above the new level of payability would soon be obliged to close down. It is therefore not likely that a fall in the price of gold would be followed, even temporarily, by a rise in output in the world as a whole, though a temporary rise might well take place in the output of certain mines, or even of certain fields.

To complete a study of the causes of changes in the output of gold some reference must be made to the effects of Government action. The subject is a wide one, and raises many interesting and difficult questions. Here it is possible only to attempt to classify the main types of

Government action and to give some examples of their possible results.

Types of Government action which affect the output of gold fall into four main classes : (1) taxation and restrictions on movement, etc., which affect the prices of factors ; (2) methods of general direct taxation ; (3) special taxation of (or subsidies to) gold mines ; (4) regulations prescribing the conditions under which mining properties can be acquired and worked.

The first of these requires little elaboration. Government action is one of the various causes which determine the local prices and supplies of factors of production. The intervention may, for instance, take the form of import duties or quotas on the stores required by the mines, or of high transport rates on State railways for the requirements of the mines. In South Africa the gold mines have at various times made strong complaints against both these practices. It may take the form of a State monopoly of an essential requirement, such as the dynamite monopoly which proved such a source of friction between the gold mines and the Government of the Transvaal before the Boer War. It may take the form of restrictions upon the movement of labour, either by local or by foreign Governments. The recent curtailment of supply of native labourers from Mozambique to work in the Union might in other circumstances have been a serious embarrassment to the mines. Another example is the rule, imposed by the South African Government in order to reduce mortality among Transvaal mine natives, whereby the mines were forbidden to employ natives coming from north of latitude 22° South. The mines now claim that improved methods of hygiene have eliminated the former risks for tropical natives, and the results of the present experimental quota are said to have borne out this claim. If this restriction is relaxed it will go far towards assuring to the mines at existing wages the supply of labour which they are equipping themselves to employ.

Secondly, methods of general direct taxation may affect the supply of capital to mines, and conceivably even the policy of the mines, in so far as they discriminate against income earned from wasting assets. In the United Kingdom, for instance, the whole of mining dividends are treated as income for purposes of income tax and surtax, although a substantial proportion (in the case of mines with short lives, a very large proportion) of the income should be used to amortise the wasting asset. The methods of taxation in use in the United Kingdom therefore tend to divert the flow of capital from mining into other investments, and to restrict mining development. They further tend to discriminate against mines with short lives, and to make the extension of the life of a mine beyond its optimum point profitable for British shareholders, and especially surtax-paying shareholders. If such shareholders are both aware of where their advantage lies and in a position to influence the policy of the company, there will be a further tendency for the current output of minerals, including gold, to be reduced.

If any form of special direct taxation is imposed on gold mines, it must necessarily have a deterrent effect on the development of new mines or the investment of additional capital in old ones, though this effect may be reduced by suitable concessions, such as the complete or partial exemption of new mines from taxation for a period, the privilege of allowing capital expenditure out of income as a deduction from profits for purposes of taxation, an increase in permitted rates of capital depreciation, etc. While, however, a general expansion of output can be secured only by some form of subsidy, such as that given to Australian gold mines from 1930 to 1932, it is possible to frame a tax in such a way that it induces such mines as are developed to mine ore of lower average grade than they otherwise would. The present form of gold-mining excess profits taxation in South Africa is designed to have this effect. It was originally introduced, in a different form, to divert to the Government a large share of the immense increase in profits which the mines obtained from the devaluation of the South African pound, and at the same time to maintain their demand for factors at as high a level as possible, while lengthening their lives.

In its present form the tax is both simple and ingenious, and it might well be applied by other Governments which desire to induce industries to give increased employment. In addition to normal income tax at a rate of 3s. in the pound, or 15 per cent, the mines must pay an excess profits tax equal to 35 per cent of their gross receipts less 40 per cent of their costs, or, to put the same thing another way, a total of 50 per cent of their profits less 5 per cent of their costs, with a minimum of 15 per cent. This means that the more costs the mines can incur in earning a given profit, the better off they are; and that it is worth their while to earn a slightly smaller profit if by so doing they can have larger costs and a larger deduction from their tax. Its effect is, therefore, the opposite of that of indirect taxation, which raises the cost of factors employed, and increases the amount paid in tax as working costs rise. The general effect of such a tax is to reduce the incentive to install labour- and material-saving equipment, and to raise working costs relatively to capital costs. In the particular case of the gold mines, it also encourages the milling of ore of a lower grade than would otherwise be profitable. It thus tends to lengthen the lives of the mines, while in the short run, and possibly also in the longer run, it tends to cause a greater reduction in the annual output of *gold* than an ordinary tax on profits would have done. Thus the form which South African taxation has taken has tended to intensify the effects on output of the mines' policy of milling the average grade of the mine.

Finally, the general structure of mining law necessarily has some effect on the rate of output. If, for instance, gold deposits are of a kind which it is possible to work on a small scale, a mining law which encourages their working as public diggings, by a large number of independent miners, each working a small claim with very little equipment, will probably cause the annual rate of output to be higher and the life of the deposit shorter than if they are worked on a larger scale and by more capitalistic methods.

Again, where the undermining rights of gold-bearing ground are owned by the State, the output of gold may be greatly affected by the terms on which the State is willing to sell or lease the ground. In such a position the State may act like a private land-owner, making the most profitable arrangements possible for the mining of the ground, and only withholding mining areas from development if it believes that their value to itself will appreciate so rapidly as more than to offset the loss of interest. On the other hand, if its object is to secure the continuance of mining activity at its present level for a long period, it may deliberately withhold land from development for a time in order to replace existing mines when they become exhausted.

The actual terms and conditions of the leases may also affect the rate of output of the mines after development. The size of the individual mines will depend largely on the State's judgment as to what area constitutes " a workable proposition ", and the larger the size the longer will the life of the mine tend to be. Secondly, the lease may be drawn in such a way that the interests of the shareholders are different from what they would have been if they had owned the mine completely. If the royalty is a fixed payment per ounce of gold produced, or per ton of ore milled, it will increase costs per ounce or per ton, raising the minimum grade of payable ore and shortening the life of the mine. If it is a uniform proportion of the profit, the position of the State will be similar to that of any shareholder, and the lease payment will have no effect on the rate of output. But if, as is the case with most of the South

African leased mines, the Government's share of profits increases as the ratio of profit to output of gold rises, it will pay the shareholders to decrease this ratio at the expense of a diminution in total profits — in other words, to mine ore which would otherwise have been below the limit of payability, decrease output, and extend the life of the mine. Thus the policy of the South African Government, both through taxation and the terms of its leases, is to check the immediate expansion of the output of gold in order to prolong the lives of the mines. It is to this policy, as well as to that of the mines themselves, that the delay in the rise of South African output is due.

With regard to the future, the prospects of developments in other spheres of economic activity are too uncertain to permit of any definite forecasts; but certain of the conclusions reached in the foregoing discussion may be usefully applied to the consideration of the probable reactions of gold production to the various possible developments elsewhere.

If the conclusions reached above are justified, the rate at which a new deposit of gold will be exhausted will depend upon the rate at which total costs increase as the annual output is expanded. This, in turn, depends largely upon the amount of durable and specific equipment needed per unit of output, so that those mines which need most capital equipment will, generally speaking, be those with the longest lives. But such mines are also those which will generally take longest to reach their optimum rate of output, so that the rate at which output is expanded is often a guide to the period for which the increased output is likely to be maintained. If this is so, those areas where production has responded most rapidly to the stimulus of the higher price of gold are likely also to be those where the deposits will be most rapidly exhausted.

Even if, therefore, the general level of prices and gold-mining costs remain in the vicinity of their present level, we may expect to see the rapid rise in output in most countries checked within the next few years, and perhaps succeeded by a gradual fall.

This development becomes still more probable if prices from now onwards assume an upward trend and gold-mining costs tend to rise. In this case we may well see a repetition of the experience of 1850–60 and 1900–1914, when a rapid expansion of gold output was in most countries brought to an end, and in many of them succeeded by a decline.

To this general rule, however, South Africa is likely to provide a striking exception. Owing partly to the depth of the ore deposits and the long delay and heavy cost involved in providing the necessary shafts and other fixed equipment, partly to the policy of the mines in reducing the average grade of ore milled, and partly to the reinforcement of this policy by Government action, South African output has not yet increased greatly above the 1932 level. That from now onwards the expansion will be both large and persistent is highly probable, especially if the difficulty of augmenting the supply of native labour can be overcome by recruiting in tropical Africa. Once heavy capital costs have been incurred, it is likely that output will be maintained at a high level even though working costs should rise. Indeed, a really sharp rise in costs, or a fall in the price of gold, which would probably cause a rapid fall in the output in other parts of the world, might well cause a temporary increase in South Africa, owing to a rise in the average grade of ore milled unaccompanied by a corresponding reduction in tonnage. Further, South African output could easily be assisted in maintaining a high level either by a reduction in gold-mining taxation or a change in its form. A rapid rise in prices, which would have the effect of increasing the South African Government's revenue from other sources, would certainly give rise to strong demands for a reduction in gold-mining taxation.

N

TABLE I

WORLD GOLD PRODUCTION
Millions of fine ozs.

Average Annual Output	U.S.A.	Canada	Australia	S. Africa	Russia	Other	Total
1841–50	0·5	..	..	..	0·8	0·4	1·7
1851–60	2·7	..	2·5	..	0·8	0·4	6·4
1861–70	2·3	0·1	1·9	..	0·9	0·9	6·1
1871–80	1·9	0·1	1·4	..	1·2	1·0	5·6
1881–90	1·6	0·1	1·2	0·1	1·0	1·2	5·2
1891–1900	2·5	0·4	2·2	1·9	1·2	2·0	10·2
Annual Output							
1901	3·8	1·2	3·3	0·3	1·1	3·0	12·7
1902	3·9	1·0	3·5	1·7	1·1	3·3	14·5
1903	3·6	0·9	3·8	3·0	1·2	3·3	15·9
1904	3·9	0·8	3·8	3·8	1·2	3·4	16·9
1905	4·3	0·7	3·7	4·9	1·1	3·8	18·5
1906	4·6	0·6	3·5	5·8	0·9	4·1	19·5
1907	4·4	0·4	3·2	6·5	1·3	4·2	20·0
1908	4·6	0·5	3·1	7·1	1·4	4·8	21·5
1909	4·8	0·5	3·0	7·3	1·5	5·0	22·1
1910	4·6	0·5	2·7	7·5	1·8	5·0	22·1
1911	4·7	0·5	2·5	8·3	1·6	4·9	22·5
1912	4·5	0·6	2·3	9·1	1·1	5·1	22·7
1913	4·3	0·8	2·2	8·8	1·3	4·9	22·3
1914	4·5	0·8	2·1	8·4	1·3	4·2	21·3
1915	4·8	0·9	1·9	9·1	1·2	4·8	22·7
1916	4·4	0·9	1·7	9·3	1·1	4·6	22·0
1917	4·0	0·7	1·4	9·0	0·9	4·3	20·3
1918	3·3	0·7	1·3	8·4	0·6	4·3	18·6
1919	2·9	0·8	1·1	8·3	0·5	4·1	17·7
1920	2·4	0·8	1·0	8·3	..	3·8	16·3
1921	2·4	0·9	0·8	8·1	..	3·8	16·0
1922	2·3	1·3	0·8	7·0	0·1	4·0	15·5
1923	2·4	1·2	0·7	9·2	0·3	4·0	17·8
1924	2·4	1·5	0·6	9·6	0·9	4·0	19·0
1925	2·3	1·7	0·6	9·6	1·0	3·8	19·0
1926	2·2	1·8	0·5	10·0	1·0	3·8	19·3
1927	2·1	1·8	0·5	10·1	1·0	3·9	19·4
1928	2·1	1·9	0·5	10·4	1·0	3·8	19·5
1929	2·1	1·9	0·4	10·4	1·0	3·8	19·6
1930	2·1	2·1	0·5	10·7	1·0	3·9	20·3
1931	2·2	2·7	0·6	10·9	1·2	4·4	22·0
1932	2·3	3·0	0·7	11·6	1·5	4·8	23·9
1933	2·2	2·9	0·8	11·0	2·2*	5·5	24·6
1934	2·8	3·0	0·9	10·5	3·8*	6·3	27·3
1935	3·2	3·3	0·9	10·8	4·5*	6·9	29·6
1936	3·8	3·7	1·2	11·3	5·5*	7·7	33·2
1937	4·1	4·1	1·4	11·7	6·0*	8·2	35·5

Sources :
   U.S.A. Bureau of Mines Economic Paper No. 6 (1929). Gold Production of All Producing Countries.
   Imperial Institute, Mineral Industry—Statistical Summary.
   Union Corporation, Ltd.   * Estimated.

TABLE II

COSTS, RECEIPTS, AND OUTPUT IN THE GOLD-MINING INDUSTRY OF THE WITWATERSRAND

	Costs per ton of Ore milled				Gross Receipts		Ore milled (Mn. tons)	Average Grade of Ore milled (dwts. per ton)	Output of Gold (Mn. ozs.)
	White Wages	Native Wages	Stores and other Costs	Total	Per ton of Ore milled	Per oz. of Gold produced			
	s. d.	s. d.	s. d.	s. d.	s. d.	s. d.			
1911	7 2	4 10	6 0	18 0	27 11	83 11	23·9	6·6	7·9
1912	6 5	4 8	7 7	18 8	29 0	83 10	25·5	6·8	8·7
1913	6 2	4 5	7 4	17 11	27 9	83 9	25·6	6·5	8·4
1914	5 7	4 2	7 4	17 1	26 6	83 8	25·7	6·2	8·0
1915	5 6	4 3	7 8	17 5	26 3	83 8	28·3	6·2	8·8
1916	5 8	4 5	8 0	18 1	26 8	84 7	28·5	6·3	9·0
1917	6 3	4 2	8 9	19 2	27 1	83 8	27·3	6·4	8·7
1918	7 2	4 6	9 11	21 7	27 11	84 0	24·9	6·6	8·2
1919	7 11	4 7	10 5	22 11	31 7	93 7	24·0	6·7	8·1
1920	9 5	5 0	11 3	25 8	35 3	107 3	24·1	6·5	7·9
1921	9 1	5 1	11 6	25 8	35 2	104 7	23·4	6·7	7·9
1922	5 11	5 9	11 10	23 6	31 4	90 8	19·5	6·9	6·8
1923	5 2	5 0	9 10	20 0	29 5	88 4	26·5	6·7	8·9
1924	5 3	4 8	9 8	19 7	29 10	91 0	28·2	6·5	9·3
1925	5 4	4 5	9 5	19 2	27 11	85 5	28·3	6·5	9·3
1926	5 2	4 5	9 5	19 0	27 9	85 3	29·5	6·5	9·7
1927	5 6	4 6	9 7	19 7	28 3	85 3	29·1	6·6	9·7
1928	5 7	4 7	9 7	19 9	28 0	85 5	30·0	6·5	9·9
1929	5 7	4 6	9 6	19 7	27 9	85 6	30·5	6·5	10·0
1930	5 6	4 7	9 4	19 5	27 10	85 5	31·1	6·5	10·2
1931	5 7	4 6	9 3	19 4	27 5	84 9	32·2	6·4	10·4
1932	5 3	4 4	9 5	19 0	27 4	85 4	34·6	6·3	11·0
1933	5 4	4 4	9 7	19 3	35 6	123 1	36·6	5·7	10·4
1934	5 8	4 4	9 3	19 3	34 8	138 7	39·4	5·0	9·8
1935	5 10	4 4	8 6	18 8	32 6	142 4	43·7	4·6	10·0
1936	6 0	4 5	8 1	18 6	31 0	140 6	47·5	4·4	10·5
1937	6 4	4 4	8 3	18 11	31 4	140 9	49·9	4·5	10·8

Sources:
South African Year Book.
Department of Mines (Union of South Africa) Monthly Statistics.

Whether the continued rise in South African output will more than offset the declines which in due course may be expected elsewhere is doubtful. On the whole, it is probable that, with stationary or slowly rising prices, output from the world as a whole (excluding Russia, where prospects are incalculable) will continue to expand for a considerable time, with South Africa producing an increasing proportion of the total; with rapidly rising prices or a substantial reduction in the price of gold, world output would probably begin to fall fairly soon, despite a probable increase in output in South Africa, and a great increase in its share of the total.

TWENTY YEARS OF THE FLOATING
DEBT [1]

I

POST-WAR ADJUSTMENT (1919–23)

ALTHOUGH the Treasury were empowered as early as 1877 to finance the temporary requirements of the Consolidated Fund by the sale at a discount of Treasury bills of up to twelve months' currency, and although in 1902 the power was extended to cover the requirements of the Supply Services, the use made of these powers, up to August 1914, was, by post-war standards, exceedingly small. The highest total of Treasury bills recorded in those years seems to have been £41 millions in April 1910, consisting of £36·7 millions issued by tender to the market and £4·3 millions issued direct to Government departments. In July 1914 the total outstanding was £15·5 millions, of which only £6 millions had been issued by tender.

During the war the Floating Debt expanded enormously. On January 4th, 1919, it stood at £1545 millions, of which £1098 millions was in Treasury bills and £447 millions in Ways and Means Advances. The very high figure for Ways and Means Advances seems to have been due to two causes. In the first place, a system had grown

---

[1] Originally published in *Economica*, August 1939. Acknowledgment is due to the Economic Research Division of the London School of Economics, without whose assistance the extraction and calculation of the Floating Debt figures would have been impossible ; also to Mr. W. T. C. King for permission to consult important unpublished material on Treasury bills prior to 1930.

up during the war whereby the banks and others were encouraged to place their surplus cash reserves on interest-bearing deposit account with the Bank of England, which re-lent them to the Treasury on Ways and Means Advances. These interest-bearing deposits, which in January 1919 may have amounted to as much as £200 millions or £250 millions, were not mentioned in the Bank of England statements, and the obvious emergence of large surplus cash reserves was therefore prevented. They could, however, be converted very rapidly into non-interest-bearing Bankers' Balances, and so gave the banks, in fact, an almost unlimited power of expansion.

The second cause of the high total of Ways and Means Advances was the fact that a large part, perhaps as much as £150 millions, of the Government Securities then held as backing for the Treasury notes in circulation was apparently in the form of Ways and Means Advances.

It is impossible to say how much of the Treasury bill total was in the possession of the banks and other non-official holders, and how much in the hands of the Savings Banks and other Government departments and perhaps of the Bank of England, though later developments suggest that official holdings were substantial. During the war the issue of bills by tender was discontinued, first in April 1915, and again, after a brief resumption, in June 1917. Instead, Treasury bills were kept on permanent offer, or on " tap ", to all applicants, official and other, at fixed rates of interest, which were altered only when the demand for bills at the fixed rates became either inadequate or excessive. At the beginning of 1919 bills were available in two usances, three months and six months, and the rate of interest on each was $3\frac{1}{2}$ per cent per annum.

The history of the Floating Debt since 1919 can be divided into three main sections, which are clearly discernible in Charts 1 and 2. First there is a period of post-war reduction, from 1919 until about the middle of

1923 ; then there ensues a period of stability, from 1923 until the departure of sterling from the gold standard in the autumn of 1931 ; and finally there is the period of managed currency and the Exchange Equalisation Account, from 1931 to date. This last period should probably be subdivided into the period of gold acquisition (September 1931 to March 1938) and the period of gold sales and heavy rearmament expenditure (March 1938 to date).

The first step towards getting the Floating Debt under control was the Victory Loan of July 1919. In order to facilitate the conversion of the Floating Debt in the hands of the banks, the sale of bills was suspended at the end of May, and the money to meet the maturing bills borrowed (indirectly from the banks) on Ways and Means Advances, so that by July 12th the total of Treasury bills had fallen to £628 millions, and that of Ways and Means Advances had risen to £930 millions. The loan was only partially successful. The total of the Floating Debt was reduced from £1559 millions on July 12th to £1181 millions on August 2nd, but under the pressure of the heavy Government deficits it soon began once more to rise, though it never again reached its former level. More important, the opportunity was taken to discontinue the system of borrowing from the banks, via the Bank of England, on Ways and Means Advances. By November 1919 Ways and Means Advances had fallen to just over £200 millions, and thereafter appear to consist of three elements only — advances from the Currency Note Commissioners, advances from other Government departments, and advances from the Bank of England. Not until 1922 were advances from the Bank distinguished in the Treasury statements from other advances.

In consequence of the renewed rise in the total Floating Debt, and of the reduction in Ways and Means Advances, by the end of the year the Treasury bill total had recovered to about the level of a year before. Broadly speaking,

CHART I

BRITISH FLOATING DEBT

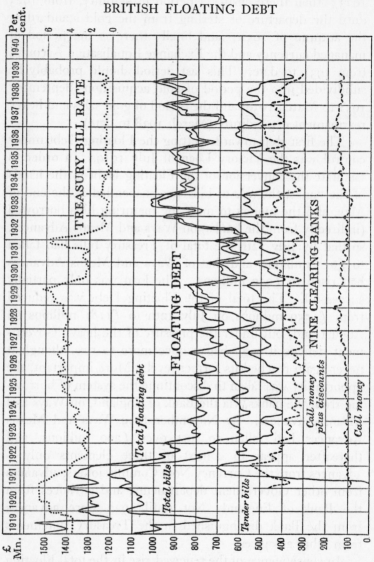

NOTE.—The figures used in constructing the Floating Debt, Treasury bills, and Treasury Bill Rate curves in this chart are monthly averages of weekly figures. For weekly figures of Treasury bills see folded table opposite p. 218.

therefore, the cash receipts of the Victory Loan of 1919 were almost entirely devoted to current expenditure and to eliminating the surplus cash reserves of the banks.

It was two years before the next effort was made to reduce the total of the Floating Debt. The large Budget surplus of 1920–21 was devoted to paying off other debt, principally Treasury bonds, and until the middle of 1921 the Floating Debt was fully maintained and, indeed, rather increased than diminished. Of the constituent items, Ways and Means Advances were reduced further, and by June 1921 Treasury bills had risen to a new high level of over £1200 millions. Nevertheless, in view of the fact that monetary conditions were at last becoming definitely easier and interest rates beginning to fall, the Treasury had ventured, at the end of April 1921, to re-introduce the system of selling bills by tender. As the system then inaugurated is that which exists to-day, it is worth while to examine it in some detail.

On each Friday the Treasury announces in the *London Gazette* the total value of the Treasury bills which it will offer for sale by tender on the following Friday. Tenders have to be made on special forms, obtainable from the Bank of England, and must be lodged at the Bank before 1 P.M. on the day on which the bills are offered. The minimum amount for which a tender will be considered is £50,000, and the tenderer has the right to specify on which day or days in the following week he wishes his bills to be dated and paid for. The bills are normally allotted to the highest tenders, and divided proportionately, where necessary, between those submitting equal tenders ; but the Treasury is under no obligation to accept any particular tender or to allot the whole of the bills offered. Under-allotment of bills by amounts of from £2 millions to £5 millions is not infrequent. A preliminary statement, giving the rate of the lowest tenders accepted, and the proportion of applications allotted to those tendering at this rate, is issued early on Friday afternoon, and a fuller statement is issued later in the day, giving in addition the total amount of applications received, the total of bills allotted, and the average discount rate for the whole issue.

This system differs from that in use before the war in three main particulars. Firstly, the fixation of the high figure of £50,000 for the minimum tenderable quantity, which in effect restricts applicants to banks, discount houses, bill brokers, and other large institutions. Secondly, applicants are allowed to spread the dates of their bills and of their payments over the whole of the following week, or to choose the days which suit them best, instead of having to tender for bills of a given date and to pay for the whole issue at once. And thirdly, all bills issued by tender are now of three months' date. They follow the same rules for determining the day of payment as do ordinary commercial bills, except that there are no days of grace.

Since all bills are of three months' date, it follows that by totalling the bills issued during thirteen consecutive weeks, the total of outstanding bills originally issued by tender can be approximately (and on many dates exactly) determined for the close of business on each Saturday. By calculating a thirteen weeks' moving total, changes in this total can be deduced. Further, since, except at the ends of quarters, the total of Treasury bills outstanding is published for each Saturday, by deducting the calculated total of " tender " bills from the published bill total, the outstanding amount of bills issued otherwise than by tender can be approximately determined. It should be noted that this method holds good only when the Treasury bill total refers to a Saturday ; for we have no means of knowing how much of a week's tenders is dated on each day. When, therefore, the total bill figure is given for the end of a quarter which does not fall on a Saturday, it cannot be related to the calculated total of " tender " bills.

The issue of bills by tender was not, at first, the exclusive method of issue to non-official purchasers that it is now. Until the middle of 1921 twelve months' bills continued to be obtainable through the " tap ", and for some years three months' bills, known as " additional " bills, were available for purchase through the " tap " at prices fixed slightly above the average rate of the previous week's tender. The issue of these appears to have been gradually restricted by reducing the number of days per week on which this offer was open, until in 1925 it ceased altogether. For the period for which these " tap " issues to the public continued, it is difficult to draw any clear deductions from the relative changes in the " tap " and " tender " totals. This is particularly unfortunate since in the two years following the resumption of issues by tender, changes of great importance occurred in the Floating Debt. In the second half of 1921 the Government began to tackle in earnest the task of reducing the greatly expanded Treasury bill total. To some extent out of Budget surplus, but mainly out of the issues of Treasury bonds, the Floating Debt was reduced by more than 40 per cent in two years :

	" Tender " Bills	" Tap " Bills	Total Treasury Bills, £ Mn.	Ways and Means Advances	Total Floating Debt
1921, July 30th	660	542	1202	154	1356
1922, July 29th	603	152	755	159	914
1923, July 28th	450	152	602	199	802

It will be seen from the above figures, and in more detail from Charts 1 and 2, that in the first of these two years the great bulk of the decline was in " tap " bills, while in the second it was entirely in " tender " bills. Over the whole period the decline in " tap " bills was much the greater.

While the continued sale to the market of an unknown quantity of bills otherwise than by " tender " renders impossible any definite statement, it seems probable that

CHART 2

BRITISH FLOATING DEBT

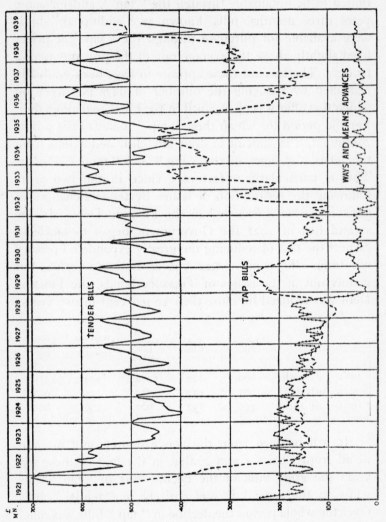

NOTE.—The figures used in constructing this chart are monthly averages of weekly figures.

the amount of " tap " bills sold to the market was small, and that the " tap " bill total consisted mainly of bills held by the Issue Department of the Bank of England, the Post Office, the Currency Note Commissioners, and other Government funds and departments.[1] If this is so, then the greater part of the great decline in the Floating Debt in 1921–22 consisted merely of substituting bonds for bills in the portfolios of the Departments. The smaller reduction from 1922 to 1923, on the other hand, seems to have taken place wholly in bills held by the market, and therefore to have been in fact much more important.

This view finds some confirmation in the figures given in the Macmillan Report of Treasury bills discounted by the clearing banks :

| | Nine London Clearing Banks' Discounts of Treasury Bills | | Treasury Bills issued by " tender ". 12 months' decrease | Total Treasury Bills. 12 months' decrease |
	Total	12 months' decrease		
	£ Mn.	£ Mn.	£ Mn.	£ Mn.
July 1921 . .	252·7	..	..	..
July 1922 . .	206·7	46·0	57	390
July 1923 . .	144·6	62·1	153	153

It is clear that the decline in the banks' holdings of Treasury bills was much more closely related to the fall in " tender " bills than to the fall in total bills. It seems reasonable to deduce that the great bulk of the " tap " bills was in official hands.

II

STABILITY AND THE GOLD STANDARD (1923–31)

By the middle of 1923 the process of reducing the Floating Debt had been virtually completed, and for the

---

[1] In this article the phrase " the Departments " will refer to all official holders of " tap " bills (including the Bank of England) apart from the Exchange Equalisation Account, except where it is made clear in the context that the Bank of England is not included.

next five years, apart from seasonal fluctuations, little further change took place. The Floating Debt as a whole showed a slight downward trend from 1923 to 1928, but as both Ways and Means Advances and "tap" bills diminished, "tender" bills showed an increase over the period of about £50 millions, the rise occurring chiefly in 1926, the year of the General Strike. This period of relative stability offers a good opportunity of observing the purely seasonal movements of the Floating Debt.

From a minimum about the beginning of the financial year, the Floating Debt (Chart 1) usually showed little change during April, and rose slightly in May. In June it rose sharply with the heavy interest payment on War Loan due on the first of that month. It usually showed a further small rise in July, a moderate decline in August and sometimes in September with the second instalment of income tax collections, and a moderate rise in October and November. In December it again rose sharply with the second half-yearly interest payment on War Loan, to the highest point of the year. In the last three months of the financial year the heavy inflow of revenue from Income Tax and Super-Tax caused a very sharp decline to the lowest point of the year, usually reached towards the end of March.

The seasonal movements in Treasury bills, both for total bills and for "tender" bills only, differed slightly from those of the total Floating Debt. The peaks were usually less marked and the minor decline in August was usually absent. This was because the sudden heavy requirements for meeting War Loan interest were too great to be met out of one week's expansion of the Treasury bill issue, and were therefore met by means of an expansion in Ways and Means Advances, partly from the Bank and partly from Government departments. These Ways and Means Advances were subsequently paid off either out of the gradual expansion of the Treasury bill issue or, especially in the case of the December expansion, out of the surplus of revenue. Thus the sharpest movements in the total Floating Debt were absorbed and the outline of the Treasury bill curve smoothed.

The phenomenon of the rise in Ways and Means Advances (Chart 2) at the dates of the War Loan interest payments is still apparent on occasion, though in recent years it has been neither so marked nor so regular: the first, because, since the War Loan Conversion of 1932, the amount involved is reduced; and the second, because the calls on the various conversion loans issued in recent years have usually been so timed as to ensure substantial receipts from the loan on either June 1st or December 1st.

It also appears that in recent years the Treasury has on certain occasions obtained its temporary advances, not from the Bank of England at all, but entirely from the Departments or the Exchange Equalisation Account. On many of these occasions it has obtained the money by the issue of " tap " bills instead of on Ways and Means Advances. The occasions when it thus finances its exceptional requirements by issues of " tap " bills frequently seem to coincide with periods when the Exchange Equalisation Account is believed to have been making substantial net sales of gold, and therefore has sterling available for investment.

When the Treasury obtains the money it requires either from the Exchange Equalisation Account or from the Departments, it is necessary for these to accumulate the necessary funds in advance. On these occasions, therefore, for a period of some weeks before the date of the interest payments, there is a rise in Public Deposits at the Bank of England and a consequent fall in Bankers' Deposits (for the Bank, even at the height of the cheap money era, has never pursued the policy of preventing such temporary declines in Bankers' Deposits); while as soon as the interest payment is made there is a fall in Public Deposits and a rise in Bankers' Deposits. On the other hand, when a substantial part of the interest payment is financed by Ways and Means Advances from the Bank, there is a smaller prior rise in Public Deposits and a temporary subsequent rise in the Bank's holding of Government Securities. Thus the former method of financing interest payments causes a tendency towards exceptional financial stringency in the period preceding an interest payment, and the latter towards exceptional financial ease in the period following the payment.

About July 1928 preparations began to be made for the transfer of the Treasury note issue to the Bank of England, which eventually took place towards the end of November in that year. As part of the preparation it was considered desirable to convert the Ways and Means Advances, which formed part of the security behind the note issue, into Treasury bills — a form presumably regarded as more suitable for holding by the Issue Department of the Bank. Consequently, between July and November, during which period the total of the Floating Debt was virtually unchanged (£760 millions on July 7th and £752 millions on November 24th), Ways and Means Advances by Departments fell by £163 millions to £13 millions, and total Treasury bills rose by £155 millions to £739 millions. Of the fall in Ways and Means Advances about £40 millions or £50 millions was seasonal, and this was reflected in a rise of £49 millions in "tender" bills. The remainder was exceptional, and was reflected in a rise of £106 millions in "tap" bills. Since 1928 Ways and Means Advances have rarely exceeded £50 millions, as compared with the £100 millions to £160 millions in the years 1920 to 1927.

In the first quarter of 1929 the seasonal decline in the Floating Debt was unusually small, owing to a net repayment in February of over £50 millions in Treasury bonds. These appear to have been held partly by the market and partly by the Departments, for on the date of repayment the rise in Treasury bills was shared fairly equally between "tap" and "tender" bills.

The total of "tap" bills remained at the relatively high level of £220-£250 millions until November 1929, when the 5 per cent Conversion Loan was launched, partly for the repayment of Treasury bonds, and partly for the reduction of the Floating Debt. The latter consequently shows an unusually small rise in the last quarter of 1929 and an unusually heavy fall in the first quarter of 1930. By the middle of April it had been reduced to £616 millions, as compared with £745 millions twelve months earlier. It would seem, however, that a substantial proportion of the loan had to be taken up "inside", for over the year (April 1929 to April 1930) there was a fall of about £50 millions in "tap" bills out of a total fall in Treasury bills of about £140 millions.

From April 1930 to September 1931 there was little change, other than seasonal, in the total of the Floating Debt. There was, however, a non-seasonal rise of some £40 millions in "tender" bills, and a corresponding fall in "tap" bills, which may have been due to an excess of expenditure in certain funds, and notably the Unemployment Funds.

III

MANAGED CURRENCY AND THE EXCHANGE EQUALISATION ACCOUNT (1931–39)

The period between the departure of sterling from the gold standard in September 1931 and the inauguration of the Exchange Equalisation Account at the end of June 1932 constitutes a kind of interregnum during which the effects of international capital movements were controlled, in so far as they were controlled at all, by various extemporary devices.

o

To begin with, the Treasury had to dispose of the proceeds of the foreign credits raised abroad and drawn upon in the effort to remain upon the gold standard. In the first instance the bulk of the sterling so received was used to pay off " tap " bills, which, between September 12th and October 10th, fell by £50 millions.[1] What the Departments did with the sterling for the moment is not certain, but it seems likely that, like the Exchange Equalisation Account in 1938, they used a substantial part of it to buy up " tender " bills in the market, and so enabled the banks to maintain their cash reserves. This interpretation is confirmed by the sharp fall in bank discounts at this time.

Between October 10th and the end of the year, " tap " bills recovered sharply to their former level, while the seasonal rise in " tender " bills was unusually small. It is likely that this was due to the Departments' replacing the bills purchased earlier from the market with new " tap " bills. Thus, in effect, the Treasury used the sterling proceeds of its foreign credits to meet its seasonal excess of payments in the last quarter of the calendar year.

In the first months of the new year the heavy return of capital from abroad enabled the Treasury to make provision for the repayment of its foreign credits. It financed this by using a large part of the seasonal excess of revenue to repay " tap " bills, thus placing sterling funds in the hands of the Departments for the purchase of foreign exchange. When the repayment of £61 millions of foreign credits became due at the end of February, the Treasury bought most of the necessary foreign exchange from the Departments, owing them for it £17 millions in additional " tap " bills and £35 millions on Ways and Means Advances. There are no such obvious signs of the repayment of the £24 millions of foreign credits made at the end of

[1] The movements during this period are so sharp and temporary that the figures of monthly averages, reproduced on Charts 1 and 2, do not adequately reflect them.

March and the beginning of April. As this was a period of especially large imports of capital, the requisite exchange may have been bought at the time in the market, and paid for out of the seasonal excess of revenue. The effect of the repayment of £85 millions of foreign credits is seen in the reduction in the magnitude of the seasonal falls in the Floating Debt and in " tender " bills, which otherwise would have been exceptionally large.

After February the Bank of England seems to have played a large share in checking the unwanted rise in the value of sterling. Between the end of February and the end of June the Bank increased its holdings of " Other Securities " (presumably foreign exchange) by £33 millions, and, in addition, bought £15 millions of gold (costing about £20 millions at market price). These increases were only partially offset by reductions in its holdings of Government Securities, and therefore resulted in a rise in Bankers' Deposits, thus initiating the " cheap money " policy. The part played by the Departments in controlling the foreign exchanges seems to have been small after February. The considerable decline in " tap " bills and Ways and Means Advances in the second quarter of 1932 can apparently be attributed to their conversion into Treasury bonds, of which nearly £100 millions was issued during the quarter. The seasonal rise in " tender " bills was diminished for the same reason.

Meanwhile the Government had found inconvenient its makeshift methods of controlling the exchange value of sterling, and had obtained authority to set up the Exchange Equalisation Account. At the end of June the Account was formally installed with a capital of £150 millions in " tap " Treasury bills, plus the £25 millions remaining in the old Dollar Exchange Account, but minus the loss of £8 millions incurred on the repayment of the Bank of England's foreign credits, and apparently also the nominal loss incurred on the Bank's recent gold purchase. The initial capital of the

Exchange Equalisation Account was therefore £167 millions, of which about £5 millions was already locked up in the Bank's gold. It seems at once to have taken over about £30 millions of foreign exchange from the Bank, transferring Treasury bills in payment, while it is not unlikely that part or all of the remainder of the old Dollar Account, which was presumably in sterling at the end of September 1931, had, by June 1932, been re-invested in foreign exchange or gold. Thus, of the initial capital, something approaching £50 millions may have been in the form of foreign exchange or gold, £5 millions in the form of a contingent claim on the Bank's gold, and perhaps £115 millions in Treasury bills.

The methods by which the Exchange Equalisation Account finances its purchases of gold and invests the sterling proceeds of its gold sales, have been too frequently discussed to require more than a brief outline here. When the Account requires sterling to pay for gold, it generally seems to allow a portion of its holdings of " tap " bills to run off, thereby obliging the Treasury to supply it with cash, either out of a seasonal surplus of revenue or out of additional sales of bills by tender. Conversely, when the Account sells gold and has sterling to invest, it normally seems to take up more " tap " bills, thus enabling the Treasury either to meet a seasonal surplus of expenditure or to reduce its issues of " tender " bills. Thus purchases of gold by the Account usually cause a fall in " tap " bills and a rise (or the absence of a seasonal fall) in " tender " bills, and sales of gold a rise in " tap " bills and a fall (or the absence of a seasonal rise) in " tender " bills.

In cases where the sales of gold by the Fund are very large and rapid, this procedure is sometimes too slow, and interim effects may appear. There have been times when the Account seems to have been unable to re-invest its sterling receipts rapidly enough, with the result that they have accumulated in Public Deposits at the Bank, thereby reducing Bankers' Deposits and leading to a temporary tendency towards stringency. This accumulation of funds may on occasion have been deliberate, in preparation for heavy Treasury requirements for the payment of interest. (See pp. 197-8.)

Recently the Account seems on some occasions, and especially during the summer and autumn of 1938, to have tried to accelerate the return to the banking system of its accumulated sterling funds by buying " tender " bills directly from the market. When this method is used, the relative figures of " tap " and " tender " bills obviously give no immediate reflection of the Account's dealings, though since the " tender " bills thus acquired by the Account seem usually to be converted into " tap " bills when they mature, the time-lag before the results of its dealings once more become apparent is not more than three months.

The difficulties of interpreting the meaning of changes in the floating debt figures is greatly increased by the fact that, though in recent years the operations of the Exchange Account have been the most important cause of fluctuations in the total of " tap " bills, they are far from being the only cause. The " tap " bill holdings of other Departments may vary with any excess of their receipts or payments, while both the Departments and the Bank of England may vary their investments between bills and other types of securities. These fluctuations have been greatly increased by the methods used, especially in recent years, for issuing funding loans. The practice has grown up for the Departments (including the Issue Department of the Bank of England) in effect to underwrite these loans, taking up any amounts not subscribed for by the market, and making payments for their share of the calls by surrendering " tap " bills to an equivalent amount.

Thus the immediate effect of such loans is to reduce the outstanding total of " tender " bills only in so far as the loans are taken up by the public, and to reduce " tap " bills in so far as they are taken up by the Departments. But since the real purpose of these funding loans has been to reduce the outstanding total of " tender " bills (from 1932 to 1938 periodically inflated by the cost of buying gold, and in 1937-38 by the cost of buying arms), the redemption of " tap " bills is merely an intermediate stage in the operation. The full objects of the issue are achieved only as the Departments replenish their holdings of " tap " bills, either out of a surplus of revenue, or out of sales of the recently acquired or other securities, and so enable the Treasury to pay off " tender " bills. In effect, therefore, the Treasury is able to spread its sales of long-term securities over a period of several months, and presumably to get a better average price for them than if they had all had to be placed in the market at once. The bill holdings of the Departments thus tend to show a gradual increase in anticipation of a loan, a rapid fall as the new loan is paid for, and a gradual replenishment as this in turn is digested.

Where the loan is for the conversion of a maturing long-term loan the symptoms are different. Now the purpose of the Departments will be to acquire as much as possible of the maturing loan in order to prevent its falling into the hands of holders who will regard it as a " short " and will therefore not be willing to convert it into a long-dated security. The Departments will therefore tend to *reduce* their bill holdings before the issue in order to buy up the security to be redeemed.

Another possible cause of changes in the " tap " bill total is the purchase or sale of gold by the Bank of England. If, on the occasion of a purchase of gold from the Exchange Account, the Bank pays for it wholly by a transfer of bills, there is clearly no change in the bill totals. If, however, it pays for part of it in cash—*i.e.* by an issue of additional notes and a corresponding credit to the Account's balance at the Bank — the Account can use these new resources to buy more bills from the Treasury through the " tap ". In this case the total issue of " tap " bills is larger and of " tender " bills smaller than if the Bank had not bought the gold. Conversely, if the Bank sells gold to the Account and is paid for it entirely by a transfer of bills, there is no change. But if the Account pays part of the price in cash, its power to buy gold or bills is reduced, and the total issue of " tap " bills is smaller and of " tender " bills larger.

It will be seen from the foregoing outline that in recent years the total of the Floating Debt and its constituent items have been subject to the influence of a considerable number of independent, or partly independent, forces, the most important of which, for convenience, are summarised below :

A. CHIEF CAUSES OF FLUCTUATIONS IN TOTAL FLOATING DEBT

(1) Excess of Treasury income or expenditure.

(2) Funding loans issued by Treasury, or loans repaid by issue of Treasury bills. Unless new loans are issued in exchange for existing loans, or for their immediate repayment, all large loans, even those issued to provide for increased expenditure, act temporarily as funding loans.

(3) Moneys lent by Treasury (of which the most important have been issues to the Exchange Equalisation Account), or repaid to the Treasury.

B. CHIEF CAUSES OF CHANGES IN CONSTITUENT ITEMS OF FLOATING DEBT

(1) *Changes in " Tap " Bills*

(a) Issue of bills to Exchange Equalisation Account (and repayments by the Account, if ever made).

(*b*) Sales or purchases of gold by Exchange Equalisation Account (not to or from the Bank of England).

(*c*) Excess of income or expenditure of Departments.

(*d*) Expansion or contraction of Government Securities in Bank of England otherwise than in exchange for gold sold to or bought from Exchange Account.

(*e*) Bank's changes in gold holdings not compensated by opposite changes in holdings of Treasury bills.

(*f*) Sales or purchases of longer-dated securities by Bank or Departments.

(*g*) Replacement of " tender " bills held by Account, Bank, or Departments with " tap " bills (and conceivably, though improbably, vice versa).

(2) *Changes in Ways and Means Advances*

Increases in Ways and Means Advances are usually made to finance a large and sudden expenditure, and are subsequently paid off by increased issues either of " tender " or " tap " bills, or out of an excess of revenue.

The seven years of the operations of the Exchange Equalisation Account may be divided into two broad phases — the period of 1932 until early in 1938, when the Account was on balance buying gold heavily, and the period 1938–39, when it was selling gold. While, however, the period 1932–38 saw on the whole an immense increase in the country's gold stocks, it contained two minor periods of substantial gold sales — during the second half of 1932 and from early in 1934 to early in 1935. The years in which it gained gold were therefore 1933 and 1935–37.

THE PERIOD OF GOLD ACQUISITION

(1) *July–December 1932. First Period of Gold Sales*

After the inauguration of the Exchange Account at the end of June, only seasonal changes in the Floating Debt occurred until the middle of August, when there was a net repayment of nearly £60 millions of Treasury bonds. Something like two-thirds of these seem to have been in the hands of the Departments (presumably largely purchased during the period of falling " tap " bills in May and June) and the total of " tap " bills outstanding rose from £229 millions on August 13th to £268 millions on August 20th. In the first week in September the final £28 millions of the Treasury's foreign credits was repaid, presumably out of the foreign exchange resources of the Exchange Account, and the " tap " bill total, which had fallen to £258 millions on September 3rd, rose again to £295 millions on September 17th.

The final repayment of the credits seems to have depleted the gold holdings of the Account so seriously that it was unable to offer much resistance to the pressure on the exchange which developed during the last quarter of the year, with the result that sterling depreciated fairly sharply. In order to pay the December instalment on the United States debt the Treasury had to use £19 millions (at par) of the Bank's gold, apparently paying for it in " tap " bills.

While the August bond repayment helps to account for the rise in " tender " bills in the third quarter, it does not account for the rise over the whole year, for it merely offset part of the effects of the issue in the second quarter. The rise of about £125 millions in " tender " bills between December 1931 and December 1932 is due partly to the fact that the seasonal rise in the last quarter of 1931 had been reduced by about £50 millions by the temporary use of the sterling proceeds of the foreign credits, and partly to the loss of over £40 millions on the repayment of the foreign credits. There was also, however, a sharp fall in " tap " bills between September and December for which there is no obvious reason. The most likely explanation seems to be that the Departments were facilitating the War

Loan conversion by supporting the gilt-edged market. The effect of this fall in " tap " bills was to induce a corresponding additional expansion in the " tender " bill issue, which on January 7th, 1933, reached a total of £666 millions, the highest figure which had been recorded since January 1922 and which has not since been equalled. It should be emphasised that little of this exceptionally high total can be attributed to the requirements of the Exchange Account for the purchase of gold; the additional issues had been used partly to finance the loss on repaying the credits and apparently partly to purchase longer-dated securities.

(2) *December 1932–January 1934. First Period of Gold Acquisition*

From the middle of December 1932 the pressure on sterling ceased and was replaced by a heavy inflow of capital. The Exchange Account began to acquire gold on a large scale and the total of " tap " bills fell sharply. By the end of January the Exchange Account was already in a position to re-sell gold to the Bank of England, thereby augmenting both the Bank's diminished reserves and its own supplies of sterling. Between the middle of January and the end of June these sales of gold to the Bank totalled about £70 millions, at the old parity, or just over £100 millions at market price. £33 millions of the increased gold holdings of the Bank was offset by a decline in Government Securities (in both Departments) and a further £6 millions by a decline in Other Securities. Notes in circulation, however, rose by £20 millions and total Deposits by £9 millions. In so far as the transfer of gold to the Bank was offset by a decline in the Bank's holding of Government Securities, it presumably represented merely a transfer of bills from the Bank to the Exchange Account and had no effect on the " tap " bill total. But in so far as it was accompanied by a rise in liabilities it presumably represented a transfer of cash to the Account, and so enabled the Account to increase its holdings of bills, thus tending to increase the total of " tap " bills and decrease the total of " tender " bills. In other words, part of the national gold holding had now been financed by monetary expansion instead of by borrowing.

In spite of the tendency of the foregoing transaction to increase the volume of " tap " bills, the amount outstanding actually fell by £64 millions between December 24th and May 13th, indicating an increase of over £90 millions in the non-sterling assets of the Account, or of £60 millions in the gold actually in its possession (since about £30 millions represented the nominal " loss " on the re-sale of gold to the Bank). The total value of the gold bought by the Account during this period, including re-sales to the Bank, was therefore about £160 millions. It is possible that even this figure under-estimates the amount of the gold acquisitions, for it is quite possible that the other Departments were simultaneously increasing their holdings of bills in preparation for the $2\frac{1}{2}$ per cent Conversion Loan launched in October. In any case, by the middle of May the sterling reserves of the Account had become so depleted that the Treasury was obliged to issue to it a further £200 millions of bills.

In the second half of the year the " tap " bill total at first declined further, and then rose fairly sharply for a few weeks, partly in consequence of a passing weakness in sterling and sales of gold by the Account, and partly perhaps because of continued purchases of bills by the Departments. With the issue of the new loan in October the trend was sharply reversed. A large proportion of the £100 millions issued for cash was taken up by the Departments and " tap " bills fell sharply on the date of each call; while at the same time the trend of sterling changed, so that the Exchange Account was probably acquiring more gold. Consequently between September 23rd and December 23rd, while the total Treasury bill issue fell by £54 millions, the "tap" bill total fell by no less than £91 millions and the "tender" bill total rose by £37 millions.

(3) *1934. Second Period of Gold Sales*

Early in 1934 the dollar was finally revalued and capital was withdrawn from Britain, both to U.S.A. and, later, to the Continent. At first sterling was allowed to fall sharply, but thereafter the Exchange Account apparently sold substantial quantities of gold to check the decline. In the first quarter the Floating Debt fell seasonally by about £130 millions and the total of "tender" bills by about the same amount, while the "tap" bill total showed little change. In the second quarter the "tap" bill issue rose by about £20 millions, in spite of the fact that the Departments apparently had to take up part of the £150 millions 3 per cent Funding Loan issued in April. The bulk of this issue was for the purpose of funding Treasury bonds and only about £30 millions was available for reducing the Floating Debt. Even this amount was enough to make the seasonal rise in the total Floating Debt obviously smaller than usual, and the increase in "tap" bills made the rise in "tender" bills still smaller. In the second half of the year the seasonal rise in the total Floating Debt was exceeded by the rise of some £80 millions in "tap" bills, so that "tender" bills showed a contra-seasonal fall. The rise in "tap" bills may be ascribed partly to the reinvestment by the Account of the proceeds of sales of gold and probably partly to the replenishment of the portfolios of the Departments.

At the end of December the total Floating Debt was only about £40 millions lower than twelve months before, and total Treasury bills about £50 millions lower, but, since "tap" bills had risen by nearly £100 millions,

" tender " bills fell by nearly £150 millions to £451 millions, the lowest end-December figure on record. This decline, and the consequent " bill famine ", were probably due partly to the delayed effects of the conversion loan of the autumn of 1933 and to a small extent to the funding loan of 1934, but it is clear that its chief cause was the heavy gold sales and the use of the sterling proceeds to pay off " tender " bills.

(4) *1935–38. Second Period of Gold Acquisition*

At the beginning of 1935 a short period of firmness of sterling was followed by a still shorter period of weakness, and during the first quarter the net changes in the Exchange Account's gold holdings were probably small. The total of " tap " bills at the beginning of April was actually slightly lower than at the beginning of January, but the seasonal decline in the Floating Debt was sufficient by itself to bring the total of " tender " bills down to the extremely low figure of £358 millions on March 16th, thus intensifying the shortage of bills. In April, however, there began the great inflow of capital from France and other parts of the Continent which was to continue, with only temporary pauses, for nearly three years. In addition, the improving trade of many of the sterling bloc countries enabled them to accumulate large amounts of sterling in London and so add to the inflow of capital. As a result, between April 1935 and April 1938 the Exchange Account is believed to have bought something like 65 million ounces of gold at a cost of about £450 millions, of which it re-sold about 31 million ounces to the Bank of England for £134 millions. Of the Bank's purchases, nearly £100 millions was financed by an expansion of the note circulation and less than £40 millions by a net reduction in Government Securities. Thus the amount of finance which had to be provided by the Treasury was probably rather over £350 millions.

The process by which this finance was provided was the now customary procedure, first, of issuing more "tender" bills to pay off the "tap" bills held by the Exchange Account and so providing it with sterling to give in exchange for gold, and then periodically of funding the additional bills so issued. The first part of the process is well illustrated in the period from April to November 1935. During that period, while the total Floating Debt showed a normal seasonal expansion of rather under £100 millions, "tap" bills fell by over £100 millions and "tender" bills rose by about £200 millions. Gold purchases are likely to have been the cause of the fall in "tap" bills, for it is unlikely that the Departments were reducing their bill holdings; in fact, they were probably increasing them.

At the beginning of December 1935 an issue was made of £200 millions of 2½ per cent Funding Loan, of which £100 millions was required to redeem Treasury bonds, leaving £100 millions for funding bills. From the movements of the bill figures on the dates of the calls, of which the last was not until the end of March, it seems probable both that a large proportion of the loan was taken up by the Departments, and that the bulk of the maturing bonds were in the same hands. Meanwhile the Exchange Account apparently continued to make substantial purchases of gold, thus preventing the total of "tender" bills from being reduced more than seasonally as the result of the public subscription of some part of the new loan. Consequently the effects of the new loan on the "tender" bill issue seem to have been confined to a reduction in the December peak, while the fall from December 1935 to April 1936 was if anything smaller than usual. Of the fall of £116 millions in "tap" bills between the end of November and the end of April, rather over half may probably be ascribed to a decrease in the holdings of the

Departments, and rather under half to the Exchange Account.

During the next four months, from the end of April to the end of August 1936, the Account apparently continued to gain gold rapidly and the " tap " bill total fell by a further £60 millions, from £225 millions to £165 millions, while the " tender " bill total rose to the high figure of £630 millions. During October the movement was temporarily reversed as a result of an outflow of capital following upon the French devaluation of September 28th, and by the beginning of November the " tap " bill figure had risen to £235 millions, or £10 millions more than at the end of April. It is, however, unlikely that the additional bills were held by the Exchange Account ; it is more probable that the Departments had been expanding their holdings on a substantial scale and that, despite the losses of September and October, at the beginning of November 1936 the Exchange Account held appreciably more gold and less bills than six months before.

Although the autumn outflow of gold had checked the seasonal rise in " tender " bills, the total of " tender " bills still stood above £600 millions, and at the beginning of December 1936 the Treasury issued another £100 millions Funding Loan at 2¾ per cent, of which £28 millions was needed for the repayment of bonds, leaving £72 millions for funding bills. Their action in so doing seems to indicate their scepticism about the permanence of the recent firmness of the franc, for if a further outflow of capital to France was to be expected, a reduction in the " tender " bill issue would take place without a funding loan. A further indication of the official view is seen in the transfer of £65 millions (at par) of gold from the Exchange Account to the Bank, and the simultaneous reduction of £60 millions in the fiduciary issue. As the reduction in the Bank's holdings of Government Securities was almost equal to its increase in gold, there was no appreciable effect on the figures of the Floating Debt.

A substantial proportion of the new loan was again taken up by the Departments, and between the end of November 1936 and the beginning of February 1937 " tap " bills fell by £50 millions, of which a large part was probably due to the reduced holdings of the Departments, though the Account had apparently been gaining gold again since November. Any increase in " tender " bills due to this was, however, apparently more than offset by sales of the new loan to the public, and " tender " bills showed an unusually heavy seasonal fall, from £622 millions at the end of December to £500 millions at the end of March.

The end of March 1937 is notable for two events. It introduced the first financial year in which the Treasury was obliged to borrow for rearmament, and it was the date of the first official figure for the Exchange Account's gold holdings (though this was not actually published until three months later). Henceforward the six-monthly changes in the Account's position are a matter of knowledge, though intermediate changes must still be estimated. The official total as at 31st March 1937 was 26·6 million ounces, so that, including 42 million ounces re-sold to the Bank, the Account's total purchases between June 1932 and March 1937 had been about 68 million ounces, costing about £450 millions.

During the second and third quarters of 1937 the Exchange Equalisation Account continued to gain gold rapidly, and, despite some further sales of gold to the Bank, its sterling resources had to be augmented at the end of June by the issue to it of a further £200 millions of Treasury bills. Meanwhile the seasonal rise in the total Floating Debt had been checked by the issue in May of £100 millions of National Defence Bonds. A large proportion of these seems to have been taken up initially by the Departments, thus accentuating the fall in " tap " bills due to the purchases of gold, so that by June 26th, before the new issue of bills, the " tap " bill total had fallen to the very low level of £132 millions.

In the third quarter the " tap " bill total continued to fall in consequence of further purchases of gold, and at the end of September stood at £296 millions. The decline of £36 millions during the quarter is probably a good deal less than the cost of the Exchange Equalisation Account's purchases of gold, for it is likely that the Departments were increasing their holdings of bills as they disposed of their share of the National Defence Bonds. For the two quarters together the Account's gain of gold was about $13\frac{1}{4}$ million ounces, costing about £94 millions, in addition to about 3 million ounces re-sold to the Bank.

With the autumn of 1937 the period of large gold purchases ceases. In the last quarter of the year it seems likely that the Exchange Account lost some gold, and, though it more than recovered it in the first quarter of 1938, the increase in its holdings for the half-year was little more than $2\frac{1}{2}$ million ounces, costing about £18 millions. As the total of " tap " bills was almost the same at the end of March as it had been at the end of the previous September, the Departments seem to have been replenishing further their bill portfolios in preparation for the next loan.

By the end of March 1938 the gold holding of the Account had reached its highest point of $42\frac{1}{2}$ million ounces, worth nearly £300 millions. On the same date the Bank of England held nearly 77 million ounces (valued in its books at £326·4 millions, but actually worth about £540 millions), of which about $48\frac{1}{2}$ million ounces, worth about £340 millions, had been bought from the Exchange Account. The combined total of gold held by the Account and the Bank amounted to nearly 120 million ounces, worth about £840 millions. The finance of this gold had been approximately as follows :

P

	£ Mn.	£ Mn.
Gold originally held by Bank of England :		
Value at par	121	
Rise in value	79	200
Net Gold Purchases of Bank of England from 31.3.32 to 31.3.38 :		
Financed by expansion of credit . .	172	
Financed by reduction in " Other Securities "	34	
Total price paid by Bank . . .	206	
Difference between par and market price, charged to Exchange Account . .	117	
Total value at prices ruling on dates of purchase by the Bank	323	
Rise in value since purchase by Bank .	17	340
Gold held by Exchange Account on 31.3.38 :		
At estimated cost	280 [1]	
Estimated rise in value since purchase .	20 [1]	300
TOTAL . .		840

From the foregoing table it will be seen that the share of the cost borne by the Exchange Account had been nearly £400 millions (£117 millions + £280 millions). Of this, about £60 millions had been raised by the increase in the issue of Treasury bills by " tender ",[2] while perhaps another £20 millions had been obtained on " tap " bills and Ways and Means Advances from the Departments. It would therefore appear that the balance of some £320 millions had been financed by long-term loans.

THE PERIOD OF GOLD LOSSES (*April 1938–March 1939*)

The effects of the conservative financing of the increase in the country's stock of gold were clearly seen during the next year, when the heavy withdrawals of foreign balances

---

[1] These figures include an estimate of the " jobbing " profits of the Account, but make no allowance for interest on Treasury bills (which does not seem to be paid to the Account though it is paid to other holders of " tap " bills) or for administrative costs.

[2] From £454 millions on March 26th, 1932, to £512 millions on March 26th, 1938.

from London obliged the Exchange Account to sell nearly 40 million ounces of gold in order to check the decline in sterling. The strain on sterling began with the heavy reflux of capital to France after the final stabilisation of the franc early in May, and there is little doubt that the Exchange Account sold a large quantity of gold at this time. This was reflected at the moment in an accumulation of sterling to the Account's credit in Public Deposits at the Bank of England, but surprisingly little in the total of " tap " bills, which rose only from £282 millions on May 7th to £311 millions on June 11th. This disproportionately small effect is believed to have been due to large purchases of " tender " bills by the Account, which for the time being effectively prevented the effect of the gold sales from being seen in the " tap " bill figures. At the end of June there was issued the National Defence Loan of £80 millions. This seems to have been taken up mainly by the public, and the total of " tender " bills fell from £585 millions on June 18th to £560 millions on August 6th, despite the continued heavy expenditure, while " tap " bills rose slightly.

During September further heavy withdrawals of capital from London occurred in consequence of the international crisis, and " tap " bills rose from £294 millions on August 27th to £362 millions on October 1st, while " tender " bills fell from £555 millions to £521 millions. The rise in " tap " bills for the whole six months, however, was only about £60 millions, which is something like £90 millions less than the proceeds of the 20·8 million ounces of gold sold by the Exchange Account during the period. Even if allowance is made for a possible decrease in bills held by the Departments, it is clear that the Account was still holding a substantial amount of " tender " bills.

The full effects of the gold sales only became visible in the following half-year. Further heavy sales of gold, estimated at not less than 14 or 15 million ounces, were made during the last quarter of 1938, while the " tender " bills held by the Account were apparently at last replaced by " tap " bills, with the result that the rise of about £136 millions in " tap " bills was greater than the seasonal rise of about £100 millions in the Floating Debt, and " tender " bills fell contra-seasonally from £521 millions on October 1st to £488 millions on December 31st. In the first quarter of 1939 gold sales were on a much smaller scale, and the " tap " bill total showed little change; [1] but the seasonal decline in the Floating Debt, following upon the absence of the seasonal rise in " tender " bills in the previous quarter, brought the " tender " bill total down to £346 millions on March 4th, the lowest post-war figure on record, and occasioned an acute " bill famine ". After March 4th the Floating Debt began to rise in response to the high Government expenditures, but for some time the increase probably did little to relieve the shortage; for the Exchange Account was obliged to sell gold fairly heavily in March and April in order to support the pound in the face of capital withdrawals inspired by the new international crisis, and seems to have invested the proceeds mainly in " tender " bills. The sharp rise in " tap " bills in June, at a time when gold sales were probably insignificant, may have been due, at least in part, to the replacement with " tap " bills of these " tender " bills held by the Account.

The net effect of the sale of gold during the year ending March 31st, 1939, was that the Government was able to finance a considerable excess of rearmament expenditure over the loan of £80 millions raised in June 1938 to meet it, and in addition to repay about £142 millions of Treasury bills issued by " tender ". Since the purchase of the gold had been financed largely by long-term loans, the result was to reduce the " tender " bills issue to a figure well

---

[1] The transfer of gold from the Bank of England to the Account and the revaluation of the Bank's gold resulted only in transfers of " tap " bills between the Bank and the Account, and had no effect on the total.

11	40	41	42	43	44	45	46	47	48	49	50	51	52	53
..	980	685	685	695	705	705	705	700	695	695	690	690	690	..
555	585	590	585	585	585	584	577	577	581	581	581	581	567	..
500	459	467	470	475	480	483	488	493	497	496	500	499	495	..
433	440	450	455	457	457	457	457	455	465	480	485	490	490	..
421	475	482	486	490	494	499	502	509	510	509	513	518	516	..
436	512	517	527	532	537	542	547	547	552	554	559	558	557	..
485	519	527	530	535	535	540	545	555	556	561	566	566	561	556
458	513	518	518	518	523	523	530	535	540	545	555	560	560	..
489	530	535	540	545	545	550	555	560	565	570	573	573	573	..
418	476	476	481	486	491	496	501	508	518	528	535	545	550	..
445	496	496	499	499	494	499	504	509	519	524	529	529	535	..
444	578	578	583	584	585	595	605	610	625	640	650	655	659	661
577	560	563	568	570	575	580	585	585	585	590	595	597	597	..
470	424	424	423	424	424	422	423	425	435	441	449	451	451	..
358	545	549	550	550	550	550	555	560	565	565	565	565	565	..
505	519	619	615	608	603	603	603	603	608	613	617	617	614	..
505	573	581	595	610	612	612	612	612	612	617	622	622	622	..
517	521	521	526	526	522	517	517	522	522	517	507	500	493	488
356	3	..	..	..	..	..	..	..	..	..	..	..	..	..

..	482	465	434	429	422	417	415	408	405	396	394	398	370	..
341	344	143	152	155	156	158	152	155	155	153	152	153	152	..
141	171	169	164	160	157	155	154	153	149	150	149	150	*	..
155	163	162	161	162	161	157	159	167	159	148	148	154	*	..
150	155	154	150	147	143	142	140	137	137	136	133	131	*	..
132	*	135	133	129	126	125	121	119	118	118	115	119	*	..
118	*	112	111	109	105	104	103	102	101	100	99	98	*	95
84	32	136	145	155	169	180	190	204	206	212	224	226	*	..
223	244	252	253	249	248	245	237	229	232	240	232	232	*	..
197	187	180	181	177	178	178	171	167	164	172	171	168	*	..
142	*	104	109	111	119	127	122	117	119	144	153	154	157	..
132	*	290	289	282	273	261	245	261	254	238	247	276	278	267
199	426	410	404	383	381	377	358	357	329	336	342	346	342	..
341	405	407	409	413	422	428	427	431	435	438	440	441	*	..
430	358	353	348	347	351	350	346	341	341	343	333	333	*	..
257	2	214	224	224	228	235	235	223	220	203	205	202	*	..
173	17	297	299	278	283	290	290	290	287	302	305	317	320	..
284	28	379	384	379	386	405	407	404	404	445	465	474	495	498
506	5	..	..	..	..	..	..	..	..	..	..	..	..	..

[facing p. 218

below that ruling before the gold purchases began. In view of the heavy Government expenditure, the " tender " bill total is now rising rapidly. But even at the present rate it will not reach a normal seasonal level until the autumn. In other words, rearmament is still being financed out of the proceeds of the sale of gold bought in previous years out of long-term loans; or, from another point of view, out of the long-term loans raised in previous years and invested temporarily in gold. The effects of this, and of other changes in the Floating Debt, upon the banking and economic position is discussed in the following article.

BRITISH FLOATING DEBT POLICY [1]

THE history of the British Floating Debt during the twenty years from 1919 to 1939 falls into three sharply divided parts. During the first, from 1919 to 1923, the total Floating Debt was reduced by nearly half, from £1500 millions to £800 millions, though it seems likely that a large part of this reduction occurred in bills held by the Bank of England and Government departments. With these we are not now concerned, for the details of financial arrangements between Government departments, though sometimes interesting and occasionally revealing, do not throw much light upon the working of economic principles. The second period, from 1923 to 1931, is the one which is richest in discussions of policy. Though during this period the total of Treasury bills issued by tender to the public, which alone need be considered here, remained, apart from seasonal fluctuations, at an approximately constant level, the question of whether this level was a desirable one was discussed in detail before two important Government committees — the Colwyn Committee of 1925 and the Macmillan Committee of 1931 — as well as in numerous articles in newspapers and periodicals. Among the latter, the articles in the *Midland Bank Review* must be regarded as the most authoritative.

In the third period, after Britain's departure from the gold standard, the methods used for the financing of the gold purchases of the Exchange Equalisation Account have had the incidental effect of causing the total of Treasury bills issued by tender to show much wider fluctuations.

[1] Originally published in *Economica*, August 1940.

During this period new considerations emerge, which will be discussed in the latter part of this article.

From the discussions of Floating Debt policy during the second of the periods mentioned above there emerge three main criteria of policy. These may be conveniently described as (1) the liquidity of the Treasury; (2) the liquidity of the remainder of the system; (3) the cost to the Treasury. Unfortunately the meaning of the term liquidity has been so circumscribed in recent economic literature that before it can be used in the present context it is necessary to pause for a moment to free it from some of the shackles which have been riveted upon it.

The concept of liquidity has for many years been used in ordinary business parlance in two somewhat different senses. In the first place, it is used of an asset, signifying the ease, speed, certainty, etc., with which it can be converted into cash; and, secondly, it is used of the general financial position of individuals or firms, signifying the ease with which they may be expected to meet their obligations. In neither of these uses of the word has it any high degree of quantitative definition. It is often impossible to decide even which of two assets may be regarded as the more liquid, until we have before us other information, such as the period of time which is to be reckoned as available for the process of liquidation. If, for instance, the period is short, an asset which can be sold rapidly even at the cost of a possible heavy fall in price, such as a Stock Exchange security, must be regarded as more liquid than another, such as a good but unmarketable debt due at notice, which can certainly be turned into cash without loss, but only over a period of time. Further, the liquidity of an asset will often depend on the point of view of the person taking the decision. A creditor, prepared to force his debtor, if necessary, into complete liquidation, need have regard only to the actual marketability of the asset in question. But its owner, in making his own decisions, must have regard not only to its marketability, but to its relation to his other assets and to his own earning power. If the sale or pledge of an asset would entail the extensive immobilisation of other assets, he cannot regard it as easily available for meeting his impending obligations, and in his scale of liquidity it will probably rank below other assets less capable of rapid realisation but also less essential for the continued conduct of his business.

In the wider application of the term liquidity to a whole financial position, the point of view of the judge is of even greater importance. A creditor will often be justified in confining his attention to existing liquid assets and current liabilities, and in expressing the liquidity of his debtor in terms of the ratio of the former of these to the latter ; though even a creditor will, on occasion, find that it pays him to take account of other factors, such as the expected earnings of his debtor, the probability of his being able in need to raise capital or borrow money elsewhere, the probability that he will not in fact be called upon to meet some part of his legal obligations, and so forth. But the controller of a business, or even a private individual, if he is to form a clear idea of the liquidity of his position, must take into account the expected flows of the whole of his receipts and payments during the period for which estimates are possible. If he can see his way clear, in all probable circumstances, to meet not only his legal debts but also all other payments which he wishes to make, with a margin for unforeseen contingencies, then he can regard his position as liquid. Perhaps, indeed, the best definition of liquidity is in terms of the margin over foreseen payments of foreseen receipts plus dispensable liquid assets.

If the result of such a consideration of a financial position reveals an insufficient margin for contingencies, various steps may be taken to increase it. Earnings may be increased by harder work, anticipated expenditure may be reduced, less liquid assets may be exchanged for more liquid assets, or money may be borrowed on long-term. In any case the results will take one of two forms — either liquid assets will be increased, or current liabilities reduced (as compared with what they would otherwise have been).

That a reduction of current liabilities may be quite as effective a method of increasing liquidity as is an increase of liquid assets is clear if we regard the current liabilities as immobilising part of the liquid assets and rendering them unavailable for other uses. This is most obvious where the assets are pledged as security for a loan, or where the continuance of the loan is contingent upon the debtor retaining possession of the assets. But even where the debtor is under no actual obligation, he will necessarily survey his assets in relation to his liabilities, and will be the less willing to see any shrinkage in his liquid assets the more they are balanced by current liabilities. A reduction in these liabilities therefore sets him free to reduce his liquid assets if occasion should require.

In recent years economists have made increasing use of the concept of liquidity, especially as an approach to monetary problems. But in giving precision to the term, they have generally amalgamated the two senses in which it is used in business terminology. They have applied the term to the general financial position, but have generally confined their consideration to changes in the distribution of assets, or even to the single item, cash. This limitation is unfortunate, since, if maintained, it would prevent us from applying the valuable concept of liquidity to many problems where it appears to provide the most convenient method of approach.

The extension of the concept of liquidity to cover changes in the distribution of liabilities through time enables us to apply it to the financial position of the British Treasury. The British Treasury held, until the inauguration of the Exchange Equalisation Account, virtually no liquid assets of its own. Its balance at the Bank of England at the dates of its weekly financial statements rarely exceeds two or three million pounds, and to meet temporary excesses of payments over receipts it depends on short-term borrowing. The bulk of its short-term borrowing is in normal times from the banks and the money market on three months Treasury bills. It also borrows on Treasury bills from other Government departments and from the Bank of England. These latter borrowings can be allowed to fluctuate more rapidly than its borrowing from the market; in anticipation of exceptionally large payments by the Treasury the other departments frequently accumulate increased balances in Public Deposits at the Bank of England, which they place at the disposal of the Treasury in exchange for bills when the date of payment arrives.[1] The Treasury also borrows on open account (Ways and Means Advances) both from Government departments and, in emergency, from the Bank of England.

From the foregoing it is clear that, like a firm operating on overdraft, the British Treasury depended for its liquidity on its power to borrow on short-term from the market, from other Government departments, or, in the last resort, from the Bank of England. Until 1932 there was, however, this difference. A firm operating on overdraft normally holds liquid assets substantially in excess of its debt, out of which, in emergency and at some cost in convenience or output, the debt can be reduced or liquidated. The Treasury had no such assets, and, to meet a demand for repayment by one section of its creditors, had no recourse in the short run but to increase its borrowings elsewhere. Since the resources of the departments at that time were limited, the ultimate guarantee of its ability to meet its debts as they fell due was its power of borrowing from the Bank of England.

If a demand for the repayment of Treasury bills was due merely to a demand for increased holdings of idle

[1] For a fuller description of these operations see pp. 197-8.

money within the country, this guarantee was adequate. Such a demand could be satisfied either by an increase in Bankers' Deposits at the Bank of England, which could be provided at the Bank's discretion, or by an increased supply of Bank of England notes, which could be provided by an increase in the fiduciary issue. A relatively small increase in one or both of these would very rapidly restore the clearing banks' ability to resume their purchases of bills, and so bring the period of stringency to an end. If, however, the demand for increased cash for internal use was for supporting a rising trend in prices which the Bank of England considered undesirable and wished to check, the existence of a large amount of short-term Government obligations in the hands of the public might prove an embarrassment to the Bank in the carrying out of its policy. This would not be due merely to the natural reluctance of the Bank to impose on the Treasury an additional cost by reason of a rise in rates of interest, such as would occur in the absence of a Floating Debt. At such times the direct effect of a moderate rise of the Bank of England rate and other short-term rates of interest in checking business activity is probably small. Much more important is the quantitative limitation on loans which a rise in the Bank rate causes banks and others to impose on their debtors, whether in the form of higher margin requirements or otherwise. By such means an incipient inflationary boom can often be checked with a relatively small rise in published rates of interest. But if there exists a large amount of Government Floating Debt in the hands of the public, maturing week by week, such methods of quantitative limitation lose much of their efficiency, for, by a refusal to renew its bills, the Treasury can be forced to provide the banks and the market with enough additional cash at the Bank of England to offset the previous restrictions. The only way to prevent this is for the Treasury to pay such rates on its bills as will by themselves provide a sufficient incentive to their holders to renew them, or for others to buy them. This rate may well be substantially higher than the rate which, in the absence of the Floating Debt, would have been charged for such short-term loans as were still granted. In other words, the Treasury is a short-term borrower whom its Bank cannot ration. Its short-term obligations to the public may therefore cause the rationing system to break down, and may compel a rise in short-term interest rates to a level sufficient by itself to check the expansion of business activity.

In the event of an increased demand for cash for the purchase of foreign exchange, the difficulties created, in a country on the gold standard, by the existence of a large Floating Debt are even greater. Unless rates of interest are allowed to rise to a level sufficient in itself to check the outflow of capital (and where confidence in the future of the currency is shaken this level may be very high indeed), the Treasury can be compelled to provide large weekly amounts of cash at the Bank of England, thus furnishing those wishing to withdraw gold with the necessary sterling funds. If gold reserves are inadequate to meet the demand, the Bank may have to choose between refusing the request of the Treasury for additional facilities and itself running the risk of being unable to meet its own obligations to pay gold. Thus the Bank's power to lend to the Treasury in this type of emergency is largely dependent on the size of its gold reserve; while the likelihood and probable severity of the emergency itself depends largely upon the proportion of Treasury bills held either by foreigners or by institutions with large sterling obligations to foreigners. Before 1932 the ultimate guarantee of the liquidity of the Treasury was therefore the Bank of England's gold reserve; and the possibility that this guarantee would be needed depended largely upon the volume of foreign money in London.

In the light of these considerations, the attitude of the Treasury, as revealed by the evidence of its representatives

before the Colwyn and Macmillan Committees,[1] is easy to
understand. With an inadequate gold reserve at the Bank
of England, large amounts of foreign funds in London,
much of them probably invested in Treasury bills, and a
persistent tendency towards an adverse balance of payments,
the Treasury, both in 1925 and in 1930, might well feel
uneasy at the size of its short-term commitments and wish
to reduce them. Its forebodings were to be only too well
justified by the events of 1931, when the Bank of England
had to choose between defaulting on its own obligations to
pay gold, and compelling the Treasury to default on its
obligation to meet its bills on maturity. Given the other
conditions present at the time, it is, of course, not im-
probable that the Bank would have done the same even if
the Treasury's Floating Debt had been much smaller; but
it is certain that, whatever the other circumstances, the
existence of so large a public Floating Debt would have
made it extremely difficult for the Bank to make effective
the stringent measures which alone might have enabled it
to continue to meet its obligations.

In spite of the wishes so clearly expressed by the
Treasury's representatives and of the recommendations of
the Colwyn Committee, we find that during the whole
period from 1923 to 1931 the total of the Treasury's short-
term liabilities to the public (that is to say, of Treasury
bills issued by tender) showed no decline on balance,
while, throughout the period, the fluctuations in the total,
apart from seasonal movements, did not exceed about £70
millions.[2] The reasons why, in face of its expressed wishes,
the Treasury failed to make any net reduction in its total
of " tender " bills, must be sought partly in its own financial
position, and partly in the repercussions which a policy of

---

[1] *Colwyn Committee: Evidence*, pp. 288, 394, 622, 623, 668. *Colwyn
Committee Report*, p. 35. *Macmillan Committee: Evidence*, vol. i, p. 32;
vol. ii, pp. 9, 10.

[2] See Chart 2, p. 194.

drastic reductions would have had on other parts of the economic system.

In the first place, the Floating Debt was not the only threat which existed to the liquidity of the Treasury. In addition, at the end of the War of 1914–18 the Treasury had some £2000 millions outstanding of medium-term debt — Exchequer bonds, War bonds, and Treasury bonds — of which substantial amounts matured each year. The task of funding or replacing these issues presented a constantly recurring problem, for at any moment a failure to float the necessary loan would involve an automatic increase in the Floating Debt. Such an increase, though a small one, in fact occurred in the spring of 1929. It can be understood that these constantly recurring periods of pressure, each threatening a rise in the Floating Debt, helped to make it difficult for the Treasury to float additional loans for the reduction of the Floating Debt itself. Actually, by reducing its medium-term debt from nearly £1600 millions in 1925 to little more than £600 millions in 1931, the Treasury did in fact succeed in substantially improving the liquidity of its position despite the unchanged amount of its short-term debt.[1]

Even if the Treasury had been able, without difficulty, to issue long-term loans between 1923 and 1930 of sufficient size to effect large reductions in its Floating Debt, it would probably have been deterred by consideration of the probable effects of its action on the other parts of the system. It is, of course, not peculiar in the fact that changes in its own liquidity normally have converse effects upon the liquidity of others. Normally every person who increases his own liquidity, without increasing the aggregate margin between his total assets and his total liabilities, decreases the liquidity of someone else. Where he exchanges a less liquid for a more liquid asset this is obvious. It is just as true in the case where he substitutes a long-dated for a

[1] See *Macmillan Committee: Evidence*, vol. ii, p. 9.

short-dated liability. A short-dated security is a better substitute for cash than a long-dated security issued by the same debtor, so that when the supply of short-dated securities is reduced and that of long-dated securities increased, the normal effect is to increase the demand to hold cash. It is most desirable in such cases to realise that the demand for increased liquidity does not come from the actual persons who are demanding more cash, but from those who, by their action in changing the form of their liabilities, have deprived their former holders of cash substitutes.

There is only one exception to the general rule that a person who increases his own liquidity decreases that of the rest of the system. If by paying off part of his short-term debt he so improves the credit standing of the remainder that it becomes a better substitute for money, the decrease in quantity may be more than offset by the increase in quality, and the liquidity of the remainder of the system may be increased. Conversely, if an increase in his short-term liabilities impairs their credit standing, the liquidity of the remainder of the system may be reduced. Broadly speaking, therefore, the system as a whole may become more liquid either when the short-term liabilities of the financially strong are increased or when those of the financially weak are reduced, and less liquid either when the short-term liabilities of the financially strong are reduced or when those of the financially weak are increased.

Since the British Treasury can normally be regarded as an extremely credit-worthy borrower, it follows that any conversion of its short-term liabilities into long-dated securities tends to reduce the supply of money substitutes and to increase the demand for money. Further, since it is by far the largest single borrower on the short-term market, it must, unlike most other borrowers, take account of the effects of its policy upon the rest of the system. It must do this for two reasons : firstly, because of reactions upon its own position of changes elsewhere; and, secondly, because the Treasury is not an independent entity, but merely represents one aspect of a Government charged with the care of the interests of the whole community. It cannot, therefore, regard with equanimity loss or inconvenience caused by its actions in other parts of the system, even though no repercussions on its own financial position are distinguishable.

The effects upon the system of changes in the volume of Treasury bills are greatly magnified by the fact that they are largely exercised via the banking system. Banks have much more definite conventions concerning the distribution of their resources than have other types of business concerns. The ratios which the larger London clearing banks now appear to regard as the lowest desirable are 10 per cent of their deposits in cash and 30 per cent in cash plus money at call and short notice, plus discounts. This means that discounts and short loans are normally regarded as complementary to cash only when the cash ratio is at or near its conventional minimum, while when the cash ratio is well above 10 per cent, discounts and short loans are regarded as substitutes for it.

The conventional minima are not in fact rigidly maintained. Even though the published total of the combined cash reserves of the clearing banks has never fallen perceptibly below 10 per cent of their deposits, the apparent maintenance of this ratio has frequently been achieved only by resort to a greater or less amount of " window-dressing ", and the true ratio has at times fallen below the conventional minimum by an unknown amount, probably on occasions to well below 9 per cent. For the combined total of " quick assets " such methods of inflating the published figures are not available,[1] and these have frequently fallen well below the 30 per cent level.

[1] Since window-dressing consists of the apparent conversion of discounts and call money into cash.

The contention of the banks [1] is that at such times the shortage of quick assets has a similar effect on their willingness to hold long-term assets — securities and advances — as a shortage of cash has upon their willingness to hold all assets other than cash. Unless, therefore, they are provided with additional cash reserves in substitution for the inadequate supply of bills, they feel obliged to restrict both advances and purchases of securities, thus raising their cash and quick assets ratios immediately by means of a fall in deposits, and later through an increase in cash rendered possible by a reduction in the demand for currency by the public. It is not clear how much additional cash is required to make up for a given shortage of bills — *i.e.* whether the 30 per cent quick assets ratio is an unchanging minimum, or whether, for instance, a 29 per cent quick assets ratio would be acceptable if accompanied by an 11 per cent cash ratio.[2]

---

[1] See *Colwyn Committee: Evidence*, pp. 106, 283, and 288. *Macmillan Committee: Evidence*, vol. i, p. 33 ; vol. ii, pp. 176, 177. *Midland Bank Monthly Review*, September–October 1933 and September–October 1934.

[2] While the effect of a shortage of bills at a time when cash reserves stand at above 10 per cent is clearly to tend to cause a rise (or check or prevent a fall) in long-term interest rates, its effect on short-term interest rates is less certain. If bills are regarded as a perfect substitute for cash so long as the cash ratio is above 10 per cent, the effect will be to drive down short-term rates of interest. But if, from the point of view of liquidity, bills are regarded as an imperfect substitute for cash, so that, say, an extra £1 million of cash will compensate for a deficiency of £2 millions of bills, the effect on discount rates will depend on the degree of competition between the banks and on the elasticity of the supply of bills to the banks as a whole. If the banks are in competition, so that the supply of bills to each bank regarded separately is elastic, the short-term rate will be forced down as each bank endeavours to attract bills away from its competitors by offering higher prices. But if the banks combine to fix the rates, they will raise their prices only if they think this will have the effect of enabling them to purchase sufficient additional bills to restore their minimum ratio. If they consider that the supply of bills to them will be highly inelastic, they will instead endeavour to increase their cash at the expense of a further reduction in discounts by selling bills to the central bank (or, in London, by calling in loans from the market), thus raising short-term interest rates. Thus, if the banks have 11 per cent of their deposits in cash and 17 per cent in call money and bills, they can reach a satisfactory position either by increasing their bills and

Q

If the banks' contention is correct, that a shortage of bills compels them to restrict their advances and holdings of securities, one might hope to find some statistical confirmation of it in the movements of figures in the clearing banks' monthly returns. Unfortunately there are considerable difficulties in the way of obtaining such confirmation. In the first place, the banks' figures cannot react instantaneously to changes in conditions, and before the reactions to a temporary change become visible their cause may have disappeared; further, short-period comparisons between different months of the same year are rendered impossible by the very strong seasonal movement in discounts (mainly in consequence of a similar movement in Treasury bills). It is not known how far the banks take this seasonal movement into account in fixing their minimum — whether, for instance, they would be more affected by a fall in the quick assets ratio below 30 per cent in October than in April. It would seem *prima facie* reasonable that they should be caused some concern by a fall in the ratio below the normal for the time of year unless they expected the position to be adjusted before the next seasonal low; that is to say, a foreseen fall below 30 per cent in a coming month should have an effect on policy before it becomes actual.

Secondly, the banks change their own views on the question of desirable minimum ratios, both suddenly, in moments of crisis, and gradually over long periods. An example of the former occurred at the outbreak of the war, when the cash ratio rose from 10·5 per cent of deposits in July 1939 to 11·8 per cent in September, while discounts and short loans fell from 19·6 per cent to 16·9 per cent. These movements occurred, not be-

short loans to 18 per cent of deposits, leaving cash unchanged at 11 per cent, or by reducing bills and short loans to 16 per cent while raising cash to 12 per cent. Which they will choose will depend on calculations about the relative amounts of interest earnings sacrificed in the two cases.

cause of an increased demand for cash engendered by a shortage of bills, but because the minimum desirable cash ratio suddenly became a good deal higher than 10 per cent.

The gradual change in the banks' conventions over time is shown by an inspection of the figures over a period of years. Thus for the five years ending 1927 the average cash ratio was 11·7 per cent and the quick assets ratio 32·7 per cent, while for the corresponding years of the following decade the average ratios had fallen to 10·7 per cent and 32·1 per cent respectively.

It would seem, therefore, that any comparisons must be made between :

(1) similar periods of different years ;

(2) years not far separated in time ;

(3) periods when the banks' normal views as to the relative liquidity values of cash and other short-term assets were not seriously disturbed. The following table shows the clearing banks' average ratios of cash and of short loans plus discounts to deposits for the three months when discounts are normally lowest (March, April, May) in each of the years 1933 to 1939 :

| | Clearing Banks' Ratio to Deposits | |
	Cash	Short Loans + Discounts
	%	%
March–May 1933	10·9	23·4
1934	12·0	18·6
1935	11·2	17·9
1936	10·3	20·6
1937	10·2	18·8
1938	10·7	18·1
1939	11·1	15·7

These figures give some support to the contention that the banks hold a higher cash ratio when their other quick assets are low; but to show that the inadequacy of the quick assets induces them to restrict advances and securities we need more than this. For when discounts fall, deposits necessarily fall correspondingly, unless the discounts are replaced by other assets. The ratio of cash to deposits will therefore rise automatically in years when discounts are low. Thus, if we start from a position where cash is 10·5 per cent of deposits, and other quick assets are 20 per cent, a fall in the latter to 17 per cent (of the reduced level of deposits), unless offset by a rise in other assets, would automatically raise the cash ratio to 10·9 per cent. To conform with the contention that a change in holdings of short loans and discounts has a tendency to cause holdings of long-term assets to change in the same direction (*i.e.* that short-term assets are complementary to long-term assets), it is necessary for the change in the cash ratio in the opposite direction to be greater than can be accounted for by this automatic rise; if it is equal to it, this would be consistent with the view that short loans and discounts are merely neutral to long-term assets.

Of the three most marked changes shown in recent years (from plenty to scarcity of short-term assets in 1933–34, from scarcity to plenty in 1935–36, and from moderate scarcity to acute scarcity in 1938–39), the first two show changes in cash reserves appreciably, and the third slightly, larger than the changes to be expected to occur automatically as a result of a fall in deposits equal to the fall in short loans and discounts :

	Cash Ratio			
	Expected		Actual	
	Rise	Fall	Rise	Fall
1933–34	0·7	..	1·1	..
1935–36	..	0·5	..	0·9
1938–39	0·3	..	0·4	..

These movements are consistent with the view that the banks normally regard call loans and discounts as a substitute for cash when the cash ratio is well above the minimum.[1]

It remains to be shown that Treasury bills have since 1918 formed so large a proportion of the banks' discounts that changes in their total seriously affect the banks' position. While no strictly accurate comparison can be made of the banks' statements after 1918 with those for 1914 and earlier years, an examination of such figures as can be compiled seems to indicate that between 1914 and 1927 bank discounts increased by about 80 per cent. Further, from the statistics quoted in the Macmillan Report it appears that in 1927 more than half the total of discounts consisted of Treasury bills. It therefore would seem that the total of commercial bills held by the banks was rather lower in 1927 than it had been in 1914. It seems clear that, but for the increase in the Treasury bill issue, either the banks would have been compelled to show a fall in their " quick assets " ratio far more drastic than the decline from 43 per cent to 32 per cent of deposits which actually occurred, or the expansion in bank deposits would have been much less than the rise of 130 per cent which occurred between 1914 and 1927, or both. It is probably true to say that the British banks were enabled more than to double their deposits after 1914 largely in consequence of the expansion of the Treasury's Floating Debt, which took the place of an expansion in the volume of commercial bills.

If, therefore, the Treasury had taken steps drastically to reduce its Floating Debt, it would have put the banks in a difficult position. Unless the volume of commercial bills had simultaneously shown a permanent expansion — a development which, though much desired,[2] did not in fact take place — the banks would have been obliged either

---

[1] In view of the many other factors involved, it is, of course, impossible to say that they afford *proof* of it, especially in view of the fact that from 1934 to 1935, and from 1936 to 1937, falls in the ratio of call loans and discounts were accompanied by falls in the cash ratio.

[2] See *Colwyn Report*, p. 36. *Colwyn Committee : Evidence*, pp. 111, 623. *Macmillan Committee : Evidence*, vol. ii, p. 11.

to make a further drastic revision of their standards of
liquidity, or to take steps to reduce the totals of their
long-term assets.

To this it may be objected that such a tendency towards
deflation could easily have been offset by a suitable increase
in the banks' cash reserves, induced by additions to the
assets of the Bank of England.[1]   To make such a policy
fully effective, however, the Bank would have to buy either
long-dated securities or gold from the public or from abroad.
For the Bank of England to buy bills would increase the
shortage of bills available for sale or pledge to the banks, and
so, by intensifying the bill famine, necessitate still further
creations of cash.   In post-gold-standard conditions, for the
Bank to buy gold from the Exchange Account would have a
similar effect, since it provides the Account with sterling
with which to pay off bills.   In the days of the gold standard,
it was clearly easiest for the Bank to offset the monetary
effects of a reduction in Treasury bills if the funding occurred
at a time when gold was flowing into the country.

This conclusion is reinforced by a second contention,
put forward with much force by Mr. Keynes in his cross-
examination of Sir Richard Hopkins before the Macmillan
Committee.[2]   The argument is roughly as follows : — If,
at a time when large quantities of funds are attracted to
London, because it is the most convenient centre for short-
term investment, a great proportion of the most suitable
channels of investment disappear and are replaced by
long-term securities, it must be anticipated that much of
these funds will be diverted to other centres.   The result
will be that gold will flow out and the initial fall in short-
term interest rates will be checked and reversed ; the ultimate result will presumably be that, while long-term rates
of interest may be forced appreciably higher, short-term

---

[1] See *Colwyn Report*, p. 36.

[2] See *Macmillan Committee : Evidence*, vol. ii, pp. 9-11.   Also *Barclays
Bank Monthly Review*, March–April 1930.

rates cannot show an appreciable fall, unless the funding operation occurs at a time when the balance of payments is active and short-term funds can be withdrawn from London without causing an outflow of gold. In other words, the British Government was in effect borrowing on short term the foreign funds the inflow of which had enabled the Bank of England to obtain or retain its gold ; and if the British Government ceased to borrow these funds on short term, they would be withdrawn, unless an alternative investment (in the form of an increase in the available supply of commercial bills) appeared, and they could only be withdrawn without causing difficulty if their withdrawal was offset by an active balance of payments.

If the validity of the foregoing argument is accepted, the course of events following upon a large Treasury funding operation between 1925 and 1931 would probably have been somewhat as follows, unless its effects had been offset either by the development of a large favourable balance of payments or by a rapid expansion in the volume of commercial bills, or by both.

Let us assume (what is by no means certain) that a substantial Funding Loan could have been issued without causing any very serious rise in long-term interest rates. The money subscribed to the loan might have come from any of four sources :

(1) From the conversion of bills owned by foreigners. In this case the foreign owners of London funds would have voluntarily accepted the burden of decreased liquidity, and no problem would arise. Unfortunately it would seem that the owners of such funds attached a high value to their liquidity, and would be unlikely to invest them on long term.

(2) From new foreign funds attracted to London by the rise in long-term interest rates. This development would also have solved most of the problem, but was almost equally unlikely.

(3) From the conversion of the British banks' holdings

of Treasury bills. This would mean that these banks were prepared not merely to maintain their long-term assets despite a decrease in their short-term assets, but to see a substantial increase in them — in other words, that they regarded bills as a substitute, not for cash, but for securities. As we have seen, this is unlikely.

(4) From existing balances held in British banks. This last source is by far the most likely. The effect on the economic system of the repayment of Treasury bills out of funds subscribed from existing bank balances would depend partly upon the identity of the holders of the bills and partly upon the use to which the funds subscribed would otherwise have been put by their owners.

(*a*) Balances used to repay bills held by the general British public. There is a strong presumption that funds received in repayment of bills, and unable to find a similar suitable investment, will be held on deposit account or otherwise inactive. If these funds were originally subscribed from inactive accounts there will be no change; if from active accounts, there will be an increase in inactive accounts at the expense of active accounts, and a fall in the velocity of circulation.

(*b*) Balances used to repay bills held by the banks. If the banks cannot find a suitable alternative short-term investment, total bank deposits will fall; if the banks regard bills as a substitute for cash and have to realise securities to increase their cash ratios, deposits will fall by more than the decrease in their discounts. In so far as the balances used to subscribe to the Treasury's loan and to buy the securities sold by the banks were formerly inactive, there is no decrease in active balances; but in so far as active balances are used, there will be a fall in the effective quantity of money in circulation.

(*c*) Balances used to repay Treasury bills owned by foreigners. The initial fall in short-term interest rates will tend to cause these foreigners to withdraw their balances from London. The resulting drain on the cash reserves of the banks will compel them to offer increased deposit rates to foreigners in order to induce them to abstain from withdrawing their funds. If the funds subscribed to the conversion loan were originally active, there will be a fall in velocity of circulation.

The effects on interest rates would appear to be as follows :

(1) An initial rise in long-term rates as a direct result of the Treasury's loan.

(2) A possible secondary rise as a result of the banks' sales of securities.

(3) An initial fall in short-term rates of interest as a result of the reduced supply of bills.

(4) A subsequent rise in short-term rates (possibly confined to foreign-owned balances) in order to prevent foreign withdrawals of funds from London.

In total, therefore, it would seem likely that the net effect of a large-scale funding operation in the conditions ruling between 1925 and 1931 would have been a reduction in the total of bank deposits and a fall in their velocity of circulation, a rise in long-term interest rates, and a smaller, perhaps negligible, fall in short-term rates. There is even a possible case in which short-term rates would actually have risen (see p. 231, footnote 2).

So far we have seen the Treasury's concern for its own liquidity in conflict with its interest in the liquidity of the remainder of the system. We must now glance briefly at the third aspect of the question, that of the direct cost to the Treasury. The problem of comparing the interest cost of long and short borrowing presents certain difficulties. In the first place, it is misleading merely to compare short-term interest rates with the current long-term rates. Once a long-term loan has been raised, the borrower can

ignore changes in long-term interest rates until such time
as the loan falls due to be repaid. In making up his mind
as to the relative cost of the two methods, he must compare
the present long-term rate with expected future short-term
rates during the whole period of the proposed long-term loan.
It is sometimes said that he compares the long-term rate
with the average of expected future short-term rates. This
is only true if the average is weighted in a particular way.
A short-term rate of 2 per cent for ten years, to be followed
by a 4 per cent rate for ten years, is obviously preferable
now to a 4 per cent rate to be followed by a 2 per cent rate.
What in fact we are comparing is the discounted present
value of the expected future interest payments on the two
methods of borrowing. The most convenient rate to use
in discounting is the present long-term rate, though strict
accuracy probably demands the use of the expected short-
term rate for each period.

If we assume foresight on the part of the borrowing
authority, we therefore have to compare the relative costs
of long-term and short-term borrowing, not between the
averages for the period lent, but between the long-term
rate on a particular date and the various subsequent short-
term rates, both discounted back to the date upon which the
long-term loan could be raised.   It may very well be that it
would pay to borrow on long term at a particular date, even
though long-term rates are expected to be persistently higher
than contemporaneous short-term rates ; and it is quite
probable that the most profitable time for converting short-
term into long-term debt is when current long-term rates
show their largest excess over current short-term rates.

Until 1932, the apparent saving in interest charges by
borrowing on short term was comparatively small. If, at the
beginning of 1923, the Treasury had issued a long-term loan
at 4½ per cent to fund £400 millions of Treasury bills (*i.e.*
practically the whole of the tender issue apart from that
required to even out seasonal movements), the extra interest

cost, from 1923 to 1931, assuming that the operation had no effect on either long-term or short-term rates, would have been about £27 millions, or an average of £3 millions per annum. The 1923 discounted value of the extra cost would have been about £22 millions. The great bulk of the extra cost would have been incurred in two years — 1923 and 1930. For the years 1925 to 1929 inclusive the cost would have been trifling.

The foregoing estimate, however, assumes that the demand both for long-dated and short-dated securities was extremely elastic, so that a large long-term loan could have been raised and large amounts of Treasury bills funded without appreciably affecting either rate of interest. As we have seen above, in the conditions which existed between 1925 and 1931 a really large funding loan would probably have caused a substantial rise in the long-term rate of interest, though perhaps little fall in the short-term rate. The cost to the Treasury of such a rise in the long-term rate cannot be judged merely by the higher rate paid on the Funding Loan itself — indeed, it is possible that most of the rise might have occurred in consequence of the repercussions of the reduction in bills, and therefore would not have affected the rate paid on the Funding Loan. The Treasury would need to take account of its expected borrowing requirements for a considerable time ahead, and especially of its need to fund maturing Treasury bonds (see p. 228). The total cost to the Treasury of a major funding operation would therefore have been very much higher than the apparent cost computed on the basis of the interest rates which actually existed during these years. Even if the Treasury had had regard solely to its own financial position, it might well have hesitated before attempting to reduce its Floating Debt to a figure merely sufficient to take care of seasonal fluctuations in revenue and expenditure. If we add to the cost of additional interest charges the probable fall in tax revenues following upon the higher level of long-term interest rates, the arguments, even on the narrowest grounds, against a drastic funding operation appear to be very strong.

We find, therefore, from the application of our three criteria, that the effect of the financial expedients and credit expansion of 1914–18 had been to place the British Treasury in a position where it was forced to choose between, on the one hand, continuing what it considered to be its own unsound position and, on the other, imposing a serious deflationary movement on the rest of the system and at the same time adding considerably to its own interest burden. It is not surprising that it found itself compelled to choose the former and temporarily easier of these alternatives, with results which were seen in September 1931.

This frustrated desire of the Treasury before 1932 for an increase in liquidity by means of a reduction in its short-term debt to the public may perhaps help to explain what otherwise appears to be its irrational behaviour after that date. Although the Bank of England was no longer under compulsion to redeem its notes in gold at a fixed rate, and therefore one of the greatest difficulties in maintaining the solvency of the Treasury in the face of foreign withdrawals had disappeared (see p. 226), the Treasury proceeded enormously to increase the liquidity of its position. Between 1932 and March 1938, the Treasury accumulated $42\frac{1}{2}$ million ounces of gold in the hands of the Exchange Equalisation Account, and during the same time enabled the Bank of England to add $48\frac{1}{2}$ million ounces to its previous holding of $28\frac{1}{2}$ million ounces. Meanwhile the price of gold had risen from £4 : 5s. per fine ounce to about £7, so that the value of the combined gold holdings of the Treasury and the Bank had increased from £121 millions to nearly £840 millions.

That this expansion of the combined gold stock of the authorities had been rendered possible largely by an inflow of short-term funds from abroad is irrelevant from the

point of view of the liquidity of the Treasury. A withdrawal of foreign funds would involve sales of gold by the
Exchange Account in exchange for sterling, which would
automatically go to reduce the size of the Floating Debt
in the hands of the public. Thus even if the whole of the
addition to the authorities' gold stock had been financed
by an expansion in the Floating Debt in the hands of the
public, and had subsequently had to be sold in order to
permit the withdrawal of foreign balances, the final position
of the Treasury would have been no weaker at the end of
the operation than before the foreign balances were transferred to London; while, during the period when the
balances were still in London, the liquidity of the Treasury's
position would have been greatly increased.

By its method of financing its purchases of gold, the
Treasury enormously exaggerated the automatic increase
in its liquidity which the inflow of gold to London would
in any case have caused. Of the increase of over £700
millions which occurred in the value of the authorities'
gold stocks, only about £60 millions was financed by an
increase of the Floating Debt in non-official hands. Of
the balance, about £320 millions was financed by long-
term borrowing, £172 millions by expansion of the Bank
of England's note issue and deposits, and the bulk of the
remainder represented the profit on old and new gold
holdings due to the rise in the price of gold.[1] A comparison
of the position at the end of March 1938 with what it
had been ten years earlier, makes clear the enormous
increase in the liquidity of the Treasury's position :

	March 1928, £ Mn.	March 1938, £ Mn.
Value of gold held by Bank of England	158	540
Value of gold held by Exchange a/c	—	300
	158	840
Total of Treasury bills issued by tender	443	512
Ratio of gold to " tender " bills	35%	164%

[1] See pp. 215-16.

The extreme conservatism of the Treasury's method of financing the purchase of gold involved some risk of inconveniencing the banking system whenever large quantities of gold needed to be re-sold. Since the sterling proceeds of such sales went automatically to reduce the total of bills issued by tender, at times when foreign money was being withdrawn from London (or rather, at the times of seasonal minimum following such withdrawals) the total of " tender " bills outstanding fell to abnormally low levels. The withdrawals of 1934 and 1938 were followed by falls to £358 millions in March 1935 and to £346 millions in March 1939. Unless these declines had been rapidly reversed, in 1935 by the reversal of the flow of gold and in 1939 by the needs of rearmament, the banks might well have been obliged to curtail their holdings of longer-dated assets.

In looking for alternative explanations for the Treasury's action in so greatly increasing the liquidity of its own position, we can presumably eliminate the possibility that it wished in this way to prevent the remainder of the system from securing a dangerous increase in liquidity, leading to the risk of inflation. After the inauguration of the " cheap money " policy in 1932 the whole trend of its policy was the other way. But in fact it ran a serious risk of a clash between the two aspects of its policy — on the one hand, to increase its own liquidity and, on the other, to expand bank credit and force down long-term rates of interest. The conflict between these two policies was resolved only by the willingness of the clearing banks to submit to a marked decrease in their own standards of liquidity, by permitting a decline in their usual " quick assets " ratio and at the same time greatly expanding their holdings of long-dated securities. The Treasury thus secured the increase in its own liquidity partly by reducing that of the banks. There can be no doubt that the " cheap money " policy could have been carried out with much less friction and anxiety to the banks if rather more of the

Treasury's gold purchases had been financed on short term and rather less on long term.

A more likely explanation of the Treasury's policy may perhaps be found in the relative costs of borrowing on long and short term. It is true that never before has the gap between long-term and short-term rates been so wide for so long a period. Since 1932 the gap between the Treasury bill rate and the gilt-edged yield has rarely been less than 2 per cent, and has for long periods exceeded $2\frac{1}{2}$ per cent. Nevertheless, the decline in prices of long-dated securities after 1936 was so marked that the Treasury's Funding Loans of 1935 and 1936 were made on very substantially better terms than could have been obtained later. If Treasury bills were to be funded at all, it was more profitable to fund them then, even at the cost of several years of increased interest payments, than to wait until yields had risen and issue prices fallen. Whether or no the Treasury foresaw the rise in long-term rates, it can be congratulated on obtaining a substantial part of its long-term borrowings at the top of the market.

There remain two other possible explanations of the apparent immense increase in the Treasury's " liquidity preference " since 1932. One, which it is to be hoped may be rejected forthwith, is that the Treasury regarded a yearly average of round about £500 millions as " reasonable " for the issue of " tender " bills, and that, regardless of other circumstances, it viewed with distrust any tendency for the average to rise much above that level. Such an attitude would be as intelligent as for a business man to regard £1000 as a " reasonable " figure for an overdraft, regardless of the amount of security he had to offer or of the liquid assets he held.

The other is that, as long ago as the spring of 1933, the Treasury foresaw the possibility that at some future date an abnormal expenditure would require urgent finance, and that this increase in potential obligations necessitated increased liquidity to offset it.   The possibility of a war is, of course, one of the factors which the Treasury must always bear in mind.   As long ago as 1925 Sir Otto Niemeyer, in his evidence before the Colwyn Committee, expressed apprehension as to the effect on short-term interest rates should the country be involved in a European war while carrying a large Floating Debt, and feared that " we should have great difficulty in renewing our bills and might be forced into very undesirable courses ".[1] But it is not unreasonable to suppose that, at least since 1935, the Treasury has been increasingly concerned with this possibility, and has deliberately followed a course directed towards securing for itself a position of extreme liquidity — a course analogous to the building up of " war chests " in bullion by monarchs of earlier centuries.

In doing so, the Treasury has incurred the risk of inconveniencing the banking system whenever the gold, bought with money borrowed on long term, has had to be sold and its sterling proceeds used for paying off short-term debt. Both after the temporary withdrawal of foreign funds in 1934 and the larger and more permanent withdrawals of 1938–39, the resulting falls in the volume of Treasury bills issued by tender constituted a serious embarrassment to the money market and the banks.   Had a large and permanent withdrawal of foreign funds occurred at a time when no exceptional Government expenditure was necessary, the result might have been the almost complete disappearance of the Treasury bill from the market, and probably a very substantial fall in bank deposits.   To prevent this, either the Exchange Equalisation Account would have had to use the sterling proceeds of its gold sales to buy long-dated securities, or, alternatively, the Issue Department of the Bank would have had to release Treasury bills to the Account, replacing them with long-dated securities.   Either of these methods, used on a large scale, would have had a

[1] *Colwyn Committee: Evidence*, pp. 622-3.

disturbing effect on the securities market, and might have involved the Treasury in substantial losses due to the purchase of securities at temporarily inflated prices.

As it was, however, the temporary bill shortage of the spring of 1939 was rapidly remedied by the rising trend of rearmament expenditure. Later, the effects of the further withdrawals of foreign funds immediately before the outbreak of war were almost exactly offset by increased war expenditure, so that the total of bills issued by tender was almost stationary from mid-July to mid-September, while the total Floating Debt rose by over £100 millions. The net effect of the Treasury's financial methods was thus, that it borrowed on long term several years in advance sufficient money to finance the deficit for the rearmament period and the first weeks of the war, invested it temporarily in gold, and realised its investments at a large profit just when the money was needed. To its previous policy must be attributed the ease with which the war was financed during its first six months without either the issue of a war loan or any serious expansion of bank credit.

R

CAPITAL VALUE AND INCOME[1]

I T would appear that the approach to the question of how far a change in the capital value of an asset without a change in the income derived therefrom improves the financial position of the owner could be appreciably simplified by the use of the following technique.

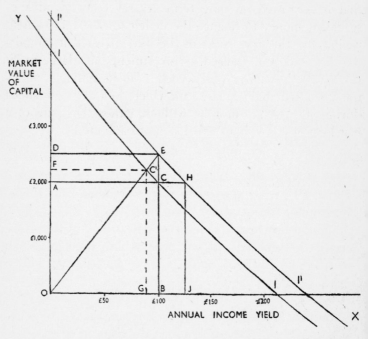

In the foregoing diagram, an investment with a market value equal to OA gives an annual income equal to OB. The point C, where the perpendiculars from A and B

[1] Originally published in *Economica*, November 1940.

248

meet, indicates the value to the owner of the combination of capital value and income yield.

Through C construct an indifference curve (I I) between capital value (yielding no income) and annual income (having no marketable value).

If the owner is completely indifferent to the annual income and is concerned only with capital value, I I will be parallel to the X axis. If he is concerned only with the annual income, then it will lie parallel to the Y axis. It is unlikely that either of these limiting cases would in fact occur. A very large capital sum will finance a substantial annual expenditure for a long time, and would therefore be preferred to a small perpetual income even by the most conservative of rentiers. Conversely, it is unlikely that even an extremely short-term speculator would fail to feel recompensed for the loss of £100 of capital value by an increase in income of £100 per week. It is therefore highly probable that the indifference curve will slope downwards and to the right and that it will cut both axes.

Now let the percentage rate of interest fall from $\dfrac{100 \ OB}{OA}$ to $\dfrac{100 \ OB}{OD}$. The capital value of the security therefore rises to OD, $=$ BE. Through E draw a second indifference curve, I'I', lying above and to the right of I I. From E draw a line to the origin.

If the owner of the security sells a part of it and consumes the proceeds, he will reduce both the capital value of his asset and his annual income, and his position will move along the line OE in the direction of O. If he stops at C', where OE cuts I I, his position will be exactly as favourable as before the fall in interest occurred. But at this point he has spent less than the amount of the rise in the capital value of his asset, since some increase (AF) in capital value is needed to offset the fall (GB) in annual income. His true profit from the rise in capital value is therefore not AD but FD, since FD is the additional amount which he can spend without making himself worse off than he was originally.

From the foregoing analysis it is clear that a distinction requires to be drawn between a capital gain due to the capitalisation of an increased income at an unchanged rate of interest, and that due to the capitalisation of an unchanged income at a reduced rate of interest. In the former case the whole of the capital gain can be spent without making the position worse than it was originally, in the latter only a part of it.

On the same diagram can be shown how much in terms of annual income the service of the availability [1] of the additional capital value is worth to its owner. If AC is extended to cut I'I' at H, then CH (= BJ) is the annual income equivalent of the rise in capital value. This does not of course mean that the owner can spend this additional amount per annum and still maintain his income at the new level. His position is similar to that of someone who receives the gift of a durable consumption good, from which he receives direct services by reason of which he is better off. If he now spends part of his capital and so reduces his money income, he will gradually return to another point on his original indifference curve, having a smaller money income but enjoying more direct services.

It can similarly be shown that if a man wishes to restore his financial position after a decline in the market value of his capital owing to a rise in the rate of interest, he must save until he has restored a part, but not the whole, of his capital loss. He will then still receive a smaller direct service from the availability of his capital, but will receive compensation for this in the form of a larger annual income. If, however, he wishes to restore his position after a decline in capital value due to a fall in the income yield, interest rates being unchanged, he must save until he has restored the whole of the former capital value.

[1] See W. H. Hutt, *The Theory of Idle Resources*, pp. 63-4.

The effect of changes in income yield, without a change in capital value (as for instance in consequence of a fall in interest rates accompanied by a conversion operation), can be similarly ascertained. If the yield of an investment falls, while its capital value is maintained, its owner, to restore his former position, must save enough to replace part, but not the whole, of his lost income. If the yield rises, without a rise in capital value, he will be no worse off than before the rise in yield if he spends a part of his capital, provided that he leaves his income still sufficiently above its former level to compensate him for the reduced market value of his capital.

Finally, this approach provides a convenient definition of the phrase " maintaining capital intact ", at least where the capital of an individual is concerned. Clearly, an individual owner of a security or other asset has maintained his capital intact if he is indifferent between his present combination of capital value and income yield and a former combination, *i.e.* if he is anywhere on the same indifference curve. Definitions of the phrase to mean the maintenance either of market value only or of annual income only can now be seen to be true only in the limiting cases where the indifference curve is parallel to one or other of the axes. Where, however, a corporation is concerned, its application is less obvious, since the indifference curves of the various shareholders may show great dissimilarities. It may therefore well be that movements in opposite directions of the market value of the securities and their yield will cause some shareholders to feel better off and others worse.

ECONOMIC INCENTIVE IN WAR-TIME[1]

The effect of taxation upon the amount of paid work which the taxpayer will prefer to do has been frequently discussed in economic literature; but in view of the unprecedented level to which direct taxation in this country has now risen, the subject has attained a degree of practical importance which is thought to justify the following attempt to re-examine some of the issues involved.

The simplest way to approach the question of the effect of taxation upon willingness to undertake paid work seems to be to look at its effect upon the demand for "leisure", that is to say, upon a man's demand for the use of his own services. The type of income change which has most usually been studied is one involving an equal change in aggregate and in marginal remuneration, such as is produced by a change in rates of hourly wages or by a change in a flat rate income tax. In such cases it has been shown[2] that the result may be either to increase or to decrease a man's demand for leisure. This indeterminacy is due to the fact that this type of income change gives rise to two distinct and opposing incentives, either of which may prove in any given case to be the stronger.

The first of these arises from the change in aggregate income. Since leisure is normally complementary to other goods, it is highly probable that the income elasticity of demand for it is positive, so that, when a man can afford fewer other goods, he can also afford less leisure. Thus a

---

[1] Originally published in *Economica*, August 1941.
[2] See L. Robbins, " On the Elasticity of Demand for Income in Terms of Effort " (*Economica*, June 1930), and D. Black, *The Incidence of Income Taxes*, ch. xii.

decrease in aggregate income will normally be followed by a decreased demand for leisure, the extent of the decrease being dependent on the income elasticity of demand.

Secondly, a change in hourly rates of pay or in a flat rate income tax will also increase or decrease the marginal income per hour, or, in other words, will decrease or increase the marginal cost of leisure. Thus a fall in income per hour at the margin will reduce the cost of additional leisure and will tend to increase the demand for it to an extent which will depend upon the individual's elasticity of demand for it.

We thus have two effects pulling in opposite directions. The income effect of a rise in a flat rate of income tax will be to cause a decreased demand for leisure, while the price effect at the margin will be to cause an increased demand for it. Which effect will prove the stronger in any particular case can be determined only if we know the demand schedule for leisure at every level of income, though it seems likely that in the majority of cases the income effect will prove more important than the price effect, and that the demand for leisure will increase as income rises. It may be noted that this difficulty is not peculiar to the case of leisure. It occurs for every commodity of which a part is consumed by the producer. The direction of the change in the consumption of butter by butter producers as a consequence of a change in the price of butter is equally difficult to predict.

From the foregoing analysis it is clear that we should expect a fall in aggregate income, without a fall in marginal income, to be followed by a decreased demand for leisure and an increased willingness to work for pay, while conversely a fall in marginal income, without a fall in aggregate income, would tend to induce an increased demand for leisure and a decreased willingness to work for pay. We can probably go further, and say that the larger the decrease in aggregate relatively to marginal income the more likely it is to reduce the demand for leisure, while the larger the decrease in marginal income relatively to aggregate the more likely it is that the demand for leisure will be increased.

The relationship of the changes in aggregate income to changes in marginal income can conveniently be shown by first expressing the aggregate and marginal incomes remaining after tax as percentages of their pre-tax levels, and then dividing the resultant figure for marginal by the resultant figure for aggregate. The higher the figure thus obtained, the more likely it would be that the tax would decrease the demand for leisure and increase the willingness to undertake paid work. For example, the result of a £10 poll tax on different levels of income would be as follows:

Original Aggregate Income	Tax as % of Original Aggregate Income	Remaining Aggregate Income as % of Original Aggregate Income	Remaining Marginal Income as % of Original Marginal Income	Remaining Marginal Income as % of remaining Aggregate Income
£100	10	90	100	111
200	5	95	100	105
500	2	98	100	102
1000	1	99	100	101

This table illustrates the well-known fact that a poll tax is more likely to induce increased offers of work from a poor population than from the well-to-do.

The results of applying similar calculations to the present rates of income tax and surtax on earned incomes are shown in the accompanying charts. Chart 1 refers to a single man, and Chart 2 to a married man with two children. For the purpose of these charts, the marginal rate of tax has been defined as the rate payable on a small addition to income. No account has been taken of the promise to repay after the war the 1941 reductions in allowances. It is difficult to estimate the present value placed by taxpayers on this future repayment, but it seems likely that it is small.

INCOME AND SURTAX (AT 1941 RATES)

(1) SINGLE MAN. ALL EARNED INCOME

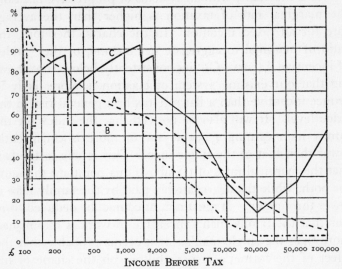

(2) MARRIED MAN WITH TWO CHILDREN. ALL EARNED INCOME

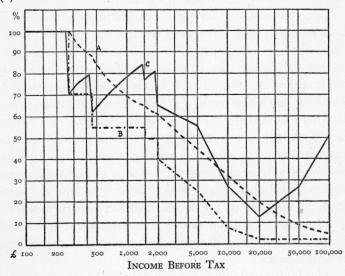

CURVE A = *Aggregate* income remaining after tax expressed as a percentage of *aggregate* income
    before tax.
CURVE B = *Marginal* income remaining after tax expressed as a percentage of *marginal* income
    before tax.
CURVE C = Curve B expressed as a percentage of curve A.

As is inevitable with all systems of progressive taxation, the marginal rate of taxation is higher than the average rate for all taxed incomes. In the charts, therefore, the ratio of marginal to aggregate net income, or the " index of incentive " (curve C), lies consistently below 100, showing that our existing system of taxation is more likely to reduce incentive than a flat rate tax or a general rise in the price level. It will also be noticed that the index for the family man earning £450 a year or more is consistently lower than that of the single man. This is due to the fact that the marginal rates of tax above this point are the same for both, while the aggregate tax paid by the family man is lower throughout. It must not, of course, be deduced from this that the family man's incentive to work is diminished more than the single man's, for it seems probable that the effect of the former's responsibilities on the shape of his income demand schedule for leisure will more than offset the effects of his higher aggregate income.

The charts show that the index fluctuates considerably and irregularly with changes in the level of income. It has three distinct low points : (1) Where tax first becomes payable (£110 for the single man, £267 for the family man) ; (2) where the full rate of tax first becomes payable (£272 for the single man, £450 for the family man) ; and (3) where total marginal tax becomes stabilised at $97\frac{1}{2}$ per cent (£20,000). Only at the first of these points can it be said with certainty that incentive to undertake additional paid work will be diminished, for at that point aggregate income is still unchanged, while marginal income is diminished, in the case of the single man very sharply indeed. At other points all that can be said with certainty is that the probability of a decrease in incentive is greater the lower the index.

The high points of the curve, where the diminution in incentive will tend to be least, lie (1) shortly before the taxpayer becomes liable for tax at the full rate ; and (2) shortly before earned income allowance ceases at £1500. The whole curve from about £500 for the single and £800 for the family man to nearly £2000, where surtax begins, stands high. From £2000 to £20,000 it falls sharply, and though with the stabilisation of the marginal rate of tax at £20,000 it begins to recover, it does not again rise to its earlier levels until the income becomes truly astronomical. It is doubtful whether the effects on the incentive to work of taxpayers earning over £2000 a year are very important, though the repercussions in the field of risk-bearing of a system of taxation which makes sixpennyworth of capital appreciation the equivalent of a pound's worth of dividends are likely to have considerable significance. This question is, however, outside the scope of the present enquiry.

The points at which the deterrent effects seem likely to be most appreciable are at £110 a year for the single and £450 for the family man. For the former especially the deterrent effect is likely to be serious, for while he pays no tax at present he is asked to pay no less than 75 per cent of the next £10 he earns — a marginal rate of tax which is not again encountered until income reaches £5000.

For most people the deterrent effect of high marginal taxation is probably substantially reduced by the present British system of assessment, whereby the income earned during the year ending April 5th is the amount upon which tax is paid during the year commencing the following October.[1] Thus an increase in earned income does not normally begin to be reflected in increased tax payments until after the lapse of from six to eighteen months, and continues to affect them until from eighteen to thirty months after it is earned. This average time-lag of eighteen months between increased earnings and increased tax payments probably prevents many taxpayers from realising clearly how much of their marginal earnings goes

---

[1] Surtax becomes payable only in the January of the next year but one, and for this tax the average time-lag is therefore twenty-seven months.

in taxation. The increased tax, when it comes to be paid, is probably often felt as an aggregate rather than a marginal tax, and may even tend in some cases to increase the incentive to earn, regardless of the fact that larger earnings now will mean still heavier taxation later on.

On the other hand, the fact that, for administrative reasons, direct services rendered by the taxpayer to himself or his family, and in many cases the goods produced by the taxpayer for his own or his family's consumption, are exempt from taxation tends to exaggerate the effect of high taxes at the margin on his willingness to undertake additional paid work. Although the value of the goods or services so produced may be lower than the gross additional income which could have been earned, it may be higher than the net addition to income after providing for tax. There must, for instance, be a certain number of middle-class married women who are induced by the high level of marginal taxation to stay at home and do their own housework, instead of going out to work and employing a domestic at a lower salary than they could earn themselves. Thus there is a social loss of the difference between the values of the services of the housewife and the domestic respectively in non-domestic employment. Similarly, high marginal taxation may cause work on a garden or allotment to be preferred to an increased amount of more valuable paid work.

The deterrent effect of high taxation at the margin is also likely to be increased when it is accompanied by an increase in wage rates greater than the increase in the cost of living. Since the percentage fall in marginal incomes due to the tax will be greater than the percentage fall in aggregate incomes, it follows that an increase in wage rates which leaves the taxpayer better off in the aggregate may still yield him a lower net wage at the margin. This is the case where, given any elasticity at all in either the demand or the income demand schedule, there must be some increase in the demand for leisure; for, with a higher aggregate income and a lower marginal income, both price and income effects are pulling in the same direction.

Where the rise in the cost of living exceeds the rise in wage rates, it cannot be stated with certainty whether the demand for leisure will be increased or decreased. Both aggregate real income and the real price of leisure are reduced, and the result will depend on the shapes of the two schedules. In most cases, however, one would expect that a rise in the cost of living would tend to offset the deterrent effects of increased taxation at the margin. Where there is a rise in wage rates exactly equal to the rise in the cost of living, the only result is to shift the taxpayer into a higher income group, and the effect on incentive will depend on the relationships between aggregate and marginal taxation in his new and old groups.

The effects of high taxation at the margin would have been seen in a most extreme form if the proposal for a 100 per cent Excess Income Tax had been adopted, on the analogy of the Excess Profits Tax. This proposal does not seem to have received serious consideration; but there is a possibility that somewhat similar results may follow from a wide extension of the system of rationing. Even with the present partial rationing system, marginal earnings have lost a considerable part of their purchasing power. In addition, the fixation of maximum prices, even without rationing, has a very similar effect in demonetising marginal earnings. As soon as prices are fixed at a level below that at which the whole of the demand can be met, supplies are distributed, not according to the amount people are willing to spend on them, but either by some unofficial rationing system, or according to the time buyers have free to stand in queues, or by superior local knowledge, or by sheer luck. As the area covered by price-fixing and rationing extends, the demonetisation of marginal earnings becomes increasingly effective for all incomes above the level sufficient for buying the official and unofficial rations, a level which itself is kept down by the subsidisation of prices of necessaries. Should the exigencies of war finance necessitate the imposition of a system of universal rationing, whether global or by individual commodities, the effect would be in many ways similar to the imposition of 100 per cent compulsory saving for all earnings in excess of the amount necessary for buying the full ration for the tax-payer and his family.

Such a system would differ from an excess income tax, or a scheme of compulsory loans to the Government, only in that the taxpayer would be able to invest his savings as he liked or to give them away to those who otherwise could not have afforded to buy the full ration. It would help to extend the effects of " cheap money " not only to Government Securities but to other types of investment, including such direct investment in durable goods as other war-time restrictions allowed. It would also favour debtors as compared with creditors, for the debtor would be enabled to pay off his debt with money which neither he nor his creditor could spend. The debtor, at least for the duration of the war, would be no worse off than if he had never contracted the debt, and after the war would find himself released from his indebtedness. " Cheap money " plus strict rationing thus has an effect on the relationship of debtors and creditors very similar to that of a normal inflation.

For some people, then — for those with monetary obligations, or who have particular investments which they are anxious and permitted to make, or who cannot afford the whole permitted ration for themselves and those dependent on them — even the completest system of rationing will leave some present incentive at the margin. But for the rest the effect on incentive will depend on the rate at which they discount the post-war benefits which they will derive from present involuntary saving. It seems likely that for many people this rate of discount will be high, and that the incentive provided by earnings which cannot now be spent will not be very great.

On the whole, therefore, it seems reasonable to expect some, and perhaps a considerable, loss of economic incentive to undertake additional work for pay, as a result of high marginal rates of taxation, price-fixing, and rationing. Against this there can fortunately be set the great increase which occurs in war-time in the willingness to work harder in the interest of the community as a whole. It would, however, be both unfair and unwise to rely wholly on patriotism to offset the diminution of economic incentive — unfair because it would throw the whole burden upon the more public-spirited members of the community, and unwise because even the most public-spirited are likely to find it easier to maintain a high level of output if their services receive some immediate and tangible recognition.

The necessity for offsetting the effects of taxation and rationing in reducing the cost of leisure and for increasing incentive at the margin has already led to the introduction of various measures designed to raise marginal income relatively to average income. One method is to fix a longer standard working week and then to pay a bonus for satisfactory attendance. This is very similar in its effects to an increase in overtime rates without a corresponding increase in standard rates. Let us assume that the worker receives the bonus only if he works six days a week. If he works five days at £1 per day he earns £5; if he works six days he earns £6 plus a bonus of 1s. per day for the whole week. His rate of pay for the sixth or marginal day is thus £1 : 6s., or 30 per cent more than the intramarginal rate and 24 per cent more than the average rate for the week.

An alternative is applied in those industries which have been made subject to an Essential Work Order. Under these orders absenteeism is made a punishable offence.

This has the effect both of raising marginal and of lowering intra-marginal wages. If, for instance, a man earning £1 per day, who should have worked six days, works only five and is fined £2 for his absence, his net income for the five days is only £3, or 12s. a day. The income forgone by not working the sixth day is £3. His marginal rate of earning has become five times as great as his intra-marginal rate and three times as great as his average rate.

Neither of these methods of providing additional incentive seems to be wholly satisfactory. The former, to be effective, would probably have to raise marginal costs out of all proportion to the increase in output, while the latter can presumably be invoked only in the most flagrant cases. Further, neither of them meets the difficulty of loss of incentive due to the partial demonetisation of marginal earnings by rationing, except in so far as the fines imposed under the second method reduce the remaining income below the level necessary for purchasing the full ration.

In view of this, it is perhaps worth while to consider whether it might not be possible to modify existing methods of taxation and rationing with a view to removing or reducing their undesirable effects on incentive at the margin. For instance, income tax might be levied, not upon the income actually earned, but upon the income which would have been earned had the taxpayer worked a standard number of hours. In this case, the number of hours actually worked would not affect the amount of tax paid. Should the taxpayer choose to enjoy more leisure than envisaged under the standard fixed, he would be taxed upon it as if he had been earning; [1] while if he chose to work more than the standard number of hours, he would reap the whole benefit of his extra labours. In this way, the marginal cost of leisure would be restored to equality with the amount of his gross marginal earnings, and the

[1] Allowance would of course have to be made for involuntary absences from work, due to illness or other unavoidable causes.

incentive to work would suffer no diminution.

Again, the loss of incentive due to rationing might be greatly reduced if those working overtime (*i.e.* more than the standard number of hours per week) were rewarded for their extra labours, not with higher rates of pay, but with increased facilities for spending their extra earnings. If, for instance, those working overtime were presented with extra coupons, permitting them to spend some part of their overtime pay on additional scarce or rationed goods, either at ordinary shops or at special stores provided for the purpose, there can be little doubt that a very marked increase in incentive would result. The increase in the consumption of scarce goods would be relatively small and would probably be far more than offset by the additional output obtained, while the rest of the community could hardly complain at a system whereby such small margin of scarce goods as was available went to those who were doing an abnormal amount of work.

THE END

PRINTED BY R. & R. CLARK, LTD., EDINBURGH